IF THE RIVER LETS ME

A YUKON RIVER ADVENTURE

For
Prof Robert MacFarlane

Thank You

Rich Kenworthy

RICHARD
KENWORTHY

Published by Richard Kenworthy
All rights reserved

First Edition 2022

ISBN 978-1-3999-2943-1

Designed and typeset by Ned Hoste, The Big Ideas Collective
Printed and bound in Great Britain by CPI Group

For Joshua, Callum and George.

Contents

Acknowledgements

There are numerous people I need to thank for their help and encouragement in the writing of this book. From the perspective of the actual task of writing, I would like to thank my sisters-in-law, Meriel and Kate: Meriel for initially sowing the idea that I should write up my journal from the trip – 'if not for you then for your boys and their children'; and then Kate who looked over and kindly commented on my early very raw work. The transition of my draft into an actual book only became real after I had spoken to Lily Neil, the owner of The Topsham Bookshop and champion of local writers. Lily's enthusiasm and sage advice helped me frame my work more lucidly, before she introduced me to Marcus Parry, my editor. Marcus is the first editor I have ever had to work with, and he proved to be a patient, thorough and understanding mentor and I thank him for his non-judgmental and conscientious rearrangement and correction of my text and the mistakes therein. Finally, in the production of the physical book, I must thank Ned Hoste who, with Marcus, brought my words to print, making the final product slicker and more stylish than I could have hoped for or deserve.

My thanks also need to go to all of those that I met and who helped me whilst I was on the Yukon River, especially the guys at Up North Adventures in Whitehorse who fitted me out for both my forays on the river and treated my requests and silly questions with professionalism and respect. Whilst my journey was remote and solitary, there were still many people that I met along the way, all of whom were generally interested, kind and supportive, and where applicable to my adventure I have mentioned them in my story.

I have two final thanks. Firstly, from an animistic perspective and out of pure primal respect, I must thank the Yukon River: I was a mere speck on that mighty river, another traveller, a minute particle of history that the living river was asked to carry, and whilst I was made to work for my goal, ultimately it was the Yukon that allowed me to complete my journey, so I need to thank it.

Finally, I must thank my wife Sophie for her understanding and support. For some reason she understands and tolerates my need to attempt such challenges and why, despite providing me with a comfortable and loving home, I still search to 'feed my rat'. I do not suppose for one second that it is any easier living with me and my madcap plans than it is wondering where I am when I'm away attempting them, so thank you my love for giving me the place from which to explore.

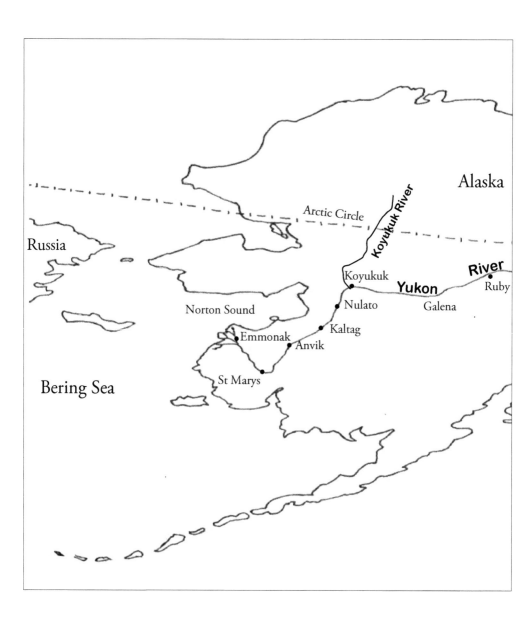

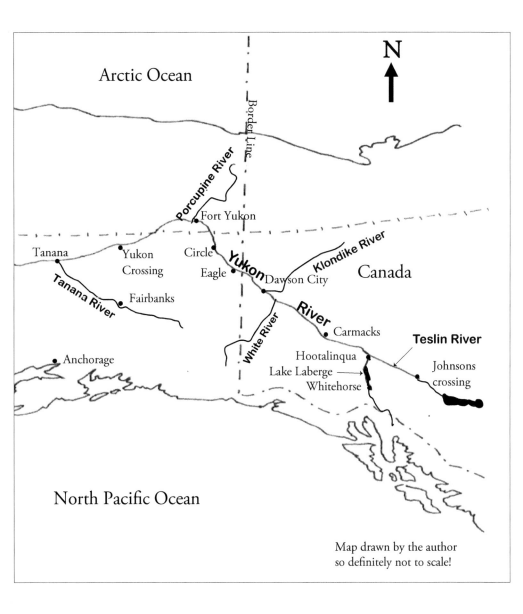

*Pulled up on a windy stretch of river somewhere
south of Koyukuk*

A Windy Afternoon
on the River

"Alaska must be viewed as having two characteristics: great beauty and implacable hostility."

James A Michener, Alaska

It was an early afternoon in mid-July 2019 and the Alaskan summer weather had taken another turn for the worse. I'd had a late start that morning, waiting for the wind to abate, and thus far that day I had made very poor progress in my 16ft canoe.

The Yukon River had been testing me for the last few days. I was now beyond the settlement of Kaltag heading south into the wind, and the brown expanse of water ahead of me was wide and angry. I was hugging the right-hand bank scanning the muddy, rock-strewn shoreline, looking for boltholes and safe havens, anywhere I might be able to pull in if the conditions became still worse. It was another of those frustrating and not so rare afternoons out on the river where to stop paddling meant going sideways, or potentially being blown to a standstill trapped between the current and the wind. I was tired, but ever the optimist, I remained convinced that the conditions around the next bend might be better, although given the capricious and unpredictable nature of the river and the winds there was also a good chance it would be impossible for me to go on.

My poor progress over the last few days made me determined to battle on for a bit longer and see what the next stretch had to offer. I was breaking one of my cardinal rules as a lone paddler, I was pushing my luck and I knew it. I hugged the shore and fought my way around the corner, trying not to bottom out on the rocks or mud; being so close meant I could gauge just how slowly I was actually going – this was silly.

The conditions were not any better around the bend, in fact, just as I'd feared, they were worse. The wind was now forcing me up onto the shore and being so focused on wrestling with the conditions and looking out and along the river I didn't notice the rather handsome black bear standing directly next to me. From my position sat in my canoe, we were at eye level about five metres apart, not a good place to be, for me at least. I didn't know if it had been there all along watching my ludicrous progress, or if it had just wandered down to the shoreline and was as shocked to see me as I was to meet it. I could clearly – too clearly – see the bear's beady brown eyes studying me with quizzical myopia from within its round, black, furry head.

I was transfixed by the bear's light brown muzzle, black twitching nose and loose lower lip rippling as it tried to work out what, exactly, I was, and how it should react. We studied each other briefly, both too surprised to say or do anything, and after what seemed like minutes but was in fact just a few seconds, my new dreadfully handsome acquaintance thankfully decided to stroll off up into the willows above the foreshore. I could breathe again. As I recovered from this unexpected close encounter, I realised that I had subconsciously moved my paddle into a position ready to parry any attack, but I knew that from my position sat in the canoe, if that bear had decided to charge this would have been utterly useless. Still slightly stunned, I relaxed my grip and desperately tried to paddle back out onto the river and get further downstream, away from the bear, but to no avail – I couldn't go any further. My canoe, with me in it, was pinned to the shore by the wind and waves just a short distance from where the bear had sauntered off into the brush.

I was left with very little choice but to step ashore and secure the canoe. I put on and buckled up my utility belt, which I always kept next to me both in and out of the boat, released the safety catch on the canister of bear spray which sat in its holster on the belt next to my dominant left hand, and subconsciously fiddled with the rather pathetic little knife on my right. It was pointless conducting my usual, fastidious patrol looking for bear signs – there were fresh tracks everywhere and I'd just seen and smelt the thing leaving them.

It was at this point that I realised that I was scared and very annoyed. The fear came from knowing that there was a wild bear nearby, a feeling greatly exacerbated by the fact that I was stuck here with it and would be until the weather improved. The annoyance was directed at me for putting myself in this position, for pushing my luck again, for not respecting the river. My mind was whirring. Where was that bear? Was it still watching me? Would it come back? How should I behave? I had been on the Yukon, on my own, since leaving Dawson City, for just over three weeks now and had seen a number of other bears along the way, but this was my first real close encounter, and I was not in control.

I remembered from all my reading and research prior to leaving the UK that black bears are said to be not as grumpy as grizzlies. A grizzly, if disturbed and feeling frightened or territorial, would likely stage a false charge and will, hopefully, halt before reaching you (providing, of course, that you have the balls to stand your ground whilst, counterintuitively, also proving you are not a threat). Black bears, on the other hand, are apparently generally less aggressive and rarely charge when surprised, preferring to run away (or perhaps saunter as my friend just did). However, if and when they do charge, they don't stop, having probably decided that you're a threat or meal and therefore need eliminating or eating. Either species, when with cubs, should be avoided at all costs. WHERE THE HELL HAD THAT BEAR GONE?

It was now late afternoon, still windy, and had started to spit with rain. The bank was too steep and rocky to put my tent up, regardless of the bear, and there was no way I was going to break out my cooker and make any tempting smells. So very tentatively, I started collecting driftwood from along the beach, reluctant to move too far from the perceived safety of my canoe. I built a small fire next to my boat on the river's edge, as far away from the shrub line as possible. I got out my camping chair and set in to wait out the weather, with one eye on the wind and water, and another nervously scanning the willow line.

The Alaskan nights were starting to get a little darker, but still remained light enough for me to see fairly well throughout, despite the drizzle. Fifteen hours later with no sleep, the safety catch on my bear spray still off, dressed in all my warm clothing and prodding the remaining embers of my fire, I was finally able to get out of there. The following morning the wind had dropped just enough to make the conditions safer and more manageable for me on my own in a canoe, but for how long? I chucked my chair in the canoe, extinguished the fire, made sure there was no sign of me having been there, and put in. I paddled stiffly in the morning chill for half a mile downstream, aiming for an exposed sandbar out in the centre of the river that I'd been eyeing up all night. I landed, put up the tent, ate some cereal bars and got into my sleeping bag desperate for some sleep.

As I shuffled in my bag, trying to find the position that would allow me to sleep, I regarded that previous night as just another part of my journey, just another obstacle that I needed to negotiate. My initial annoyance had abated overnight, but I was conflicted: on the one hand I was thankful that the bear had not returned and relatively confident that I had behaved appropriately given the circumstances I put myself in; but on the other, I also felt very privileged to have had such a personal encounter with a beautiful wild animal.

With nearly a month on the river and as desperate as I was to catch some sleep, it didn't immediately occur to me that I was rather a long way from the nearest human habitation and possible help had that encounter and evening turned out differently. I knew from my mapping exactly where I was on the Yukon and just how far I still had to go to reach my goal of the Bering Sea, but it did not register that at that moment I was camping on the same northern latitude as Iceland and as far west as the longitudinal line running south through the Hawaiian Islands. I was slightly below the Arctic Circle and now just a little closer to Russia than my starting point in Canada.

I slept well that morning, a yearned-for repose that I could feel topping up every cell in my body, but was roused by an unearthly quietness. The wind had dropped, the low Alaskan sun was out, the Yukon River was inviting me to continue my journey: it was going to allow me to go on. I broke camp, made some strong coffee, loaded my canoe, and once again pushed off into another day in the Alaskan wilderness, still heading for the sea.

A misty morning on the Yukon River

My Return to
the Yukon

"When you are where wild bears live you learn to pay attention to the rhythm of the land and yourself. Bears not only make the habitat rich, they enrich us just by being."

Linda Jo Hunter, Lonesome for Bears

Sitting at home in 2017, two years prior to my encounter with that black bear, and contemplating my first foray on the Yukon River, up north to Dawson City, earlier that year, I kept returning to the same question, 'is it possible to go further?' As the answer to this question, and many more in the same vein, kept coming back 'yes', my question then grew into, 'So, could I manage to paddle all the way to the Bering Sea?'

I had started that first trip on the Teslin River (a tributary of the Yukon and arguably the source of the longest watercourse to the Bering Sea) since in late May 2017 Lake Laberge, the 30-mile open expanse of the Yukon River below the Yukon Territory Capital of Whitehorse, was still frozen and impassable. I spent days on end paddling on my own – initially through floe ice – and got to sight bears, wolves and beavers as well as meeting a lynx. Whilst a step into the unknown for me personally at that time, the Teslin River and the upper reaches of the Yukon are well-trodden and explored. Information and guides are plentiful and the outdoor industry in the region is well set up to cater for the adventurous and nutty types. There were numerous spots recommended for camping along the way and it was possible to hire a canoe or kayak from a number of rental companies in Whitehorse who would, for a price, drop you off at the start of your trip and pick you up when you'd finished. It was all pretty well packaged and once I had settled into it I loved it, but I must admit I did get a little bored towards the end.

On that first trip, after a stopover at the Coal Mine Campground near the village of Carmacks, having taken advantage of a welcome Wi-Fi call home, a shower, a couple of beers and the best Cheese Burger I think I've ever had (hold that thought for the Yukon River Camp at Yukon Bridge, Alaska!), I was ready to take on the infamous Five Finger Rapids. It had taken me seven days to kayak the 250 miles to Carmacks (not that I was rushing) and the thought of the impending Five Finger Rapids 30 miles downstream had grabbed my attention. Prior to leaving Carmacks, I made sure all my kit was properly stowed and waterproofed in anticipation of a rough ride and maybe a cold dip. So, it was with my heart pounding that I rounded a huge bend in the river and lined up my kayak with the recommended gap in the finger rocks that span the river, ready to negotiate the rapids that form between them. Sadly, other than a swifter than usual bob through the rocks and out the other side, the rapids didn't flick my switch. As a result, I think I then, subconsciously, decided that I had cracked that particular trip. I covered the remaining 200 plus miles to Dawson City in three days, focusing more on my daily mileage than the scenery and experience.

I left Dawson that first time, heading south on the Husky Bus (the bus service that runs up and down from Whitehorse every few days or so throughout the summer) with one hell of a hangover and a bit of a 'so what' feeling. I was sure that there was more to do and experience, and began wondering if, indeed, I had it in me to potentially go any further, to 'drop off the edge of the world' as they say in Dawson and make it all the way to the Bering Sea. It was an itch that built steadily at home over the subsequent months. Perhaps I had been bitten by Robert Service's Spell of The Yukon? I wasn't interested in gold but there is certainly something about the land:

No! There's the land. (Have you seen it?)
It's the cussedest land that I know,
From the big, dizzy mountains that screen it
To the deep, deathlike valleys below,
Some say God was tired when he made it;
Some say it's a fine land to shun;
Maybe; but there's some as would trade it
For no land on earth – and I'm one.
It's the great, big, broad land 'way up yonder,
It's the forests where silence has lease;
It's the beauty that thrills me with wonder,
It's the stillness that fills me with peace.

Robert Service, 1907

Clearly the journey to the Bering Sea had been made many times before, but for me, with my own resourses – possibly on my own – was I being realistic? I spent many hours through 2018 re-reading Dan Maclean's excellent guidebook Paddling the Yukon River and its Tributaries and pondering the available online accounts and satellite imagery of the Yukon River steadily becoming more obsessive – and, as with all good obsessions, a little secretive. Was this pie-in-the-sky thinking? Was I just full of hot air and being boastful about my potential against a goal I could not realistically achieve? As always, the trick of turning an idea into reality is to lay it out, to express it, to turn it from random electrical impulses in my head and make it real by talking about it. I finally laid out my latest mad-cap idea, in its rawest terms, over a glass of wine, to my ever-understanding wife, Sophie. Let's just say she didn't say 'no', although she did make a few choice comments that I won't print here. At least I had her interest, if not her immediate approval, and it was out of the bag, so I could really start unpacking this 'beast' that I was looking at tackling.

This journey was going to be very different from my 2017 Yukon paddle. Whilst there were a few places where I could possibly find supplies along the way, there were no guarantees so I committed to take everything I would need for roughly 40 days with me. I would be crossing the international border between Canada and the USA, and would, briefly, be above the Arctic Circle; and for the last 1200 miles, there were no detailed river guides that I could find. I was also particularly nervous about the conditions I would face towards the end once in the Yukon–Kuskokwim Delta, not to mention the constant nagging thought that I would be in bear country again. I was fairly confident that I had the ability to paddle the distance, but as I planned my trip there seemed to be just so many variables, so many 'known and unknown, unknowns', to paraphrase Donald Rumsfeld.

Dan Maclean's book is the paddling equivalent of a 'thru-hiker's' guide (a long-distance hiking guide that crosses a country from one point to another) covering the five longest rivers in Alaska, including the entire Yukon and the Kuskokwim, Porcupine, Tanana and Koyukuk Rivers, with maps, information on access points, resupply options and navigation tips. In 2017, given the abundance of specific Teslin and Yukon River guides with more detailed mapping covering the Johnson's Crossing to Dawson City stretch, I used Dan's book for more generalised planning and backup information than for navigation. However, as I started to look beyond Dawson, and particularly beyond the city of Circle (so named because of its proximity to the Arctic Circle), Dan's book became my go-to reference source. The timelines he provides all the way through to Emmonak, which remained remarkably accurate regardless of the conditions, were fundamental to my planning and approach this time around.

"It does not do to leave a live dragon out of your calculation, if you live near one."

J.R.R. Tolkien, The Hobbit

Perhaps before we go any further we should discuss the elephant in the room: the bears in the woods. The thought of bears was ever present in my planning, just as it is for pretty much anyone that heads out into the 'bush' in North America. Even people living in cities in the northern latitudes think about bears. I was told by a couple from Anchorage, that I met in Tanana, that the incidents of bears entering their local back gardens was on the increase. When I asked if this was due to the bears being hungry and looking for food, I was told that it was, but it isn't rubbish that they're after, it's juvenile moose. They told me that the moose had got savvy to the idea that they are safer from predation by bears in urban areas, so more cow moose are bringing their young in, which in turn brings the bears after them, along with all the mischief that entails.

You don't have to read too far into Bill Bryson's A Walk in Woods, his masterful telling of his attempt to walk the Appalachian Trail, before you come across lurid accounts of bear attacks, as he also tries to reassure himself of the wisdom of his particular mid-life adventure. In Coming into the Country, when confronting his particular fear of bears and the possibility of meeting one during a solo trek out of the bush to be picked up on the Yukon River, John McPhee sights an old adage "when a pine needle drops in the forest the eagle will see it fall; the deer will hear it when it hits the ground;

the bear will smell it." The feeling that there is always something out there, in the bush, that could see, hear or smell you is constant and without a doubt has a real impact, practically, emotionally and spiritually. But it really was the idea that some of the critters out there, the ones that are much bigger than you and are also particularly adept when it comes to sniffing out their prey, that peaks one's attention. I was told that, amongst almost everything else, bears were particularly attracted to toothpaste. No surprise there, I guess, given its inherently strong smell, and so brushing my teeth became a task I completed only when leaving a stopover.

I am sure the locals in Canada and Alaska, and almost anywhere else in the world where bears are still wild, enjoy telling visitors gruesome and scary bear stories. In the tourist hotspots, such as Banff in the Canadian Rockies, the stories of big grizzlies 'The Boss' and 'Split Lip' abound, and at Yukon Crossing in Alaska, the story of the hibernating brown bear (in Alaska grizzlies are known as brown bears) is, again, attention-grabbing, scary stuff. I suspect that the stories, true or exaggerated, help keep visitors aware and cautious (and therefore, possibly, alive) and in turn keep the bears safe.

The fact remains that there are bears out there and, yes, they are more than capable of killing a careless human. In the great North American taiga, humans are not necessarily top of the pecking order, and if you want to survive, you need to be informed, conscientious and respectful. For me, whilst still a real concern (and not wanting to sound blasé), this dynamic most definitely added to the attraction and mystique of the Yukon. Of course, there are plenty of other creatures that could potentially do you a lot of harm out there. I saw a few mostly loan wolves lolling along the shoreline as I paddled past, and for a short stretch, after Yukon Crossing, I was aware of a small pack keeping pace with me through the wooded bank. Spending a night listening to some hungry-sounding howling whilst tucked up in my sleeping bag was pretty disconcerting. Jack London's short story The Law of Life about Koshoosh, an elderly Indian who, in accordance with tribal tradition, was left to the elements and the wolves, kept springing to mind.

For my part, I was hoping that most of the bears would be away from the river whilst I was paddling. Bears usually head up into the hills to gorge on the abundance of berries during the height of summer, then return to the river in late summer/early autumn, to take advantage of the salmon spawning. Both food sources provide them with the nutrition and fat they need for hibernation, but of late, as global warming has started to affect the seasons, the separation between the berry and salmon gluts has blurred. So rather than benefiting from both sources of nutrition, the bears focus on the berries which are both easier to harvest and provide more reserves, potentially missing out on the final, pre-hibernation, top-up of salmon. That said, I was told that later in my paddle I might witness a congregation of bears feeding on spawned-out salmon at the mouth of one or two of the smaller tributaries along the Yukon, but sadly I didn't.

In reality, the bears and other wildlife were just another potential hazard that I needed to plan for and manage. I think, ultimately, I became fairly fatalistic about the possibilities of meeting a bear: an example of the dualism I felt as part of me wanted to stay safe and keep my time on the Yukon as simple as possible, whilst another part wanted to encounter the wildlife (yes, even a bear). I believed that, provided I was conscientious and did everything I realistically could do to avoid attracting – or accidentally stumbling/paddling into – a bear, then there really wasn't an awful lot of point in becoming paranoid. If I came face-to-face with something, I'd have to manage that situation – all part of testing myself, I guess: would I be able to man-up when eye to eye with a bear?

I do think that living with the constant reality of big and potentially dangerous animals was one of the aspects of my trips on the Yukon that made them so exhilarating. The thought and reality of bears is part of the wonder of the place, part the very real and the wider existential experience. Knowing that, ultimately, I was not entirely in control, but that I had to work with, respect and understand my place within the environment, made me feel more alert and therefore, dare I say, alive. There is a tangible sense of freedom, of mindfulness, created with only having to focus on paddling and staying alive that enables you to shake off (or forget for a while at least) the day-to-day inane clutter that can become so important and all-encompassing in the comfort of our otherwise domesticated lives. It does not take an enormous leap of imagination or personal projection to understand why for many people the Yukon offers a sanctuary from the puerile pressures of prescribed modern existence.

As I look back at my early my planning, I see that whilst predominant in my mind throughout, bears were only third on my list of things that I was worried might damage or kill me. Second on the list was me, myself and my potential incompetence, in that I might drown, poison, cut or break myself, all very real possibilities that I would have to manage and consider in my planning, my approach and my actual behaviour on the river. I had a degree of confidence that I could look after myself, but I also knew from experience how quickly a few silly mistakes, a lack of concentration, or just pure laziness can escalate into unwanted and uncomfortable situations.

Top of my list of things that could harm me, above the bears and my own incompetence, were...trees. I'm terrified of trees in the bush, that's not to say that I walk around trying to avoid them, jumping in surprise and cowering at the sight of them, rather that I know how much damage they can inflict if not treated with respect. Deadfall kills and damages more people in the forests of the world than any of the pointy-toothed creatures that live in them. With regards to the Yukon, I was concerned by the very real threat of the trees that would be in the river creating obstacles, hitting the boat or forming log jams, and also the land-based overhanging, entangling and falling varieties. I'd been caught by overhanging trees on flowing rivers before and knew just how quickly you can become ensnared and how, once the weight of the water has your boat pinned in amongst the deadly limbs of timber, your options quickly run out. Both times that it happened to me previously – on the River Spey near Kingusse in Scotland, and on the River Exe in Devon during a race – I had to fight my way out of my boats and, once free, my only option was to plunge below the obstacles without knowing what was under the surface. It scared me. I was lucky both times and really did not want to try my luck again. Perhaps because of this, the idea of taking a wrong turn into a slough (pronounced locally as 'slew') or branch of the river, coming face-to-face with a log jam and being propelled into it by thousands of tons of glacial melt water, really scared me. There would have been little I could do but hope that the canoe would not be swamped or dragged under the jam pinning me to the logs, unable to extricate myself.

Maybe, if I had gone with someone else my ability to relax a little more, take a few more risks and tackle the river more confidently would have been different. One of the first questions people ask when I now tell them about my trip is 'who did you go with?' usually followed by 'were you part of an organised group?'. When I say I went on my own they generally sound more incredulous about that fact than the idea that I actually undertook the journey at all. My stock response to being asked why I went on my own was that I couldn't find anyone with the desire, time, or means to join me. In all honesty, I think all along, throughout the burgeoning idea and the more detailed planning, I knew that I was going to be going alone. It's not that I'm a particularly antisocial person (although I can't be described as gregarious either), I think it was just that I wanted to undertake the paddle in my own way and not compromise the experience.

My first trip was straightforward: I was already in Canada, Sophie wasn't inclined to join me, and my boys had work or university to get back to, so going on my own was obvious and, arguably, less risky on those upper sections of river. Second time around, and with the proposed paddle being three times the distance and far more remote, perhaps I should have given more consideration and time to finding a suitable partner or team. But I was worried about failing, scared of over-promising and underperforming, and reluctant to expose or discuss my plans too widely for exactly those reasons. I also couldn't think of anyone that I could realistically suggest it to. I knew my usual kayaking buddy, Ian, wouldn't be able to find the time and I'm sure (no disrespect to him) whilst he'd have given it a bloody good go, he would have struggled, or worse dropped out at the last minute. Re-reading Len Webster's Teslin River Guide from my first trip made me think again. Under the heading 'It's a Bear! What Do I do Now?', one line of advice offers, "Throw something onto the ground (like a camera or friend) if the bear pursues you, as it may be distracted by this, and will allow time for you to escape"; perhaps Ian would have been perfect! Mind you, looking at it from the other side, you would have to question the sanity of any poor sod that would willingly want to spend six weeks or more in a canoe with me. And then, of course, when not paddling there would be the usual arguments about the snoring. Why is it that it's always the first person to fall asleep that snores?

I had pretty much concluded that I was going on my own by the time I read Dan Maclean's comments on the pros and cons of paddling with a partner, "As anyone who has planned a long trip probably knows...partners can be enthusiastic and eager up until it's time to go, at which point they discover other priorities. Frequently, the only way to do long trips is to go alone." In the next sentence he says, "Traveling solo is not recommended," but by then my mind was made up – I would be going it alone.

Having completed as much planning as I could from home, I had to commit to a date for my trip. I was conscious of the very short Yukon summer and keen to get started as soon as possible. Sophie and I had arranged a campervan tour of Scotland's west coast in May and early June so I was trying not to give the impression that my own trip was the most important thing on my mind at that time. Additionally, as the considerate and loving husband I am, I thought it best that I wait until after our 25th Wedding Anniversary, so I booked to fly from Gatwick two days after the anniversary on 18th June. Sophie was delighted!

'Why have you chosen that particular day to leave me for your hare-brained and potentially suicidal trip?' she asked. 'But darling,' I began confidently, although that confidence was fading fast when confronted with the look on her face, 'I have purposefully and thoughtfully booked to leave two days after our anniversary so we can spend some precious time together before I go on my well planned and entirely safe trip'. I can't remember the number of times through my life where I have committed to saying or doing something with entire confidence only to realise as soon as I opened my mouth or started the task at hand that I'd got it wrong. The one abiding sense that I have always had in these situations (and I suspect that I'm not entirely alone here) is that despite my brain knowing I've got it wrong, it refuses to do anything about it and just lets me continue to talk. It is almost as if it relishes some sort of schadenfreude toward me. 'That's very thoughtful of you,' said Sophie and then after a short pause, enough for my brain to have had its fun, she asked, 'so after 25 years of marriage what day of the month do you think we actually got married on?'. After a few failed, stumbling, attempts to say the right thing I gave up. Hopefully I won't confuse the 16th and 18th June again! I quickly rebooked to fly on 20th June.

Rather worryingly, it wasn't until I was actually sitting on the WestJet Boeing 737 taking off from Gatwick that the true scale, remoteness and arguably the madness of what lay ahead really sank in. I'd managed to secure myself a bit of leg room on the plane in an emergency exit row and sat opposite me was a rather bored-looking flight attendant who having completed her pre-flight checks was buckled into her jump-seat inspecting her nails. Above her, on the bulkhead, was a TV monitor which having finished the safety brief had moved on to show the flight information and the flight path we were due to take to Calgary. As the view panned out, up and away from the UK, then west and north across the northern hemisphere, over the Atlantic Ocean and across the vast expanse of Canada, I could pick-out my 'onward destinations': Calgary, then Vancouver, and then north up to Whitehorse in the Canadian Yukon Territory. Not a problem – I'd already been there, I knew roughly what to expect. But now I was going further, much further, and for the first time I could comprehend where I was heading in a global context. The monitor's view didn't stretch far enough up north or west across the planet to show me Dawson City, the planned starting point for my trip, never mind my intended final destination, western Alaska and the Bering Sea, where I was hoping to finish, if the river let me!

Throughout my planning, as I'd been honing my canoeing skills on the Exe Estuary, in Devon, seeking windier rough days to develop my technique, or when creating my own mapping at home, I'd been focusing on the river, looking at the detailed features: the bends, turns, islands, rapids and potential hazards along the way. The things I would have to deal with face-to-face, hour-by-hour, day-by-day, in order to complete this trip. Now, as I sat on the plane climbing to 36,000ft, committed to at least reaching northwest Canada, I could finally see where I was heading and what I was planning to do from a much wider perspective, a global perspective, and to be honest it scared me. As I sat on the plane, I was acutely conscious that I had half the kit I needed with me, I'd paid for half of my canoe and I didn't have any return flights booked – what could possibly go wrong! So, for the next nine hours, every time I looked up at that monitor, I got to scare myself just a little bit more!

In hindsight, perhaps the most stressful aspect of the whole adventure was the journey to and from the Yukon. I suspect this was because my passage was in the hands of my fellow humans rather than me or at the whim of the Yukon. When travelling in June, with a 'toppers' 125 litre dry bag on my back and another 60 litre bag masquerading as cabin luggage, I was at the mercy of train and flight company timetables and their staff, most of whom were genuinely helpful (some far more than others) and fellow commuters for whom this large bloke clearing people out of the way with every lift and turn of his ridiculous baggage and sweating under the weight of his load was clearly a nuisance. Once on the river, my world would be just me in my 16ft canoe in one of the largest wildernesses on the planet, at the mercy of the river, weather and critters. But it would be for me to decide how to deal with every situation, and only me to manage and answer to.

Not untypical bear and wolf tracks next to my size 11s – the tracks were not fresh but I still didn't hang around here

*My kayak pulled up on the banks of the
Teslin River May 2017*

Whitehorse

So, after months of planning, and 24 hours travelling from the UK on two trains, three planes and a taxi, I was relieved when I finally reached Whitehorse. It was familiar as I had been here previously, both for the start of my last trip and for a couple of days 'R&R' when I finished. Whitehorse had everything I needed to complete my kit list and packing for this trip, and I knew where to find everything so two days was plenty of time. I had arrived in Whitehorse for the 21 June and the 'Indigenous Peoples Live Event', the town was buzzing.

Before I go any further, I think it important to discuss the terms used to describe the indigenous people along the Yukon River. The use of the term 'First Nations' is predominantly Canadian, whilst in Alaska, 'Alaskan Natives' is used in to describe those nations and tribes that are descended from the first known peoples to inhabit the entire region, having crossed the, then open, land bridge from Eurasia somewhere over 10,000 years ago. The evidence to pinpoint exactly when this was and who first crossed it is still disputed, but the fact that the current First Nations and Alaskan Natives are their descendants is not. They were most likely following migrating caribou and, by all accounts, found what for them at that time must have been a veritable paradise. The unique topography of the Yukon Basin at that time meant that much of it, whilst subject to annual freeze and thaw, remained relatively snow-and-ice-free. Those first humans would have found a vast, seasonal, arid grassland, intersected by the fish-rich Yukon and its tributaries, home to woolly mammoths, wild horses, scimitar lions, muskox and bison, to mention just a fraction of the fauna these First Peoples would have encountered and incorporated into their way of life. From those beginnings there are now a multitude of tribes, peoples and cultures of whom I, regrettably, have little understanding and who I am unable, here, to properly articulate and describe.

I did conduct some limited research prior to arriving in their lands and knew, in basic terms, that there are differences between the interior and coastal peoples, the difference between what were once generalised as 'Indians', in the interior, and 'Eskimos' on the coasts. The terms Eskimo and Indian remain difficult and pejorative to many of the First Nations Peoples of North America. The term Eskimo is taken from the French Esquimaux, possibly picked up from an indigenous word exkipot meaning 'an eater of raw flesh'. The term Indian is believed to derive from Christopher Columbus' belief that he had reached the Indies (Asia) rather than central America and the term has stuck for all indigenous North American peoples. The term aboriginal has been suggested but this denotes that the people originated in North America which they did not. It has also been suggested that each people or tribe should use their own names, but as some of these effectively mean 'the people of all this land' the problems continue.

Along the Yukon I could possibly meet a number of interior tribes, including the Gwich'in, the Hän, the Koyukan, the Tutchone or the Teslin, all with common Athapascan ancestral links and languages but now with their own separate histories, cultures and relationship with the land and the river. On the coast were the Inupiaq along the Arctic Ocean to the north; the Alutiiq and Unangax to the south and across the Aleutian Islands; and the Yup'ik peoples of the Yukon–Kuskokwim Delta where I was due to finish. The term Inuit can also be used to represent all the culturally similar indigenous peoples inhabiting the Arctic and Subarctic regions of Greenland, Canada and Alaska. A potentially confusing array of names and terms, but, as with anyone entering another country I would hope, I was acutely aware of my status as a visitor, a tourist and an interloper and my ignorance of the detailed history and modern-day issues concerning Canada, Alaska and the Native or First Nations Peoples. As such, I tried to remain as discrete, respectful and conscientious as possible whilst a guest in their land and will try to do the same in my writing.

I may also, occasionally, use the term 'locals' for the Native People where it is clear what is meant and appropriate, but in general when I use this term, I am referring to the non-native people that live and work along the Yukon, many of whom were born there and have family ties going back many generations, some to those that first met the First Nations. For an interesting and enlightening look at the situation and status of these Alaskan 'locals' and their backgrounds and relationships, albeit in the mid- to late-1970s, but still a seminal period in Alaska's modern development, read John McPhee's Coming to the Country. A beautifully written and acutely observed book that has influenced my subsequent view of Alaska and confirmed many of the observations I had already recorded. You may get bored of me referring to McPhee as we go along, but you won't get bored of his writing.

Back to Whitehorse, which I had previously heard described as being much like a port town but without a harbour, and which seemed particularly apt for my 48hrs there this time. Once a major staging post for the Gold Rush, it was the launching point for prospectors onto Lake Laberge downstream, and up north to Dawson City. Now the state capital of the Yukon Territory (it took the title from Dawson City in 1952), Whitehorse seems to exude a mix of aspirational state capital with the trappings of a rundown port. Like all towns across our globe that spend the majority of their existence frozen or under snow, they exude a naked starkness when exposed to the unremitting glare of the short-lived but intense summer sun. The downtown streets are wide and laid out in a grid system with a mixture of the older wooden planked buildings preserved for tourism. The former train station and the SS Klondike, one of the paddle steamers that used to ply their trade on the river between Whitehorse and Dawson, sit alongside more modern shopping complexes, hotels and local government buildings. On the edge of town are the large shopping malls, the drive-thru restaurants and the supermarkets you would expect to find in any North American town or city, all made for people with cars. The airport is conveniently close and sits up on a hill overlooking the town.

During my visits, Whitehorse seemed friendly enough but still held an edge, a feeling that maybe some places it wasn't wise to venture into. There appeared to be a 'them and us' aspect to Whitehorse. It has a number of trendier, touristy, bars and restaurants, some harking back to the Gold Rush days, some selling craft-ale and some offering vegan menus. (If you visit Whitehorse but don't fancy a trip into the 'bush' you could always check out the 98 Hotel Bar downtown where you can see pretty much all the large animals you're likely to encounter, or at least their heads, hanging from the walls).

There were also an obvious number of inebriated residents. Sadly, they were predominantly from the First Nations Peoples – more so this time during the festival – and they appeared to have their own bars or back alleys. I'm not wanting to comment on social aspects of cities and countries where

I was a guest, an obvious interloper, and despite my best intentions I was still just an adventure tourist like many others (and goodness knows we in the UK cannot point fingers when it comes to divisions and antisocial behaviour), but I couldn't help but pick up on an undercurrent of social and cultural disenfranchisement bubbling along here next to the silt in the Yukon River as it passed by Whitehorse. That said, I liked Whitehorse, it was real, and it provided me with everything I finally needed to start my trip.

At the practical level, perhaps the biggest early decision I had had to make was a bit of a no brainer, to be frank: this trip I had to make by canoe rather than kayak. If the journey were to take 35-45 days, there was no way I would get everything I'd need into a solo kayak. Whilst I had only limited experience of canoes, I knew I would want that extra capacity and steady comfort over a faster kayak and, for me in my dotage, avoid the crippling pain of being jammed into a cockpit for a protracted length of time. Two other bits of kit also came high on my 'middle-aged-comfort-list': a canoe seat with backrest and a decent camping chair. I learnt long ago that 'anyone can be uncomfortable in the field'.

I had already contacted Up North Adventures (the outdoor suppliers in Whitehorse who had rented me a kayak and some kit in 2017) and enquired about their line in used canoes. I knew that there was no way I could realistically (or cheaply) get a rental canoe back to them. So, buying was my only real option and hopefully second-hand would be affordable and suitable. It was – just. I also knew that I could get myself, my kit and the boat up to Dawson City on the Husky Bus. During my planning, cost remained a constant compromise and balancing the need to have the most suitable, safest and most reliable kit, against the expense of such was always an interesting trade-off. I could have spent a fortune, but there had to be a minimum cost that safely achieved the standard of kit that I would need. I just wasn't exactly sure what that standard was. So, although Up North Adventures would never be the cheapest, I knew that they'd be reliable and would look after me; they did.

The canoe I finally went for was a 'Nova Craft Prospector 16'. As the name suggests, it was 16ft long, but also a good 3ft wide. Weighing just 59lb, with a suggested capacity of 1000lb, it offered me plenty of room and stability. It was made of a substance branded as 'TuffStuff', a composite material made, according to the blurb, from "melted basalt rock and a polypropylene fibre, woven together into a cloth and infused with a high impact resin system". How on earth did anyone come up with that concept? Mind you, the thought that I would be paddling a boat made partly of rock did amuse me. It was advertised as a light canoe suitable for extended tripping with more than enough strength to handle lots of abuse in the back country. So ideal for me! It was red and still had the Up North Adventures decal stickers and large white rental number, 715, both front and rear which I toyed with removing, but ultimately concluded that they were part of the boat's character. I also thought, perhaps naïvely, that it would make the canoe harder to lose; hold onto that thought!

A lot of my other kit I bought from the huge Canadian Tire store in Whitehorse. For those of you who are not familiar with Canadian Tire stores, they sell everything you could possibly need for camping, fishing, boating, motoring, or your home and were as close to heaven when shopping as I thought it was possible to get! I could have bought anything from a gun, a hunting bow, an outboard motor, or a car jack to scented candles and office stationery all under one roof. It was a good job that I had to fit all my purchases into a backpack, otherwise any budget I may have had would have been easily blown, not to mention needing a bigger boat!

With all my kit purchased and packed, the evening before I left I treated myself to a 'last supper' of a large steak and a bottle of red wine in Giorgio's Cucina, just beside my hotel on Jarvis Street. During the meal I paid any outstanding debit card bills, sent my final messages and cleared any unfinished internet business from my phone in the expectation of having no need of it for the next month or more.

The Husky Bus ride the following day was thankfully uneventful. There were four other passengers, a young Canadian couple and two older women, all of whom were heading up to Dawson for a couple of days' sightseeing. Besides my boat, which our driver Mateus and I tied to the roof, and the kit and baggage of the other passengers, there were a number of large boxes being transported which made the 10-seater bus crowded. Given the indulgencies of my 'last supper' the previous night I volunteered to jump in the back, put on my headphones and promptly went to sleep. The ability to sleep at any and every opportunity was a necessary and important skill that I had learnt and adopted many years ago.

Toward the end of the bus trip the route follows the lower Klondike River with its almost lunar landscape scarred by over a hundred years of intensive gold mining. I awoke as we neared Dawson and one of the women asked me where I was intending to paddle to. Reluctantly, and predicated again by the words 'if the river lets me', I told her I was hoping to reach the Bering Sea. 'That'll be something to write home about' was her initial response followed by the bizarre observation that I would 'probably have skin like leather' by the time I finished!

Talking about writing home, and before I start the journey proper, I think it might be worth explaining why my trip has become a book. Ernest Hemingway famously said, amongst many other things, "It's none of their business that you have to learn to write. Let them think you were born that way."

Reluctant though I am to disagree with the great Ernest, I think it is worth me outlining how and why I have written this book. In the past I have found that longer journeys have a tendency to blend into a single memory, usually based around the prevailing weather conditions and day-to-day mishaps that make up the adventure. The existential experience, the personal mental pictures – those that constitute the real essence of the journey – have a propensity, like all memories, to blur, mutate or dissipate unless attempts are made to capture them as they happen. I had always intended to take some rough notes from this journey, notes that would provide my failing mind with joggers and cement memories for the future, but not a book. In all honesty, the idea that I should be writing a book for a potentially wider audience on a subject that was, I thought, already well explored (and also implicitly personal to me), seemed a little pretentious. I have, in the past, always marvelled, slightly suspiciously, at people who seem to have a story about almost everything. I guess for me my own inherent lack of confidence leads me to err away from telling people about my experiences and adventures. Surely life is about creating stories not telling them? Maybe not, maybe I'm changing!

I did not go to the Yukon River to write about it, I went to challenge myself and to experience the environment for my own, selfish, affirming, adventure. However, on my return home whenever I got anywhere near a desktop globe or a world atlas, I couldn't help but trace my route and marvel, quietly and proudly, at my achievement. I guess it's better to look back and think, 'Wow, did I really do that?', than to spend your life wondering if you could have. Whilst quietly proud of my achievement (and again not wishing to bore people with my adventure), my wife and her family did show an interest in my trip and encouraged me to write it down, initially with the thought 'if not for you, then maybe as a keepsake for your sons and their children'.

With this encouragement, I started writing, using my notes as a guide and adding some hopefully relevant details, a few favourite literary references and a smattering of personal thoughts and anecdotes with the aim of making this a little more interesting and informative. I also attempted to explain the more existential aspects of my journey and how these affected me as I tried to stay focused on my day-to-day life on the river. I have tried to keep my account light-hearted and not focus too much on the 'shitty' bits (an easy tendency when working in hindsight) but ultimately this is an account of the paddle as I saw and felt it. What it's most definitely not is a guide for future adventurers, nor is it a reference manual or an academic paper, unless you wish to read it as a dialectic study into the dangerous combination of a little knowledge, planning, know-how and determination, mixed with a worryingly prevalent level of incompetence, ineptitude and yet more stubborn determination: the recipe of my life!

To support my journal, I did endeavour to keep a photographic record of the trip but, given my level of expertise and the cameras I took, these were always going to be more holiday snaps than an artistic, insightful pictorial journal. I knew that without any real skill in photography – and with just a so-called 'smart phone' and a GoPro camera – I was unlikely to do justice to the majesty of the Yukon. And just as with the majority of my canoeing or kayaking photos (the ones my mother-in-law, bless her, always so readily bemoaned as boring), I knew that most of the picture were likely to feature the front of the boat, occasionally with a paddle blade inset for some perspective, with an expanse of nondescript water and some rolling hills or bluffs in the background. On my own, I was unlikely to give my pictures any life or perspective, although occasionally I did try filming myself and talking to the camera using a selfie-stick or small tripod. It's amazing how self-conscious you can still feel despite there being no one else within miles.

I did consider buying a small camera drone whilst in Whitehorse, thinking that this might be a way of capturing my remoteness on the river, but once I'd seen the price and was told I'd need to apply for a licence I quickly dropped that idea. Probably a good thing as I could see hundreds of dollars of equipment nosediving into the river on its first outing, never to be seen again, or sending up the drone whilst camped only to see a family of ravenous bears or a pack of wolves lurking beyond the shrubs next door. I do regret not having a decent camera and better knowledge to properly capture parts of my trip, but perhaps my biggest regret from my adventure was not taking more time to stop, study and think.

One more thing, if I may, before we dive into my story in earnest. Many years ago, I desperately tried to prove, and improve, my limited intellectual potential beyond the slack handful of 'O' Levels and CSE's I left school with aged 16. Although enough to get me into the Royal Marines as a recruit and then, four years later, to help me scrape through the Admiralty Interview Board and somehow gain a commission, it was very apparent that I needed more educating; the Royal Marines did their best, but it was clear I was always playing catch-up in the educational race. So, in 1999, I enrolled on an Open University degree course, but for a reason that still escapes me, rather than looking at a business or management degree to help me develop more role-appropriate skills, I plumped for a Humanities degree, focused on philosophy. The degree took me five years to complete, the first two years being fairly straightforward whilst in the UK, the last three (2001-2003) were a little more hectic as world events took many of us away from home for extended periods of time – some of whom sadly did not return as they left. Anyway, the upshot was that I came away with a BA(Hons) in Humanities with Philosophy – who'd have thought it!

As a result, I developed a previously underdeveloped appreciation of art, poetry and literature, 'stuff' that I had not previously been introduced to, or educated in, but I particularly enjoyed reading philosophy, with the logical enquiry of ideas and the nature of life and the human condition, perhaps something I had always been subconsciously interested in. More recently, I toyed with the idea of attempting a Masters in Philosophy and approached Professor Edward Skidelsky at Exeter University with an outline proposal to study 'Greed'. I went to Edward with this idea, partly because Exeter University is just up the road from my home, but primarily because I had just attempted to retire and had read his book How Much Is Enough, co-authored with his economist father, Robert. The book explores, from both a philosophical and economic perspective, why the economist John Maynard Keynes' 1930's prediction that by now, a century later, we would, in the west, all have the income and basic needs required to work no more than fifteen hours a week, so spectacularly failed. I found it a very enlightening read and would recommend it to anyone considering retirement or recently retired.

Edward encouraged my exploration and research into the nature of greed and inequality, but, as I delved deeper, I became overwhelmed by the scale, history and fundamentally intrinsic nature of greed; I dropped the idea. Paddling the length of the Yukon appeared to be a far easier challenge for me than trying to articulate anything useful to society about the nature of greed; maybe I should have another look at this. The point of me telling you this is that I will, without doubt, at times go off on the odd philosophical tangent, as is my wont. Please excuse me if I do – I'll try to warn you beforehand!

*View of frozen Lake Laberge from plane coming
into Whitehorse May 2017*

Inside the Westminster Hotel Bar Dawson City 2017

Dawson City

Dawson City was described to me by the Husky Bus driver when we drove back down to Whitehorse in 2017 as an 'end-of-the-road town'. It was just the two of us, the driver and me, making the road-trip south that time, so I sat up front and had an interesting and informative 8-hour chat. We discussed what she meant (apologies but I cannot remember her name) and concluded Dawson was now the sort of place that attracted people that wanted to get away from the 'mainstream'. I spent a little while mulling over the idea that people would choose to be alongside the mainstream that is the Yukon River in order to get away from their issues with the mainstream of modern western life. She added that, 'in Dawson we don't ask anyone their name or where they're from', a view that didn't appear to take the First Nation's perspective into account, since they were there long before the Gold Rush and the establishment of the current town and have less opportunity to get away from their 'mainstream', should they so wish.

In 1867, Russia sold Alaska to the US for $7.2 million, although many of the Native Peoples asserted that it wasn't really theirs to sell. In that same year, Canada (or The British Dominion of Canada as it was then) came into being setting the national boundaries that exist today. Thirty-two years later, two First Nations prospectors, Jim 'Skookum' Mason and Dawson Charlie, and a white man, George Carmack, who was married to one of their relatives, found gold in Bonanza Creek off the Klondike River. The infamous Klondike Gold Rush that followed had a short but evocative heyday. In the following two years, the settlement that was to become Dawson City went from a small First Nations fish camp to a bustling city of 40,000 people. A year later, the Gold Rush had ended, and the population plummeted to a fifth of that size. Dawson's fortunes waned after World War II; the new Alaska Highway bypassed Dawson 300 miles to the south and the city was not connected by road until 1955. Today Dawson sells itself on Gold Rush history, attracting tourists and end-of-the-road 'getaway' folks.

Dwayne, the pianist at the Sourdough Bar in Dawson, was a 'getaway' character. I first met him as I entered the bar after my trip in July 2017. The entrance from the street, from the dusty dirt-graded road, across the worn, wooden planked sidewalk was through chest high, swing doors. I entered from the bright sunlit street into the dark seclusion of the bar where

Dwayne was at his piano to the right of the door hammering out some popular tunes in that honky-tonk style redolent of classic western films. I enjoyed my entrance so much that I promptly turned around, went back out through the door, spun around on the sidewalk and entered again with my best John Wayne swagger, carefully allowing the doors to swing behind me without knocking me into the bar. I then looked more closely at the bar to see it full of rather rotund tourists wearing the ubiquitous North American tourist uniform; sandals and socks, chino shorts with bulging belts holding in neatly pressed collared T-shirts or short-sleeved Hawaiian shirts, and sunglasses propped on top of their baseball caps. Oh well, I enjoyed the initial illusion, so I had a couple of pints listening to Dwayne playing over the hubbub and watching the tourists queue to pay for the dubious privilege of drinking a shot of liquor from a glass containing a blackened severed big-toe and receive a certificate for the honour.

I had a quick chat with Dwayne during his break as he asked for musical suggestions. I resisted all the obvious 'hilarious' piano-related responses as he was clearly working the crowd for tips and probably would have completely missed the airing of the childish and inane comments rattling around in my head, most of which revolved around chimpanzees and PG Tips tea. It was only later that evening in the Westminster Hotel Tavern, a quirky but more authentic bar, that Dwayne and I struck up a proper, if drunken, conversation. Dwayne was about 5'6", skinny and probably my age (although it was difficult to tell) with thinning dark hair on top of a rather sad but mischievous-looking face. He spoke with a thick French–Canadian accent which was initially hard work for my delicate English ear (it didn't help that he was also drinking with an older 'family escapee' from Nova Scotia who spoke with a randomly mixed Scots and Irish accent). It took me a few more beers to get my ear in.

Dwayne told me he was a former concert pianist from one of the major Canadian cosmopolitan cities, I can't remember which one, and that he was now living in a shack in the woods across the river from Dawson. Each day he crossed the river to play at the Sourdough Bar and lived off his tips and a few handouts. He wasn't too specific in his reasons for quitting the metropolis, and in true Dawson fashion I wasn't going to pry, but I got the idea it was family related. He was good fun we hit it off, and had a lively evening in that drunken, stoned strangers, end-of-the-road town, sort of way. I certainly got to meet some of the more colourful Dawson characters, whether I wanted to or not. All had their reasons and stories as to how they ended up in Dawson and most, it seemed to me, had an underlying sense of sadness or loss.

On the morning I was due to catch the Husky Bus back down to Whitehorse, I popped into the Sourdough and gave Dwayne my unused and by then superfluous can of bear spray. I'd agreed to give it to him the night before and thought it would be more use to him in his shack in the woods than to anyone I would otherwise have left it with. He may still have been at his piano that evening as I set off on this trip. I think it's worth a quick note about the term Sourdough, as in the Sourdough Bar, here. The term has been used since the days of the Gold Rush to denote someone who has proven their ability to handle the hardships of the Yukon and Alaskan wilderness, particularly the winters. It was supposed that someone like this would by that point have their very own sourdough culture on the go which they would carefully and jealously nurture to help keep them fed. The opposite to a Sourdough is a Cheechakos: someone recently moved to the mining districts. Some say you need to have managed three winters (some maintain it's nearer twenty) before you can move from being a Cheechakos to becoming a Sourdough. Either way, it's clear that true life on the Yukon is really about surviving the winters and not some summer beano downstream in a canoe.

A typical street in Dawson City

So, here I was, once again, stood on the banks of the mighty Yukon River, gazing over that infamous body of tumbling silt-laden water, my intended home for the next six weeks or so. The Yukon at Dawson is only just over 200 metres wide, the same width as the Thames at Westminster, but in June, still 1340 miles from the Bering Sea, it is already powered by a host of renowned tributaries further upstream: the Teslin, the Pelly, the Stewart, the White and, here at Dawson, now also the Klondike River. For my part, my little red canoe was now loaded and ready to go at the river's edge. It sat there looking ludicrously tiny, transparent in the low evening sun, insignificant, and frankly absurd against the size and power of the river.

It was 6pm on Sunday 23 June 2019, just a few days after the solstice. It had been another brilliantly hot day; the sun was still intense and would be until very much later. It occurred to me that I could book into a hotel or bunkhouse and set off in the morning, but that would have been pure procrastination. To get back on the Yukon River was what all my planning over the previous year, and the travelling thus far, had been about. Besides, at the end of my last outing on the Yukon, I'd experienced a couple of nights in Dawson City, exploring the delights of the numerous bars and Diamond Tooth Gertie's Gambling Hall and, whilst a fun way to end a trip, the challenge that now lay ahead was uppermost in my mind.

As I stood by my boat taking a couple of photos of my still dry canoe with the rear-paddle steamer, the SS Keno, in the background I was shaking. A mixture of exhaustion and exhilaration at having finally, actually, arrived here again, mixed with the trepidation of what now lay ahead. Have I got everything I need? Will I be able to make it? Will I embarrass myself? Have I planned everything properly? All the way to this point, when anyone had asked me what I was up to, I felt reluctant to tell them. When I did, I still found myself couching my own (and therefore their) expectations in terms of 'if'; 'if everything goes to plan' or my preferred, reverential, response 'if the river lets me'. I was about to find out.

So, all I could do now, with shaking limbs, and to the cheers of a couple of slightly worse for wear locals that had appeared, like the shopkeeper from Mr Benn, alongside me on the bank, was get in my canoe and head downstream. Initially, I had just one aim in mind; not to capsize or sink within sight of Dawson City and my impromptu departure committee. If I could make it look like I knew what I was doing until I got around the bend downstream, beyond Moosehide Hill (the hill with a huge gouge in its side, shaped like a moosehide, overlooking Dawson), then I could, hopefully, relax a little and really start making things up for the next 1340 miles.

My shiny almost transparent canoe ready to launch on the banks of the Yukon at Dawson with the SS Keno in the background

That first evening I managed three hours on the river and quickly, unsurprisingly, remembered that it wasn't going to be a case of floating downstream with the odd piece of artful paddling. Whilst still relatively fresh, I was keen to work on my technique, so I started off properly, that is to say knelt down in the canoe, which, as a single paddler, I was effectively paddling back-to-front to offer better buoyancy and greater control. At least that was the idea. The first hour went fairly well: the current was swift and steady, I didn't embarrass myself within sight of Dawson and I seemed to have a degree of control over my direction and position on the river. Importantly, there was no sign of the larger craft which, occasionally, barrel up and down the river between Dawson and the town of Eagle, further downstream, up north, in

Alaska. According to my river guide these boats don't necessarily respect, or even see, lone paddlers in their little canoes. I was wary, but I wasn't going to go to the extent of wearing a tinfoil hat to make me visible to radar, as had been suggested. Dignity before safety at all times!

After an hour or so, a breeze picked up blowing in my face so, just as I'd practised back at home, I gracefully sat up and spun around on the canoe seat and then knelt down again, facing the opposite direction. This turned the canoe about and I started paddling from what would normally be the bow, which initially worked pretty well with the single paddle. However, I found that the rear of the canoe was now slewing and fishtailing behind me, making it difficult to make any real headway or keep a decent course. So, again, just as I had experimented at home on the windy Exe Estuary, I changed paddles and started to use the double-bladed kayak paddle that I'd bought in Whitehorse. Having a paddle blade working on either side rather than constantly changing the single paddle from hand to hand and side to side, certainly made it easier to hold my course and control the fishtailing, but it also meant that every time I raised the paddle I showered myself and the inside of the boat with river water, helped on its way by the headwind. Within those first three hours I'd worked out that a lot of the techniques I thought I could employ had a number of downsides and that, just as I'd expected, kneeling down to paddle for 8-12 hours a day for six weeks or more, was not a viable option for me in my dotage.

Having put in those initial few hesitant, but confirming, hours I decided to find a suitable spot to pull in for my first night ashore. I spied a likely-looking expanse of dry sand between two small, wooded islands far enough away from the forested banks of the river, I thought, to offer me a safe camping spot. I was hoping to use islands as much as possible on this trip in the hope that there would be less chance of meeting a bear than when camping in the forest along the banks. That's not to say that the bears cannot swim, they swim very well, it just meant that once I'd checked the island there would, hopefully, be less chance of a bear inadvertently wandering into my camp.

The stop commenced with the first iteration of a routine that I knew I would need to fastidiously and conscientiously conduct every time I stepped out of my boat, particularly if I was looking to stay for any length of time. Having hauled the boat up out of the water, far enough to hopefully stop it wandering off on its own, I grabbed my utility belt with bear spray and knife attached, the double-bladed kayak paddle and air horn. I gave a quick, self-conscious, blast on the horn to announce my presence and then set off to check the intended camping spot and surrounding area for any signs of recent bear activity: fresh paw prints, scat and/or scratch marks on the trees. There were plenty of tracks from a variety of critters, but none seemed fresh and there were no recent signs of bears that I could find. It became a note of ironic amusement for me throughout the rest of the trip that whenever I conducted these searches and despite my best efforts, having found no signs, shortly after setting up the tent I would invariably stumble across a huge bear paw print or two, usually too late for me to be arsed to pack everything away again.

As I started to set up camp on the sandbar with the river and spruce-lined islands on either side, I quickly became aware of a familiar tingling sensation coursing through my body and brain. This was not just the result of the days of travelling to get to this point or from those first few hours of paddling that evening, rather it was my body and my senses adapting to their new environment. My conscious mind was whirring in overdrive, working on the speed, distance, time calculations – pointless calculations – that would plague me throughout my early days. It was relating the mapping to the actual river and my surroundings; it was trying to remember where my kit was stowed and the best packing and unpacking routine to use; but most importantly, it was trying to work out what dangers were present. Beyond this and independent of any conscious control, my senses were excitedly working to support my brain's efforts. Without appreciation or control, my eyes were flicking between the close-up details of any work at hand and my immediate surroundings, and then extending their view to scan the distant tree line and further horizon. They were helping my brain answer some of its questions. What are the clouds doing? Is there anything that looks odd or dangerous? Why are there no straight lines anywhere?

At the same time, my ears were searching for different, unexpected and potentially alarming noises and my nose was sucking in the spruce-laden air, a hint of smoke, something more, something organic? The skin and fine hairs on my cheeks and the back of my hands were becoming sensitive to changes in air temperature and wind speed. My hands, still with a slight tremble, were working to feel their way and measure their strength, either to firmly grip and work the paddle without strain or quiver, or to work zips, knots, stove dials and electronic equipment confidently, dexterously and without fumbling. In my limbs I could feel the fizzing from the release of usually dormant chemicals and hormones: norephedrine, cortisol, testosterone. Readied to fight or fly, whilst still being consciously controlled to lift, push and move with purpose and direction. My stomach was tight, not full but firm within my core, which I was pleased to note felt strong and confident, and also readied for action. My spine was alert though tight at the shoulders from travelling and the paddle, tiredness and old injuries, and on the back of my head and neck, the fine hairs were also stood-to, searching the tree line behind me for hints and ideas of unwanted movement; for the notion of a bear.

In my chest, my heart was booming loudly – not quickly but strongly – and not just from the physical exertion, nor from my nervousness and sense of trepidation. It felt as if it were independently trying to understand and expand into its new environment, as if it were echo-sounding the surroundings. I could feel it almost thinking for itself, trying to connect with the nature that now surrounded it. Without checking every sensation or feeling at the time, I recognised and relished them. Despite my undoubted tiredness, I was alert, my mind and body were operating entirely as they should in an environment such as this. I knew that the conscious recognition of these sensations would subside over the coming days, beyond the three-day syndrome, those first few days as you adapt to a new environment and regime. But just then, at that moment, I was happy and confident in the knowledge that, subconsciously, my body and mind would be doing their job. They were protecting me. It felt good, very good.

That first night, once I was more settled and sitting outside my tent, was affirmative. I was glad I had set off that evening. I should have stayed there a little longer, soaking up the situation and contemplating life, but I was tired and I needed to sleep. It was nearly 11pm and while outside in the breeze it was a lovely balmy evening, inside the tent it was sweltering. In late June on the Yukon, north of Dawson City the sun doesn't rise, climb and set as it does at home. Instead, it transcribes a low circular path – an almost closed horseshoe – around the horizon, clockwise from just east of north, and back to just west of north, never reaching much higher than 45^0 in the sky to the south and only really setting behind the hills and trees. The Yukon was tilted closer to the sun than at any other time of the year and from its arc the sun was centre stage, not high, but piercing.

I tried to settle in the tent and ended up lying naked on my roll-mat, sweating. I had aligned the tent aerodynamically with the lower, foot-end, facing in the direction of the breeze so, naturally and logically, I opened the entrance flap by my head in the lee to allow in some cooler air. It certainly allowed the cool air in but with it, in the vortex created by the shape of the tent, came swirling gusts of fine sand. I quickly zipped the flap shut, spitting out a mouthful of sand and dust as I did so. Still sweating I then decided to open up the vents in the tent inner, under the fly sheet, to see if I could get enough air through that way to cool down even just a fraction. Another mistake. All that happened this time was that the wind blew plumes of super-fine sand and dust into the tent through the gauze vents. These plumes settled on my exposed skin, stuck to the sweat and formed a mucky, sticky layer of grime all over my prostrate body. I resorted to cutting up a cotton pillowcase that I had bought along for a little bit of luxury and using the two halves as sweat rags to cover my face and nether regions.

All I could do was lay there, trying to sleep, waiting for the heat of the sun to dissipate to a degree at which I could think about covering myself up more thoroughly and, hopefully, then sleep through the rest of the night. When I woke up an hour or so later, it was still light, but I was shivering. I dampened my improvised sweat rags to wipe off as much of the grime stuck to my skin as I could and got into my sleeping bag, donned an eye mask and settled in for the first such night in my tent. The sweat lodge situation lasted, on and off, well into late July and my roll-mat smelt of wet dog for the rest of the journey.

The tent I had chosen for this trip was a Vango Hydra 200, a lightweight, two-person tent with plenty of room in which I could spread my kit about and also sit up. Having the luxury of the extra space was useful, particularly given some of the extended periods I spent in it. Back in the UK, I would usually make do with a Gortex bivvy-bag, a waterproof, breathable, bag just big enough for me in my sleeping bag. While perfect for lightweight, short-term trips, it would be uncomfortable and difficult to sustain on a longer expedition, and not particularly sensible if bears are a concern. The geodesic design of the Hydra 200 made it relatively straightforward to erect and self-supporting, and therefore could be secured to the ground using whatever was available out on the sandbars and mudflats – driftwood, rocks or spadesful of mud – rather than relying on pegs and guy-ropes.

I had arranged my kit into what I referred to as 1st, 2nd and 3rd line kit. In reverse, the 3rd line kit was the stuff that I would not be needing to use day-to-day on the river: the clothes I wore flying to Canada and would hopefully wear home, along with my spares and repairs. This was contained in the large waterproof bag that I carried my kit over from the UK in and was stowed securely in the middle of my boat. The 2nd line kit was the stuff I would use day-to-day like my camping gear, tent, sleeping bag, changes of clothes, waterproofs, etc. These were spread through a number of smaller waterproof bags which I could readily grab as and when required. The 1st line kit was, effectively, the stuff I was wearing, my utility belt with the bear spray and knife attached, but also included the satellite phone, a set of spare warm clothes, a water purifying straw and the Jet Boil with a couple of days of food. The 1st line kit was stowed, when on the water, in a dry bag directly behind my seat in the hope that I could quickly grab it if, for some reason, I became separated from the boat and my other kit.

I had one other large bag in the boat, the heaviest of them all initially, which contained my food. Ideally this should have been kept in a rigid, bear-proof barrel but I made the decision that I didn't want to pay extra for one of those. This bag and the water container were stowed in the front of the canoe to counterbalance me and keep the boat trimmed as best I could. The general concept worked, but it took a few days to rationalise and sort out the daily loading and unloading to be as efficient and painless as possible.

In those first few days, as I settled into my paddle, as my body adjusted to life on the Yukon, and as I rationalised my stores and my pattern of life for the coming weeks, I remained focused on the practicalities of living and paddling in this new, wild environment. This practical focus, which I thought was important to my success and survival, was suddenly thrown into question as I rose from my slumber on my third morning on the river. I'd managed five hours reasonable sleep and felt relatively rested and relaxed, but as I threw back my tent flap to check what the day had to offer, my jaw dropped at the sight that greeted me. The morning was still and subdued with a slight chill, even though the sun had hardly dipped below the horizon that night, the hills were shrouded in fine layers of low cloud and the river was rolling gently under a wispy duvet of mist. The scene was really not much, and not necessarily beautiful, in so many ways – an expanse of sand and mud, the low nondescript spruce-covered hills and a lethargic Yukon – but in so many other ways it was stunning. It was wilderness encapsulated, an almost perfect distillation of the sublime aspects of the river, the country and the sky, all of which combined to present a picture that was, I guess, frankly to me that morning, breathtaking.

My experience and sensations up to this point had been predominantly physical and internal, based as they rightly were on making my adventure happen and staying safe, but now I was faced with a different sensation, a different experience. This was more existential and it caught me by surprise. I am not usually prone to hyperbole and generally lack the emotional intelligence and eloquence to properly digest and articulate such experiences – and I'd still not had my first coffee that morning – but what struck me very evidently, as I lay in the warmth of my sleeping bag, looking out at the Yukon River, was the fact that this trip was not going to be a simple case of doggedly plodding, paddling, along, which was my usual forte. No, there was going to be an awful lot more interaction between me, the river and the country than perhaps I had or should have anticipated. The scene which greeted me that morning, the vision of the nature that surrounded me in my little tent on a sandy island, pierced the thick body-armour protecting my soul and once compromised it was clear that the Yukon was going to pour in and saturate my being whether I liked it or not. The question that echoed about my skull that morning as I filtered my coffee and loaded the canoe was just how well equipped I was to manage the duality I now faced: could I adequately focus on my paddle and still comprehend the wonder of the world that now surrounded me?

I did promise that I would try to warn you if I was about to go off on a philosophical tangent, so here goes! Once on the water, as I gently paddled through the morning mist, idling occasionally to sup strong hot black coffee from my thermos and feeling a little more secure and settled on the gently rolling river, I had time to think and reflect and remembered, reading Edmund Burke's Philosophical Enquiry into the Origin of our ideas of the Sublime and Beautiful. In his 'Enquiry' Burke argues that "the ideas of the sublime and beautiful are frequently confounded" and this proposition seemed to resonate for me here, this morning, on the Yukon.

Burke proposed that a landscape can only arouse the idea of the sublime when it suggests power, particularly a power that is greater than our own and is also, in some way threatening, to us. This made sense to me. Whilst the country I was travelling through was not strictly beautiful in the same way as, perhaps, a formal landscape designed to appeal to our aesthetic response, it had more, much more to it, and this was the very real feeling that the river and the country held a power so much greater than my own. It chimes with James Michener's view of Alaska possessing both great beauty and implacable hostility. Burke further categorised the features that he believed constitute sublime landscapes, using terms such as 'vast', 'empty', 'dark' and 'apparently infinite', most of which certainly applied here. Although, personally, I would have added 'wildlife' to this list, especially bears, for they are part of the landscape of the Yukon and constitute a threat with power greater than my own which only added to the feeling of awe and therefore, arguably, the sense of the sublime.

As it was still late June and therefore did not get dark, the Yukon, that morning, and throughout the rest of my paddle, fitted most of Burke's concept of the sublime. One question remained for me, however, as I paddled contented and thoughtfully that day: just how, in 1757, did Edmund Burke, a young man in his twenties, that had not travelled much from his native Ireland (other than to London), never mind met a bear in the wild, manage to conceptualise and articulate an idea that seemed so apt for a country that must, in his time, have been beyond his ken?

*Midnight sun on the Yukon somewhere
between Eagle and Circle*

Why the Yukon?

Journal 25 June 2019: I have to assume that today the Yukon has been testing me! I had a steady start on a calm river in pleasant sunshine, but that soon turned into an overcast windy day with random thunderstorms. The wind was producing white tops on the water as it blew against the current. I had a couple of wobbly bits and decided to pull over, which is when the wind died down! The last few hours paddling were fairly pleasant. I did not stop at my first landing spot as there were too many tracks; moose, wolf and some old bear prints. I moved to this next island and was immediately attacked by mossies so I've jumped into the tent, and now the thunder has started again, so to sleep, hopefully a cooler night, and let's see what tomorrow brings.

At this point you may be asking yourself why this middle-aged man with a comfortable life and lovely family home within staggering distance of several friendly real-ale pubs, would want to go and put himself through all the planning, travelling and expense to be exposed to the privations of paddling and living along the Yukon River through Canada and Alaska. For as long as I can remember – probably from my days as a Cub Scout with the particularly energetic 1st Waltham Cross Pack, either on the evenings in our leaky Nisson hut next to the looming gasometer on York Road, or more likely when out on our various fun-filled camping, climbing, kayaking and hill walking expeditions – I'd been captivated by the idea of being dropped off in the middle of the boreal wilderness, particularly the North American forests, and left to fend for myself and find my way out. This was second only to wanting to be a member of crew of the Calypso and go diving with the famous French undersea explorer, Jacques Cousteau.

No doubt these ideas were partly inspired by some of the 1970s TV programmes about early 19th century North American voyageurs and fur trappers, such as James A Michener's Centennial or the iconic Canadian Beachcombers series, set amongst the inlets and forests of Vancouver Island. I remember watching these religiously with my siblings and a random selection of waifs and strays on Sunday lunchtimes in the back room of the local Conservative Club, while lime and soda and packets of crisps were passed through the hatch from the main bar where the adults were.

Back then, maybe not as a boy scout but certainly a few years later, after I'd joined Her Majesty's Royal Marines and was unintentionally and undramatically working my way through what ended up as a thirty-year career, I was confident enough that I'd have the know-how to make it work and I wanted to test myself. Sadly, whilst serving, I neither found the time nor the determination to make any of my personal plans happen. Subsequently, I was plagued by that classic cliché of 'dodgy knees' from a relatively young age, albeit I had put them and the rest of my body through the wringer a few times. Young enough for consultants to insist that it was too soon for replacements in case I wore them out, but old enough that the pain and discomfort slowly undermined my quality of life, I found myself steering away from activities that involved walking, running and (eventually) standing. As a result, I took up cycling and kayaking to try to keep fit, get out and about, seek adventure and test myself. I subsequently had a knee replacement at the tender age of 51, after leaving the Marines, and haven't looked back since. If you suffer with dodgy joints, take my advice and, if you can, get them replaced, rather than suffer a slow, insidious corrosion of your quality of life.

So, kayaking became my 'thing' and my early ambition to walk through the forest became one of wanting to paddle through it. Eventually, I was provided with the perfect opportunity in 2017, after a family holiday in Canada visiting our son, and with the permission – if not the explicit approval – of my wife, the Yukon River it had to be.

During those years, prior to retirement, and before I found the time or determination to fulfil my dream, I made do with the odd kayaking trip, either near home in the West Country, or further afield in Wales or the west coast of Scotland. But to remind me that there was still more to do, I carried with me a quote, one that I found by accident many years ago and had routinely pinned to any desk or computer that I had to work at. More recently, I had it 'Fabloned', stuck back-to-back, with a photograph of my feet warming by a campfire with a bottle of whisky, whilst pulled over on a kayaking trip around the Isle of Arran. I had the quote printed on the back of the mapping I produced for this trip, again to remind me of why I was here (as if I needed it). Having carried the words with me for many years, I only recently discovered that this passage is the work of the American author, environmentalist and anarchist Edward Abbey (1927-1989) and is taken from a speech he delivered to fellow eco-activists in Colorado in 1976. This advice has helped keep me sane and grounded through many a difficult time and place.

> *"One final paragraph of advice: Do not burn*
> *yourselves out. Be as I am, a reluctant enthusiast, a*
> *part time crusader, a half-hearted fanatic. Save the*
> *other half of yourselves and your lives for pleasure*
> *and adventure. It is not enough to fight for the land;*
> *it is more important to enjoy it while you still can*
> *and while it's still there. So, get out there and hunt*
> *and fish and mess around with your friends, ramble*
> *out yonder and explore the forest, encounter the*
> *grizzly, climb the mountains, bag the peaks, run*
> *the rivers, breath deep the yet sweet and lucid air,*
> *sit quietly for a while and contemplate the precious*
> *stillness, that lovely mysterious and awesome space."*

Edward Abbey (1976)

I could relate to this advice, and the idea of being a reluctant enthusiast, a part-time crusader and a half-hearted fanatic suited my character and my outlook on life. But I do understand that to some who cannot see beyond the words this may seem like a 'cop-out philosophy', a philosophy that offers ambiguity and commitment wriggle room and I have had more than one interesting conversation, usually with some crusty senior officer about the 'example' that being a self-confessed, reluctant, half-hearted, part-timer might offer. For sure, there has been many a time in my military career where there has been absolutely no room for ambiguity in aim, purpose or action, but just because certain circumstances dictate such focus it still doesn't follow that being a fanatic or crusader are necessarily correct or effective. Surely the more effective enthusiasts, crusaders and fanatics are those that can contextualise their cause and are able to see the different angles and aspects to their argument or fight. I think this is what Abbey is getting at because he was certainly a fanatical crusader when it came to the environment, but at the same time he loved the American southwest that he was fighting for, and he understood that to really love that land and persuade others to follow you needed to get out and understand it; any enjoyment being an added bonus.

I have read a few of Abbey's books since finding out that he was the author of this 'final paragraph of advice' that I had been carrying with me for so long and would suggest that within his fiction, particularly the anarchic environmentalist romp The Monkey Wrench Gang, he permits some of his, clearly self-reflective, protagonists to take on the roles of the unerring fanatics and crusaders, saving the more reasoned, persuasive side of his eco-activist zeal for his lectures and talks. For myself, I have always been wary of the SIFs (Single Issue Fanatics), those people that have only one idea, one approach and one solution; people who in steadfastly trying to meet their goal will usually entirely miss the bigger picture, invariably walk over other people to get what they think they want and inevitably never succeed in their singular mission; the sort of people that would happily sink the ship with all hands for their want of being the Captain. I wonder why I decided to paddle solo!

Now, retired, with self-inflicted time on my hands, I was determined to selfishly, but considerately, enjoy myself and to 'run' the Yukon River whilst I still could and whilst it is still there. I most certainly did not set off to escape from anything, or to 'find myself', although this was a worrying possibility at the back of my mind; goodness only knows what I'd find, or more pertinently, not find! It was just an adventure, a challenge; it seemed like a good idea and was exactly the sort of thing that I had always had in mind and which I took redundancy and early retirement to have a go at. Although it very nearly didn't happen. A few years back someone cunningly and thankfully sowed a brain-worm in my soggy head. I can't remember who it was and I'm not sure whether I should thank him or not, but the 'advice' stuck.

'Rich' he said, 'when you retire from the Royal Marines you will be young enough and hopefully still fit enough to go off and fulfil all those adventures you've put on hold whilst committed to your job, but there is also a very good chance that you will be offered work that will be very similar to the sort of thing you'll have been doing just before retirement. That work will be challenging enough, rewarding and well paid and you'll spend the next ten to twenty years happily working and enjoying a good steady life. However, there is then a very strong possibility that you'll hit your sixties or seventies and suddenly realise that you're then too old to do the sort of things you wished you had done and you'll be left wondering why you just wasted the opportunities of the last decade or so'.

Again, this was advice that I could also relate to and it chimed with the 'final paragraph of advice'. I was determined not to fall into the 'it's easier to work' trap. I subsequently took redundancy and fell straight into that trap. I was offered a role with a charity, initially for six months, which was enjoyable and very rewarding, but the brain-worm kept eating away at me. After four good years with the charity – years that flew past – I bit the bullet and quit, determined not to 'waste' what remained of my fifties and relatively good health but to follow that 'one final paragraph of advice' and give myself to travel and adventure.

In trying further to understand and describe my motivation, I was particularly struck by Evelyn Waugh's description of why Eric Newby felt he needed to take a Short Walk in the Hindu Kush in his introduction to Newby's book of the same name. Waugh points out that Newby was no sailor when he embarked as a merchant seaman to work 'before the mast' on the four-masted Finnish barque, the Moshulu, in 1938 heading for Australia, and no mountaineer when he decided to leave his comfortable job in the London fashion industry to climb Mir Samir in the Hindu Kush. Waugh, in a foreword to a version of Newby's book, suggests that seeking adventure is a rather English thing to do; "It was the longing, romantic, reasonless, which lies deep in the hearts of most Englishmen, to shun the celebrated spectacles of the tourist and without any concern with science or politics or commerce, simply to set their feet where few civilized feet have trod".

For me, the Yukon seemed to fit that bill as well. I didn't have a good rationale or reason to undertake my journey and I really did not want to be a tourist, it was just a longing, something that I had wanted to do for a long time, and I am, as I keep proving to myself, undeniably English and would be taking my inherent 'Englishness' down the Yukon with me.

One final piece of explanation regarding the Yukon if I may, before I return to my paddle, I think it is worth me stating that predominantly when I refer to the Yukon here, I am referring to the River Yukon and not the Canadian Territory known as The Yukon. The Canadian Yukon Territory comes with its very own 'idea' born of the Gold Rush and the words of Jack London and Robert Service, an idea that has led many a young reader to visualise a compelling but naïve ideal. An ideal of the implacable Royal Canadian Mounted Policeman establishing and upholding the law in a wild country, of courageous frontiersmen and women combating the elements to carve out new lives, of exotic natives and dangerous wildlife. The Yukon Territory is certainly some of these things, even if the reality is more prosaic than the dubious but evocative fiction.

The Yukon River is now generally accepted to begin at the Llewelyn Glacier at the southern end of Lake Atlin in British Columbia, about 100 miles south of Whitehorse. It then flows for just shy of 2000 miles, through the Yukon Territory, across into Alaska and finally joins with the Kuskokwim River to flow into the Bering Sea through the Yukon–Kuskokwim Delta. This makes it the third longest river in North America and the 23rd longest in the world. It actually travels in a north-westerly direction for it first thousand miles or so, which explains the constant confusion in saying I'm heading downstream, and up north. The river crosses the Arctic Circle for a short while at its halfway mark near Fort Yukon, before turning west across central Alaska, then heading south, and finally hooking north again around the bottom of the Nulato Hills and up into the delta and the Bering Sea.

The word Yukon is believed to be derived from the First Nation word for white water, which in turn relates to the colour of the glacial run-off that feeds the river throughout its journey, although from my experience the Yukon was predominantly the colour of weak tea. Its drainage area, the Yukon Basin, covers an area of 330,000 square miles, an area nearly twice the size of the UK. There are well over 40 rivers and tributaries that feed directly into the Yukon and many more that feed into those, which together add up to a mighty river. Despite its length and capacity, the Yukon drops just 640 metres between Whitehorse and the Bering Sea making it navigable by boat for those few precious months when it is not frozen. Whilst I did not endeavour to find out personally, the Yukon is said to be 10-15 metres deep in the navigable channels but can be as shallow as two metres in very low water conditions. In certain sections, and in rapids where swirl holes may exist, it can be as deep as 40 metres.

The Yukon Basin can be frozen for up to for seven months of the year and the whole area is underlaid by permafrost. Permafrost is a much-misunderstood substance, as it is frozen soil rather than ice, but despite this it acts like ice and spreads using a process of crystalline growth. Permafrost underlies the ground throughout the Arctic region in those areas never covered by glacial ice and varies in thickness from just a few feet to over 600 metres in parts of northern Russia. This makes the whole area prone to flash floods, as flood water is unable to penetrate the layer of permafrost. Recently this situation has become more unpredictable as steadily rising global temperatures are not only melting the permafrost but also causing more erratic melting of the snow and ice, which, in the spring, creates more flooding, erosion and damage from river-borne ice and debris. In the dry summer months, global warming manifests itself in the increased incidence of forest fires.

I was not on the Yukon long enough to be able to offer any first-hand testimony to the effects of climate change, but I did witness some exceedingly large forest fires and also the melting of the permafrost along one particular bluff where the bank had been cut away by the river. I could see the permafrost formed thousands of years ago, glistening and peaty black as it was exposed to the sun and melting into the river. Sadly, I didn't smell any rotting flesh and therefore was not lucky enough to see a newly exposed and defrosting mammoth carcass, but more and more preserved remains of these giants are being given up across the expanse of the subarctic northern hemisphere by the now melting permafrost. I'm most definitely not a fan of global warming but seeing a recently de-frosted mammoth would have been pretty cool; the pun is entirely unintentional! If you'd like to read more about the devastating effects of the spring ice melt read Adam Weymouth's account of his meeting with Andy Bassich (of TV Reality Show Life Below Zero fame) and read about how Andy lost his house, his dogs and almost his life to the river near Eagle back in the spring break-up of 2009.

A sublime misty morning on the banks of the Yukon

Getting to Know
the Yukon

JOURNAL 26 JUNE 2019: It's now 8pm and I'm sat in a towel by a fire with a blazing sun on my back, this really can mess with your head, effectively the sun here is at its highest at about 6pm. Today has been a good day, on the water at 6am with decent weather and a better attitude from me, well to start with anyway. Having to stop early yesterday forced me to have a good night's sleep and when I woke up this morning and got on the water I was more relaxed than previously. I have to stop calculating how long I think the whole trip will take based on 3 days' worth of paddling.

The Yukon beyond Dawson is very similar to the 400 or so miles south upstream from Hootalinqua, the paddle I had completed in 2017. As the river meanders and curls its way north through the 600-million-year-old landscape, it negotiates a geologist's wet-dream of bluffs, outcrops and cliffs. I won't even pretend to know what all the various formations were other than to reassert the fact that there is something about the river and its relationship with the surrounding environment that touches you at a deeply subconscious level. The emotions I felt remained compelling, but I had work to do; within its meandering path through the hills and forests, the river carries its own inner dynamic, a myriad of currents snaking and twisting within the water itself. Reading these currents and recognising the path of the main weight of water requires concentration but can really help a paddler cover the miles more easily.

In 2017, paddling a kayak with a rear rudder was a real joy, once my eye was in. I didn't need to compensate or steer with my paddle to stay on track, I just needed to maintain some forward momentum and use my feet to work the rudder levers and ride the current. Catching the current as it swept around the outside of the numerous long bends felt good, even as the mudstone bluffs above were being eroded by the river and landslides of earth and rock would roll down toward you. Occasionally these were accompanied by a tree or two sliding, still upright, from the top of the bluff, reminiscent of the landslide scene from The Railway Children. Or the times when I was escorted by squadrons of Bank Swallows that would exit the nest holes that pockmarked the bluff looking very much like Star Wars X-wing fighters scrambling from their base to see off this bizarre alien intruder that was getting too close to their homes.

Riding the current in the canoe was not so easy. As a flat-bottomed craft, without any form of skeg or rudder, it was more suspectable to the forces on and above the surface of the water, predominantly the wind. The river's current produces swirling eddies on either side of its path and without being able to stick to the flow, as I could in the kayak, the canoe was often spat out when its nose was caught in one of these vortices. Even so, the advantage of being in the flow was worth the constant adjusting and correcting; to feel the boat being propelled along was particularly good for morale. To put it the other way around, slogging your guts out and feeling as if you were stationary when not in the current was a bitch. Add to this any decent wind and the canoe was often at risk of being out of control. I used the first 250 miles up to Circle to perfect my paddling and thoroughly enjoyed the scenery, the camping, the information within the river guide and the chance to settle into an early rhythm on the Yukon. This was effectively my rehearsal and training for what lay ahead.

Over the course of the first week or so I also developed a few paddling 'rules of thumb' to support my reading of the river to aid me in quickly – and, hopefully, safely – making the right decisions as to when and whether to set off or continue. The first key rule was that I would not set out on the river if I could see that the back of the main current was up. I worked out through a little trial and error that if I could see permanent white tops on the back of the current, even if it were some way off toward the middle of the river, the conditions for paddling were probably not suitable for me on my own. Often, when the wind was against the flow, the river would appear as if it had been annoyed and it would have its back up much like that of an aggressive, snarling dog. I'm sure that if I were double-handed and paddling with a partner we could have coped with some of these conditions, but for me on my own the white tops signalled conditions that would put me in danger of being swamped or driven into places I didn't want to go.

I spent many a frustrating hour and the occasional day stood by my boat on a windswept foreshore wistfully looking out at the water, wishing for the white tops to disappear. On an early occasion (and there was only the one other, when I was, for whatever reason I cannot remember, a little desperate) when I did put out in such conditions, I experienced an exhausting, panic-ridden, rollercoaster of a ride as I tried not to let my boat get blown sideways against the swell whilst keeping on track for an island a few hundred metres downstream. It didn't take the brains of an archbishop to work out that the limited reward was not worth the risk. I had to work extremely hard to be Zen about the conditions, whilst whiling away the time waiting for the wind to drop. The frustration at watching the occasional skiff shoot up or down the river or seeing pieces of deadwood drift by as I sat stranded on the bank was, at times, almost unbearable. Mind you, when I saw just how well wrapped up the occupants of the skiffs usually were, crouching behind the improvised windshields and bouncing around wildly, I was less tempted to join them. Additionally, telling myself that I was being overtaken by deadwood (the key word being 'dead') lessened my desire to compete with the flotsam as well. The weather was going to be my guide.

In those long, hot, late June days I quickly found my stride and some peace of mind in the canoe, paddling along with just a thin layer of moulded granite and plastic between me and the rolling water of the Yukon. My body was, on the whole, adjusting to life on the river; I had my kit stowed more efficiently and my camping gear where I needed it; and I was revelling in the use of my wooden 'Grey Owl' paddle. That paddle was, without doubt, my most providential and ultimately serendipitous investment of the trip. I had initially picked up a cheap, moulded plastic paddle and the double-bladed kayak paddle from the Canadian Tire store in Whitehorse, just as I'd planned. As with most of the kit that I bought in Whitehorse, I knew I wouldn't be taking it home, so I was rather circumspect about how much I wanted to spend – a perverse incentive given my plans! However, as I was finalising the payment for my canoe in the Up North Adventures store, I casually looked over their collection of beautiful wooden canoe paddles and, being dizzy with the spending of those few days, thought I'd treat myself to a backup paddle. As dozy and short-witted as ever, my rationale for buying the lovely-looking wooden paddle was that it looked incredibly cheap for the obvious quality. It was only as I was paying for it that I realised the '60' sticker referred to its length in inches rather than the price in Canadian dollars. The actual price was probably three times as long! Having committed to buying the paddle – and not wanting to give the young lass serving me any more indications that I was, in fact, a numpty who really shouldn't be allowed to paddle the Yukon on his own – I casually handed over my credit card. I'm sure she saw right through me, and if she did, I certainly wouldn't want to play her at poker. I think she was pleased with the sale. I started using the Grey Owl paddle on my third day on the water and, compared to the cheap plastic one which was actually too short for me and whose rough moulded edges would have left my hands blistered throughout the trip, it was a revelation. It felt so natural to use and had the balance, length and finish to make paddling easier and more efficient. It is the only physical memento I brought home from the Yukon, but even that was touch and go when it didn't arrive on the baggage carousel at Gatwick.

I was starting to sleep well when the temperature allowed and was managing all my various age- and lifestyle-related aches and pains. I had also stopped constantly trying to calculate my speed and time: I was in no hurry. I had deliberately chosen not to book any return flights for the end of my paddle, partly because I didn't know where or when that might actually be, but primarily so that I would not have to work to an imposed deadline that could detrimentally affect my decision-making later in the paddle. There was no rush, life was good. I had time to think!

So, with the semblance of a routine established, and the time to think that that provided, I began to mull over some of the wider implications and experiences inherent in my journey: some of those reflective feelings I had already been experiencing; the sense of the sublime I had previously recognised. I came to realise that I was almost constantly, mentally balancing the day-to-day, hour-by-hour practicalities of my paddle – of living alongside the Yukon and my aim of getting to the Bering Sea in one piece – against the immense and potentially overwhelming experience, the sheer sense of majesty innate in the space I was negotiating. It was an all-encompassing feeling that seemed fundamentally true yet still frustratingly illusive. It was a vague sense of being part of something much bigger, much older and very real, but it was also something that I could push to the back of my mind when focusing on staying safe and keeping busy working toward my goal.

Keeping busy, or sharing a joke with friends, are the usual tactics I employ to stave off such existential thoughts and experiences, but here on the Yukon, on my own in the 'bigger' spaces, those crutches were not available to me. Here those thoughts about life, existence and one's true size could, in the quiet moments, creep up on you and catch you unawares. As such, during my trip, these thoughts became interwoven within my almost constant sense of concern, the ever-present, real and focusing fear that something bigger – the river itself, or something with big pointy teeth and claws – was out there waiting for me to mess-up. Whilst that sense was always there, it was not until I finished my trip and finally felt truly safe that, perhaps, I have been able to examine the real scope of my experience.

In those early days, as a consequence of feeling that I was at the mercy of something bigger and potentially threatening, I was extremely reverential toward my surroundings. In fact, my deference probably bordered on some form of obsessive paranoia as I thought and hoped that if I displayed sincere and obvious respect for the river and my surroundings, it would respond in kind – or, possibly, more pertinently, that any sign of disrespect would be met with suitable retribution. At that stage I was happy to take any help I could get. I would doff my hat and pay my salutations to all and any crossing ravens to seek their favour, just as we would do to the crows back home when I had the privilege of salmon netting on the Exe Estuary. Back home saying, 'G'day, Mr Crow', was a superstitious act to help with the fishing, so now on the Yukon, I adopted, 'G'day Mr Raven', as a way of seeking help and detering any unnecessary bad luck.

I did not know at the time (although I sensed it, knowing that ravens are one of the most mythologised creatures in northern cultures), but in the Alaskan Native Distant Time stories the raven is the creator of their world. In his work Make Prayers to the Raven, the cultural anthropologist Richard K Nelson quotes one of the Koyukon hunters he stayed with – the Koyukon tribal area covers the Yukon and Koyukuk Rivers centred around the settlement of Galena – as saying "It's like talking to God, that's why we talk to the raven. He created our world."

It wasn't just the approbation of the spirits of fauna I was after, though, I also found myself carefully digging up the flora, tufts of grass from the proposed footprint of my tent, and relocating them with some water to again petition the goodwill of the spirits of the Yukon. Little did I know then that a few weeks later I'd be cursing the ravens out loud for their lack of help and be furiously and impatiently kicking the vegetation away from my campsite whilst plagued by flies and mosquitoes. By which point in my journey, I was well and truly imbued with the bitter resignation that I was on my own and as such the owner of my own good or bad fortune, well most of it at least. There still remained that lingering, untouchable sense that there were bigger forces at work somewhere out there, I was just trying to ignore them! But as Richard K Nelson also wrote of the Koyukon people of northwestern Alaska, "Traditional Koyukon people live in a world that watches, in a forest of eyes. A person moving through nature – however wild, remote, even desolate the place maybe – is never truly alone. The surroundings are aware, sensate, personified. They feel. They can be offended. And they must, at every moment, be treated with proper respect".

> **JOURNAL 23 MAY 2017:** I've noticed whilst paddling that I'm starting to get used to the sights and sounds. It is strange how many times I've thought I'd seen buildings in the trees only to find that they were fallen trees. Likewise with the noises – equating them to human voices and machinery. I think that coming from a human urban environment it's what my brain expects to see and hear and therefore, initially, equates shapes and sounds to.

I remembered how long it took my rather dull senses to become accustomed to the sights and sounds of the river and forest when I undertook my previous trip. Starting from Johnson's Crossing rather than Whitehorse was a blessing, and kayaking on the Teslin River, with the last remnants of the ice from Lake Teslin, was a real treat, even if it did rain for the first few days and I was terrified that I was going to sink in my ridiculously overloaded and poorly-packed kayak. The top end of the Teslin is narrower, more enclosed and relatively slow moving with a pleasant nature – at least it was when I was on it. On the Teslin you can quickly become immersed in the surroundings, as opposed to being distanced from them or hugging the banks for comfort on the beast that is the Yukon in its latter stages. This meant that I could more quickly adapt to being on the river, and to its sights, sounds, movement and approaching conditions.

In 2017, I quickly became accustomed to the noises of the ice, whether the polystyrene 'squeak' as my kayak nosed its way through the floes floating downstream with me, or the tinkling of the icicles left dangling along the bank after the ice had disappeared and which rippled xylophonically in my wake. Before long I could gauge the impending approach and direction of the winds from the change in the texture and direction of the corrugation on the river's surface, or from the change in colour of the riverside foliage as the lighter, silver undersides of the willow leaves were exposed in the distance by the prevailing wind. This was occasionally accompanied, in the close river of the Teslin, by the eerie psithurism of the wind in the trees and the occasional deep wooden wind-chime, or glockenspiel sound, produced by the knocking together of the tops of the spruce.

More disconcertingly, once pulled over, was the sound of the water bubbling along the shoreline, particularly when camped by a creek, which, at times, sounded unerringly like people chatting, like the sometimes relaxing, sometimes irritating background hubbub at a party or in a bar. It was the sort of sound that makes it impossible to hear what a charming female guest may, for whatever reason, be trying to tell me, and usually results in me grinning inanely whilst focusing disconcertingly upon her lips in a vain attempt to nod in agreement or laugh indulgently at the right time in the conversation without a clue as to what's being said. Thanks to Gavin Pretor-Pinney's brilliant book The Wavewatcher's Companion I now understand the science as to why it's almost impossible for someone like me, with a large misshapen swede on top of my shoulders, to fully comprehend the higher pitched voice when the soundwaves get lost in the lee created by the random shaped island that is my head.

Mind you, there was one instance on my first trip, after four days without seeing anyone, when I thought I had heard voices and assumed it was the river playing tricks again only to discover it was, actually, real people! In fact, it was a couple of young German guys in a ridiculously overloaded double kayak, which made me feel better about the state of my own boat. I had pulled over at Hootalinqua, the former paddle steamer administrative station at the confluence of the Teslin and the Yukon and was in the process of drying out my kit in the purpose-built and much appreciated shelter that was situated in amongst a theme-park like array of dilapidated huts. I had concerns about bears given that Hootalinqua looked like a well-used stopover, so had a particularly good scout about and, whilst I saw some older tracks, I found nothing that worried me unduly.

The German guys, having initially said hello, told me that they were recceing the river with a view to leading tours over the forthcoming summer. They had a quick look about the station before coming back to me to tell me that they were trying to 'put the miles in' and left without further ado. I thought nothing of their quick departure until I unexpectedly met them again the following morning as I pulled in for a break further downstream. They were at one of the recommended campsites and were just getting ready to set off. Before I'd managed to land, and without offering a helping hand, they asked if I'd seen any bears the previous evening saying that they'd seen some large fresh paw prints near my location. I thanked them for so kindly letting me know the day after their sighting, whilst quietly questioning to myself their ability to lead tours if they couldn't let me know what they'd seen at the time. Not to mention their clearly limited ability to 'put the miles in' given I'd caught them in a single kayak within a couple of hours that morning. Perhaps they were hoping I would have been attacked by a bear so they would have a story for their tours!

One sound that particularly perplexed me on my first trip, and to this day I haven't successfully explained, was a thudding sound like someone trying unsuccessfully to start an outboard motor. An initial slow thud, as if the starter cord were being pulled, was followed by a quick, much faster, beating like the engine kicking in, only to abruptly come to a halt. There were no boats about and I only ever heard the sound in camp, particularly when tucked up in my sleeping bag, when it seemed to reverberate through the ground. I initially thought it must be rabbits, or hares, clearly harking back to some subconscious memory of watching Thumper the rabbit friend of Bambi! Not having seen any rabbits or hares, I thought it more possible that, perhaps, it was beavers, banging their tails, either in warning or to cement their dams, somewhere underground near where I was lying with the sound reverberating for me to hear. I only heard the sound once whilst in Alaska and I have still not confirmed its origin.

There was also a bird that sounded uncannily like a mobile phone. More than once it had me stop to look for someone receiving a call, even though I knew there was no one for many miles and there was no signal either. But perhaps the noise that startled me most and had me lying awake in my tent listening on tenterhooks, waiting for a large, clawed paw to rip through the flimsy fabric, was a very distinctive deep growling. It took me some time to work out that, whilst the noise was most definitely a low grumbling ursine growl, it was not in fact from any large predatory beast but, embarrassingly, coming from my stomach. There were also times when I thought I could hear scraping outside the tent only to realise that it was the noise of my own toes wiggling in the bottom of my sleeping bag. It amazed me how time and again I could feel so detached from my own body. My mind would be focusing on one thing, normally trying not to listen for sounds outside the tent, seemingly unaware that my body was doing its own thing without the two sharing the information. Occasionally, the two did talk, and when they did it was usually an argument in which my mind wanted to do more, but my body had decided it had had enough. Too often, of late, I have found, to my cost, that my brain still thinks I am 25. It would be fair to say, as a result, that my body thinks I'm an idiot!

Paddling and living on your own for extended periods of time in an unfamiliar and potentially hostile environment is as much a mental challenge as a physical one. Whether that be recalibrating your urban-orientated brain toward the sights and sounds of the wilderness, dealing with the isolation and feelings of being out of control when stormbound, or instilling the order and self-discipline required to push on or stop at the right time and to carry out those routines that, whilst boring, will keep you safe. Luckily for me I've never been gifted with too much imagination and still, just, have a modicum of the physical and mental rigour that was drilled into me over my years in the military. So, I was unlikely to get too het up by the imaginary 'what ifs', although those early noises 'outside' the tent and latterly the hours (and occasional days) stranded on the shores of the Yukon, did require some serious soul-searching, a degree of communion with my situation. But, ultimately, if nothing else I proved to myself yet again that I have a remarkable gift for stubborn, dogged, uneventful 'plodding on'.

The state of my canoe in the early days - it remained like this throughout

*Early days on the river following
Mike Rourke's river guide*

Crossing the Border

Back on the Yukon, it took just a couple of days from Dawson to reach the Canada–US border. The delineation between the two countries was well marked by a stark straight line on my map, but on the ground it was not so obvious. It actually appeared as an overgrown break in the forest running down from the hills to my right and continued, almost exactly opposite, off into the trees on my left. There were a few tatty flags – Canadian and American, I assumed, although again it wasn't clear – flying limply on the left-hand bank. I attempted to record my momentous international crossing by videoing and photographing the border on either side, sweeping across the river as I crossed the line, but given the speed at which the river was moving and my proven ineptitude with my GoPro camera, all I actually caught were some indistinct and distant images of the tree-covered hills surrounding me. It has only been by checking the time and date of the images that I've been able to confirm that they are of the actual border crossing point. Not that I expected any great fanfare, pomp or celebration, it was typically Canadian, and – as I was soon to discover – equally typically Alaskan.

There is a pragmatism up north that is determined by the environment. In general life and in minor bureaucratic and international matters, there appears little point in fighting against the environment which encompasses the northern climes of both countries, delineated only by the arbitrary hand of modern man. It seems to me that it is only in times of international crisis, or when it comes to exploiting the natural resources when vast amounts of money are to be made, that people really make any extreme exertions to fight, alter and to try and tame the wilderness. Otherwise, they live with it, just as they have for tens of thousands of years.

I was going to miss Canada and the Canadians. I like the Canadians. OK, so like all nations, nationalities and people there is the complete mish-mash of origins, personalities and perspectives, but the Canadians that I've met over the years have all, pretty much, been open-minded, laid back, friendly and on the whole helpfully well intentioned. I've known a French–Canadian archaeologist-cum-architect-cum-builder for a number of years and whilst highly proficient and experienced at his work (so he tells me) he is more horizontally sardonic with his mumbling gallic accent, droopy moustache and handmade rollies than anyone I've ever met; an archetype of the French Canadian?

One of my memorable early encounters with Canadians, en masse, has to be the first time I met some Canadian Army Rangers. I was on board the USS Nassau on our way up the Eastern American seaboard from Norfolk, Virginia, to Newfoundland for an amphibious exercise, part of a small Brit contingent evaluating some new technologies for detecting and clearing mines and obstacles in the 'surf-zone'. For the first few days a couple of us had a 135-man mess-deck to ourselves, 45 sets of three high bunks and a few lockers in a single compartment in the bowels of the ship. We were just getting used to the US Navy way of doing things when we were joined by a Company of Canadian Rangers, 100 plus of them. Initially, it was a bit of a shock, being surrounded by so many people with different accents but, on the whole, it was very much like being with any other embarked military force, albeit in the UK we tend to have much smaller mess-decks – and much smaller ships for that matter.

As I lay on my top bunk listening to the guys sort themselves out, I gradually became aware of an aspect of the Canadian language that has become predominant in my way of thinking of them. They can't help saying 'fuck'. In fact, they seem compelled to say it. Far from being a form of emphasis, they use it for punctuation. My dawning realisation was indelibly reinforced a day or two later when I listened to one of the Ranger NCOs briefing the guys on the mess-deck as to their role within the forthcoming landings. Whilst his brief was generally clear and well given, it was twice as long as it needed to be because every other word of his brief was 'fuck' or a variation thereof. I had to roll over on my bunk to ensure no one could see the smile on my face. The first time I was in Dawson, after my paddle from Johnson's Crossing, I was obliged to make a note of a conversation I overheard between two Canadians in the Sourdough Bar. They were talking about one of the other great Canadian obsessions – if not the greatest – namely Ice Hockey. On being told the result of a particular game, one guy replied, and I quote, 'well kick me in the nut sack, I could have done without that fucking result' – pure Canadian poetry!

Mind you, I did feel compelled to chuck in a 'fuck' myself in the very same bar when asked if I'd like to take part in the tourist attraction of drinking a shot from a glass containing a severed blackened toe, allegedly, a throwback to the Gold Rush days when prospectors and miners were regularly losing various digits to frostbite. I was told that these days they have a bit of a shortage of easily available, 'fresh', toes and they now rely on personal donations! My use of the word 'fuck' in this instance was very Anglo Saxon and was used to reinforce my point, as in 'fuck off' I'm not doing that and no I don't want a certificate to prove I've done it. I suppose I could have added that certificate to another dubious Canadian accolade, that of being an honorary Newfoundlander – a 'Newffy' – having kissed a cod whilst wearing wellies and then drinking down some 'Screech' in a bar in Stephenville at the end of the exercise where I met the Rangers, but that's another story.

From my limited experience, the Alaskans are even more laid back than the Canadians, but maybe a little less profane. They are, perhaps, also a little less officious when it comes to the outback. Whilst in Whitehorse, I was required to sign for my bear spray, buy a fishing licence and told I needed a permit to buy a camera drone. As a result, I only ended up buying the bear spray. In Emmonak, the guys I met just wanted to know if I had any firearms to sell and were incredulous that I should have been out on the river for so long without needing a weapon.

Having crossed the border from Canada, I was required to report to the US Customs and Border Checkpoint in Eagle, the first American town on the river 10 miles further downstream. The town holds a special piece of Yukon history, since it was there that late in 1905 the Norwegian polar explorer Roald Amundsen appeared after travelling hundreds of miles across the northern wastes from the Arctic Ocean, to telegraph to the world the news that he had finally found the Northwest Passage. Later in the 1970s the town also enjoyed some fame as the hub of John McPhee's magnificent book Coming into the Country. McPhee detailed the lives and motivations of a number of characters living their various chosen lives in and around Eagle in his commentary on the nature of Alaska at that time.

As a quick aside, and talking of Roald Amundsen, one of my favourite stories regarding him retells his incredulity and admiration for a character he met as he made his way back north from the Yukon to the Arctic Ocean coast with his Eskimo companions in the February of 1906, where his ship and crew were waiting for him. This is the man that five years later won the race to the South Pole and subsequently explored more of the remote frozen areas of the planet than anyone else alive at the time, but even he was completely agog when, some two hundred miles up the Porcupine River north of Fort Yukon, he met a postman. The postman, named Darrell, was an employee of the Hudson Bay Company and was hauling his toboggan by hand over the mountains from the Arctic Ocean. Amundsen later wrote "I could not believe my eyes, here was a man, hundreds of miles from the nearest human being, with not a soul to aid him in case of illness or accident, cheerfully trudging through the Arctic winter across an unblazed wilderness, thinking nothing at all of his exploit. I was lost in admiration". He continued, "I stood looking after him as he disappeared from view, and I thought, if you got together a few more men of his stamp, you could get to the moon". It has often been surmised that it was Amundsen's understanding of the Eskimo way of living in the Arctic – their dress, approach and, fundamentally, their use of dogs – that gave Amundsen the winning edge over Scott in the Antarctic.

I liked the look of Eagle, and as I approached the landing point after a good day on the water, I could see a couple of well-maintained houses with white picket fences and manicured lawns set back from the river; they looked too pristine for the environment. The landing point was at the upstream end of town, and I pulled in there despite Dan Maclean suggesting that it was possible to pull up at the newly built wharf further downstream and closer to the border checkpoint in the centre of town. The landing was easy, on a well-used gravel slipway, above which in a prominent position was a metal US Customs and Border Protection sign with 'STOP and REPORT' in bold red at the top telling me that 'All Persons and Vessels/Vehicles Arriving From Canada Must Stop and Report Their Arrival'.

Fair enough, I knew that was required, but then I read the directions to the 'Reporting Location': 'Use Golden Street and turn right on Front Street, left on Fremont, right on First Avenue, Follow First Ave. ½ mile to Eagle Trading Company and use the yellow phone in the white box at the end of the building'. I had only been on the water for a couple of days by this stage and my mind was just getting used to following a river guide downstream, so this was a bit too much. I took a photo of the sign and set off at a gentle rolling amble determined to report to customs. Given the instructions, the first thing I had to do was find a street name, Golden Street to be precise, easier said than done. Having not found Golden Street, I just took the first right then first left, it seemed to make sense. It was another scorching day and away from the river the graded roads were hot and dusty. Alongside scattered in the overgrown vegetation, there were old cars, large earth-moving or tree-cutting machines and the odd dilapidated looking shack. It was hard to tell if most of these were abandoned or still in use.

Just as I thought I'd found First Avenue (though there was nothing to confirm this, other than this road being straighter, wider and possibly pointing in the right direction) a pick-up truck came careering up the road behind me. I stepped off the road as I couldn't jump – I'd been in the boat for too long already that day and my legs were just coping with walking, never mind jumping. The pick-up was perfect, it must have been in use since the '50s, was an absolute classic, not in the well-maintained showroom type of way, but as the sort of battered American pick-up we Brit kids of the '70s used to see on imported American TV programmes; the programmes that informed our early impressions of the US and of Americans themselves.

I couldn't tell you if it was a Ford or a Dodge, or what make it was for that matter, but it seemed as apt and appropriate to its surroundings as, say, Coca-Cola and bald eagles. The pick-up halted beside me, its bonnet (or should I say hood) near chest height. I popped my head through the open window and saw that the driver was the human doppelganger for the pick-up. Tall, thin, very broad and unshaven, he had probably been driving the truck since the '50s as well and was himself a stereotypical version of an old-time cowboy from my childhood TV viewing, right down to his drawl. Another archetype? I began to realise that, for me at least, the Yukon held a lot of archetypes. Probably a condition of too much TV, or reading the works of Jack London, et al., but there was also something about the place that felt oddly familiar. The door of the pick-up creaked as I opened it to get in, a creak not from rust or neglect but from old age; I knew how it felt!

I had trouble understanding my lift, not that he said much, and I think he was slightly deaf and probably couldn't hear a word I was saying either.

Nevertheless, he seemed automatically to know where I was trying to head, I assume from my attire and my usual slightly lost expression. He took me the mile or so down the road, pulled up opposite the Eagle Trading Company and pointed out the phone booth attached to one end of the shabby looking wooden planked building. I was reluctant to get out, sitting in the huge single front seat felt like being taken back to childhood, to the days when it was a treat for kids to ride along up front. Whilst I didn't know at the time, as I hadn't read it then, I now wonder if my driver was one of the characters, one of the locals, John McPhee interviewed in Eagle back in the mid-1970s.

Sure enough, as described on the sign and in Dan Maclean's guide, the phone booth was indeed a low white canopy, an unnecessarily low canopy, covering a yellow phone on an equally unnecessarily short cable. I ducked under the canopy to pick up the phone and followed the instructions posted in the booth. There was a pause before the phone was answered by a slightly hesitant and surprised sounding voice. I imagined the phone being a bit like to one from the old Carlsberg adverts, in the complaints department, covered in dusty cobwebs. My image was reinforced when I explained that I was checking-in, having crossed the border by canoe, and was told to hang on a second while the voice on the end found the logbook. I wondered whether he had to blow the dust of that as well.

Once we were ready to go, all I had to do was give my passport number, which wasn't as easy as it sounds squeezed in under the canopy close to the phone trying to hold it at a distance where I could read it without my glasses. Along with my passport details I was asked for my date of birth and a physical description. Eternally blessed with a childish, but not necessarily funny, sense of humour the idea of giving a completely ludicrous personal description flickered briefly through the echoing cavern of my mind, just as it does when faced with any such minor officialdom. I quickly thought better of it, however, and checked my puerile impulses. 6'2", blues eyes, strawberry blonde – sorry, grey – hair and beard, no other distinguishing features! Could I declare my innate and never-diminished childishness?

I was then asked how much cash I had with me and when and where I was expecting to leave the USA. The explanation of my intended trip and the fact that I had no end date in mind, nor any return plans arranged, seemed to strike a chord of alarm with my inquisitor whose voice now took on a sterner tone. My urge to mess about increased. I explained what I was up to again but he still needed a date and a location for my departure, so I arbitrarily made up a date far enough ahead to hopefully allow for any changes to my plans and, given my choice of leaving from either Anchorage or Fairbanks, plumped for Anchorage. Then, realising that all he really wanted was to be sure that I wasn't looking to stay illegally in Alaska, I gave him my home number in the UK and told him to ring there if I didn't report in as agreed. I added that there was no way my wife would let me stay in the US and she'd be able to track me down, which got a hint of a chuckle out of him! My job was done – I was free to enter the USA.

I walked across from the phone booth to a large, newish, hotel-like building with wonderful views over the new wharf and the large bend in the Yukon as it bounces off and around Eagle Bluff overlooking the town. The entrance was on the glass-fronted lower floor and I found an empty restaurant and small shop inside. I wandered around for a bit, revelling in the feeling of being indoors for a change, then bought a cold can of coke and an apple from a rather lost looking assistant before wandering back along the hot, dusty roads back to my boat.

*The US Customs and Border Protection
sign at the landing point in Eagle*

*A typical campsite in the early days
on the Yukon*

Eagle to Circle

On leaving Eagle, the river runs through the Yukon–Charley Rivers National Preserve and, for the first time on my trip, I noticed from the river guide that there were public use cabins available along the river's edge. As it was, my journey was slightly out of sync with the locations of the cabins, but I decided to take a look at one to see if it would be worth a stopover. I set my sites on the Nation Bluff Cabin which was near the site of the former Nation River Coal Mine.

The conditions were kind, in fact it was another particularly hot day with only a slight breeze, so I could easily cross to the right-hand side of the river and try to find the cabin which was set back in the trees. As I was approaching the supposed spot, a skiff passed me heading downstream on the left-hand bank and then took a large right-hand turn across the river to pull up directly in front of me next to the point where the cabin was meant to be. My initial thought was, 'Bloody typical – just as I thought I'd do a little exploring some locals turn up!' After a few days on my own I was feeling relatively mellow and really didn't fancy sharing a cabin with strangers. However, as I approached the skiff, I noticed that it was slightly different to the few other aluminium craft I had seen up until then, with its drab green paint and more than the usual number of antennae.

Then I noticed that, of the two people on board, the one that had stepped ashore was in a sort of uniform: they were park rangers. I approached with a slight touch of paranoia, expecting them to start quizzing me on my reasons, planning and suitability for being out on the water. The guy ashore waved at me and as I was less than 50 metres away and heading straight at them, I thought it would look a bit suspect if I veered out and swerved around their boat. So I pulled up and got out as elegantly as I could, trying to give the impression of complete professionalism and easy competence; thankfully as I'd had four days practice, I think I just about got away with it.

I need not have worried, the rangers – a male and a female, probably in their mid- to late- forties (though I could have misjudged) – were as friendly, knowledgeable and supportive as anyone could have hoped for. They looked more like schoolteachers or scout leaders than Alaskan Park Rangers, not that I'd met any of the latter before. The two of them were at the cabin to give it a spruce-up and as we chatted they were unloading heavy duty strimmers, fuel cans and kit bags. At their eager and proud insistence, I left them unloading and went to take a look at the cabin which was situated about 50 metres back from the riverbank.

Stepping out of the sunlight and into the green of the trees was like stepping into a verdant otherworld: a world removed from the sun-baked mudflats, the cooling breezes, the sky and distant horizon out on the river. Usually at this latitude the banks were populated by spruce and, like all large conifers, their coverage and needle fall stunts the undergrowth on the forest floor. But here near the cabin, which had been in almost constant use for many decades, the bigger trees had been cleared and the vegetation was now predominantly secondary shrubs with a few remaining spruces. This created an incongruous world of closeness, of claustrophobia, a world where things moved, chatted, chirped and squealed right next to you.

Almost as soon as I was out of the sunlight, I was engaged at eye level by an aggressive, boggle-eyed, mangy squirrel. It was on a branch chittering noisily, flicking its almost hairless tail aggressively, spitting at me, and clearly checking out my credentials for being in its domain. I was aware of what cantankerous little buggers the squirrels were from my previous trip where, camping mostly in amongst the trees, I had a nightly wakeup call from these surly critters. They weren't shy and they certainly weren't very accepting of strangers. Then, just as my eyesight was adjusting to the chlorophyllic gloom, something brushed through the undergrowth at ankle height to my left, and once I'd looked down to see nothing there and back up again, my furry inquisitor was gone.

At this point perhaps I should point out that in my former life I spent nigh on a year working in the jungles of Borneo, a truly privileged position in an amazing environment. So, in theory, I was trained and mentally equipped to manage in these circumstances – the claustrophobic and potentially overwhelming assault on the senses that trees, close vegetation and the cacophony of critters that live there, can produce. But that was a long time ago and most recently my world had been contained within my canoe on the bright, open river. Here, at this point, I felt more prey than predator, more meerkat than monkey. I pushed on and as I approached the cabin something more substantial, about the size of a small dog (I've still no real idea what it might have been) ran off through the undergrowth, leaving a trail of disturbed and shaking vegetation in its wake. I was glad that the commotion was moving away from me instead of at me, as it was at that point that I'd realised, that assured by the presence of the rangers I'd neglected to pick up my bear spray so felt even more uncomfortably exposed than I had seconds previously.

The actual cabin, with a log cache on stilts next to it, was exactly as you would expect, a single-storey, squat, square, log-built box. I entered the cabin into a sort of small reception room which held much of the cooking equipment and a neat stack of firewood. I then opened the mosquito screen and door into the main cabin. It was unnaturally dark, darker than the woods in which it sat, particularly with the shutters still up, but I could make out a comfortable-looking bed platform, a desk, fireplace and a number of pictures, with what looked like people holding up fish although it was hard to be sure without taking down the shutters. It all looked very comfortable and potentially accommodating, but it was still only four in the afternoon and with decent conditions on the river and my newly acquired penchant for sunshine, cooling breezes and sandbars with a good field of vision, I decided I should push on.

On my way back to the river, I lost a 'Tony Hancock' armful of blood to some huge mosquitoes, ones that were adept at landing, stabbing and supping a pint or two before you noticed. Back by the river, I made my excuses to the rangers. They seemed a little disappointed by my rejection of their cabin and recommended a couple of other options further downstream. Regardless of their reaction, I did wonder if perhaps it was I that may have been potentially cramping their style or spoiling their fun, a cosy night in the cabin after a few hours work on the camp!

To my extreme embarrassment, I can't now remember their names. The guy – Ken, I think – gave me his card and asked me to drop him a line when I finished my trip, and I wrote the other ranger's name on the card to remember them both. It was only when I finished my trip and I was sorting out my gear in Emmonak that I realised that the card, which I thought had been safely stowed in the sleeve at the back of my notebook, was nowhere to be found. I've searched for it several times now such is my annoyance at not being able to drop 'Ken' a note of achievement and thanks. It was only as I got back into my boat that I noticed a huge, fresh, bear track in the mud right next to it. Once afloat I tried to pull away as competently as possible, waving confidently as I passed by their skiff, and paddled, contentedly alone, back into the open bright expanse of the river.

A few days later, prior to reaching Circle, I met a couple of other groups of kayakers out on the river. This stretch of the Yukon, through the Yukon–Charley Preserve, is an increasingly well-used part of the river, with the public use cabins available and road access to both Eagle and Circle from Fairbanks. The first group I met were three American women, two in a canoe and one on her own in a small kayak. I'd passed these guys earlier that day and noticed that the two women in the canoe were talking non-stop whilst the one in the solo kayak was whizzing all over the place like a puppy being taken for a walk. I pulled over for a cup of tea just after passing them and then caught them up again later on, at which point the puppy paddled over for a chat. She asked me if I'd seen the mother moose and calf back upstream and said they had thought that I had pulled over to get a better look. I was able to give the most English answer possible by saying that I hadn't seen the moose and that I'd just pulled over for a cup tea! It went straight over her head and I quickly understood why, perhaps, the other two women were keeping their distance from this one; I got her whole life history and the background on the other two over the next mile or so before making my excuses and heading on.

The Yukon–Charley Preserve is controversial in some people's minds. Some still see it as an artificial conceit whereby the Alaskan state has bought up, often compulsorily, land that once belonged to miners and settlers in order to protect the land and provide access for the wider public, hence all the public use cabins. The creation of the preserve is a linear result of the Alaskan state land carve-up of the 1970s motivated to enable a more 'morally principled' exploitation of the oil found in Prudhoe Bay on the northern coast in the '60s.

The building of the pipeline across Alaska to transport the oil north to south, to be shipped to the 'lower 48', the rest of the continental USA, brought to a head the long-overdue question of who owned what land in Alaska. Before the pipeline could be built the government and the Native

Peoples agreed the Alaskan Native Claims Settlement Act (1971) in which 12 Native Peoples Corporations were established to agree to the ownership and management of 180,000km² (44 million acres) of land – one-ninth of Alaska – as well as $963 million on behalf of all the Native Peoples. Under the subsequent Alaska National Interest Land Act (1980) a further 423,000 km² (104.5 million acres) – close to a quarter of Alaska – was designated for state use. The Alaskan state has thus far established 15 National Preserves on the land it owns, the Yukon–Charley Preserve being one of these. The impact of these negotiations, along with the bizarre attempts to find a new Alaskan state capital, an alternative to Juneau, in the mid-'70s, is also examined by John McPhee in Coming into the Country.

The morning before reaching Circle, I set off early and soon after getting on the water saw a couple of kayakers on an island packing after, I assume, a night's camping. We reached the landing point at Circle at the same time, an hour or so later, where they had arranged to be picked up and taken to Fairbanks. I noticed that their kayaks were familiar, they were the same make that I'd used on my 2017 trip. They in turn commented on the decals still on my canoe and it transpired that they had started their paddle at Whitehorse and had also bought their kayaks second-hand from Up North Adventures.

We had a brief, eyebrow-raising, and rather sardonic, chat about the cost of used boats from Up North Adventures (second-hand kayaks apparently cost a lot more than canoes), but we all agreed that the cost was worth it for the experience. They had arranged to sell their boats in Fairbanks in an attempt to recoup some of their outlay. More importantly, they had 'stuff' they were looking to off-load. They offered me their remaining rations, but I didn't think I'd need any more at that point in my trip. I did, however, gratefully, take a whole load of particularly gooey energy bars from them: sticky bars that I stowed in the bottom of my large waterproof food bag, and which I ravenously raided many weeks later when in need of some extra energy negotiating the lower reaches of the river and toward the sea.

Circle was established in 1893 when gold was discovered nearby and served as an unloading point for supplies shipped upriver from the Bering Sea. Before the Klondike Gold Rush a few years later, Circle, population 700, was the largest mining town on the river with a store, a few dance halls, an opera house, a library, a school, a hospital, a church, a newspaper, a mill, and a number of federal officials. I could see little of this history while I was there: to me Circle looked very similar to Eagle, if a little scruffier, insomuch as it had a substantial wharf that looked able to take some larger vessels and a huge, newer, hotel-type building overlooking the wharf, which in this case looked unfinished.

Approching Circle

The town of Circle was so named because when it was established the founding miners thought it sat on the Arctic Circle, although it's actually 50 miles south of the latitudinal line. I knew from Dan Maclean's guide that there was a communal shower, laundry and store somewhere in town, so set off in entirely the wrong direction to find them. I had a rather difficult time trying to make myself understood by two perplexed Alaskan Native chaps armed with some savage looking huskies as the word 'shop' didn't seem to register, but when I finally said 'store' with a fake American drawl, I got a begrudging nod in the right direction.

Off the river and on the hot, dusty, dirt roads of Circle, the mozzies were out in force. I had to wait for the store to open as I thought it was nearly 10am but in fact Circle is an hour behind Dawson (I hadn't checked the time in Eagle – who'd have thought?). Once open, I bought some tokens and took my washing into the communal block opposite, a large wooden plank building set off the ground on a sturdy concrete base. Outside was a drive-through water point where locals could pull up in their pick-ups and fill their huge bowsers from a large hose that hung from the top of a lean-to.

The inside of the building itself was tatty but functional. The Lino on the floor was peeling and the walls and doorways were well scuffed but the main room held two large industrial washing machines and two equally robust dryers. Two scruffy shower cubicles – one male and one female – were set off a corridor behind the main room. As I entered the building, I saw a couple of cheerful native women herding their children whilst loading one of the washing machines. One of them looked up and asked with a smile, "how do like our mosquitoes?". "They seem hungry," I replied. No more needed to be said: we had related, exchanged pleasantries and they clearly needed no more information from me.

Having a shower was good for morale. I used the female shower, as, for the life of me, I couldn't get the gents shower to work and guessed I wouldn't be disturbed even if the door wouldn't lock. Any benefit I may have received from taking a shower was immediately negated as soon as I stepped outside into the heat, dust and mossies. However, the two tangible benefits that I picked up from Circle were found in the store. I finally got my hands on some Pilot Bread, having previously searched in both Whitehorse and Dawson; I was also kindly given a large pack of paper coffee filters by the store owner who could have been my truck driver from Eagle, or at least his brother, they looked so much alike. He said he'd got the filters for his own coffee machine, but they were the wrong size. The filters would stand in for the metal filter that I'd inadvertently flipped into the river earlier that morning and the Pilot Bread would go with my lunchtime peanut butter and replace the ridiculous crumbling snack crackers I had been using up until then.

I don't know why I hadn't been able to find Pilot Bread in Whitehorse or Dawson as I had read that it was the thing to use on such expeditions, and it was. Marketed as the bread that could survive an apocalypse, if (as described to great amusement by the comedian Peter Kay) the great British Hobnob is the 'Marine' of biscuits, then Pilot Bread must be the 'Thor', a mighty God in the pantheon of biscuits and crackers. For those of you who don't know, Pilot Bread – aka 'hardtack' from its use as part of the staple diet of the Royal Navy in their days under sail – is a large cracker-cum-biscuit-cum-breeze block, the size and consistency of a cork drinks coaster, not that I've ever eaten a cork coaster. A cross between a thick savoury digestive biscuit and a compressed rusk, they are very filling, almost indestructible and when smeared with a thick coating of glutinous peanut butter are heaven for the lone, hungry, tired, paddler. Don't ever try eating one without having a drink on hand to wash it down, though.

Talking about food, for this trip I was planning to use the same ration regime as I had employed previously. Although this journey was going to be three times the length, I was confident, from a nutritional perspective, that it would keep me going. Importantly, it used provisions that were easy to buy (other than the Pilot Bread), store, prepare and eat. They were also hygienic to eat and created minimal residual mess or smell. For breakfast I would have a couple of muesli bars, washed down with lots of hot strong black coffee along with my morning Ibuprofen and associated painkillers to get me moving. Throughout the day I would munch my way through a zip-lock bag containing a trail mix: nuts, dried fruit, seeds, chocolate and, additionally, a one-a-day gummy bear multi-vitamin thrown in for good measure.

I'd had great fun buying copious bags of various trail mixes from a supermarket in Whitehorse, although the woman at the checkout wasn't so enamoured with having to work out which mix was which. They all cost slightly different amounts and I'd neglected to attach the dedicated code to each large bag I'd filled and presented to her on her conveyor belt. I managed to create quite a queue. I then took these big bags of mixes back to my hotel room and spent an evening decanting a variety of combinations, three large handfuls into each of forty individual smaller zip-lock bags. Throughout the day, or night, as I was paddling, I'd munch on my trail mix, normally pouring it directly into my mouth from the bag to avoid getting my grubby fingers involved. The amount I scoffed throughout the day was a good indicator of how hungry I was and how much energy I was using. Some daily bags were more welcome than others, particularly those that had a little more chocolate in, and the lucky-dip approach to picking a daily bag out of a big dry bag added a bit of fun; I'm easily pleased.

Lunch was a real treat, something to look forward to: peanut butter and crackers, or the Pilot Bread when I finally got hold of some. After 3 or 4 hours paddling, I would look to pull over for 'lunch', whatever time of day or night that might be. I'd set up my camping chair next to the boat – or further ashore if the boat was beached in wet mud – make another coffee or tea, grab my large, plastic, 'Spork' (yes, it's a cross between a spoon and fork), grab the Pilot Bread, unscrew the lid of a large tub of peanut butter and dig-in, smearing thick layers of the butter over the crackers before devouring them greedily. I was always very conscious of bears at this point, given their alleged sense of smell. I was sure they'd be as partial to peanut butter as I was and could sniff it out from miles about, although it would be the one thing I'd seriously think about fighting a grizzly for. Once replete with peanut butter and, if I felt secure enough, I'd put my feet up in the gunwale of the canoe and snatch a power nap.

My last meal of the day would be a sachet of dehydrated, freeze-dried, rations. Dehydrated rations have been around for decades but, in my experience, have really come into their own over the last few years or so. They used to be considered emergency rations, lightweight rations that could be easily stored, were slow to ruin and fairly quick to prepare. However, they were inevitably incredibly boring to eat and held only limited nutritional value, hence being held in reserve and used as a last resort. The dehydrated rations available today are a different kettle of fish, the recipes and types of meals on offer are far superior, some with decent imaginative flavours, so no more need to take a bottle of tabasco, or pot of chilli powder, with you to pep up your meal. Importantly, whilst not super-high, they contain a good amount of nutrition, around 600-800 calories per sachet. They are also very easy to prepare, just add boiling water, stir and wait. My journal is littered with references to my appreciation of my dehydrated meals: Wild Thyme Turkey, Peppered Beef with Rice, Teriyaki, Kung Po or Spicy Curry Chicken, to name but a few. Despite being in no rush, waiting the 10-15 minutes for the boiling water to fully hydrated the contents could be hard work particularly toward the end of a long day, but it was worth it if I wanted the contents to be edible and not end up eating crunchy freeze-dried pasta and flavoured food-dust from the bottom of the sachet.

Helpfully, there was no washing of pots, pans and/or mess tins. Much less fuss, less bulk, more hygienic and, as I have said, no potential for lingering attractive smells. Please don't mention this to my old drill instructor from my Royal Marine recruit training, he'd have a fit if he thought I'd ever leave anything other than a spotless mess tin. The poor bloke spent enough of his time making me retrieve my dirty mess tins from gorse bushes and then run up and down the Devon hills with my rifle held above my head to help me learn; it worked!

I looked forward to my 'main' meal of the day, partly out of enjoyment (I made it another case of pot-luck by not looking into the kit bag as I delved in to pull that day's meal out; most days were a pleasant surprise – it's the little things that keep you going) and partly because it generally heralded the end of that day's paddling. I would, where and when possible, pull over an hour or so before really looking to camp and have my meal on the riverbank ensuring that I'd minimised any mess. If possible, I'd burn the empty sachets or stow them in an airtight bag until I could properly dispose of them later, and generally try to ensure that there was no residual mess or odours on me before heading on toward my campsite. I did also try to ensure that there was absolutely no sign, other than a few footprints, of my presence at any of the locations I stopped at. Finally, on the occasional evening when I felt secure or thought I'd deserved it, I'd treat myself to a nip of whisky whilst sat by my tent reading or writing my journal.

Given this regime, all I really needed to eat reasonably well, stay hydrated and keep clean was to be able to find water that was suitable to boil and therefore sterilise. Most of this water came from the surrounding hills. This had worked out well on my first trip and I didn't get an upset stomach. I took my water from the clear creek water that spilled from the hillsides into the main river. Occasionally, I could smell just how fresh this water was when filling my water bottle or just when passing some of these creeks. I would catch the smell of cooler spruce-infused mountain air being washed down into the Yukon – not the sort of cloying smell you get from those pine-shaped air fresheners that hang from car rear view mirrors, this was an invigorating, oxygen-filled air that wakes you up and tingles the senses; it was Abbey's "deep the yet sweet and lucid air". I wanted to follow it to its source – perhaps it is true that happiness does indeed have a smell!

Most of the creek water could probably have been drunk straightaway but to be on the safe side I would allow it to settle and then boil it before use. As a backup I took a small but effective 'drinking straw' water filtration system. If the worst came to the worst, I could, in theory, drink from almost any source using the straw. I did have to use this a couple of times, both in the Flats and the delta, when there were no surrounding hills for creeks to run down from and I was forced to take the water straight from the Yukon itself. Both times I did this, I had to flush the straw back through with about a quarter of the clean filtered water to keep the device clear of silt. I then boiled the water and added purifying tablets before drinking, again to be on the safe side.

Having an efficient stove was helpful and for this my trusty 'Jet Boil™' cooker was my go-to choice. The Jet Boil is a simple but clever and compact stove that uses butane gas canisters and when working properly boils a pint of water in a minute or so. I spent a few weeks prior to heading out to the Yukon, whilst touring Scotland with Sophie, boiling water in my Jet Boil to work out how much I could get from a 450g butane canister. The answer, if you're interested, was 54 pints. I reckoned that I'd need to boil 6 to 8 pints of water a day for roughly 40 days, so I reckoned 5 x 450g cans of butane would suffice.

I had a 15-litre collapsible water container into which my clean, boiled water was decanted. I did manage to get this filled from public drinking sources in Dawson, Circle and Yukon Crossing, thereby saving on the butane gas by not having to boil it. In Eagle I asked a guy at the landing point and he kindly filled the container from his garden hose, one of the houses I saw with the lawn and picket fence.

All the food and clean water were important, but there was one thing that I knew I had to get right if I were to survive my trip, the one thing that I did approach with what could be regarded as some form of religious fervour; my coffee! I used to be a tea drinker, Earl Grey was my preferred breakfast beverage, but a couple of tours of duty working with the American military and I was hooked, and possibly addicted. Strong black coffee it has to be, albeit I try not to drink any after lunchtime and limit my intake to three, maybe four, shots a day; safer for everyone.

I spent an inordinate amount of time experimenting with and making sure I had the right combination of cooker, mug and collapsible field filter to be sure the coffee would be perfect, achievable and hot regardless of the conditions. In, Hougen's (a hunting store in Whitehorse), I found my ideal mug, a 'Stanley', one litre, thermal captains' mug. As well as a secure lid the mug had a wide base, which I found was important to keep it from toppling over, particularly when filling it since I had to balance the 'field coffee filter' on the neck of the mug and had previously been scalded when using less stable mugs; this was a serious business.

The fact that I dropped the perforated metal disc, the key component of my collapsible field filter overboard, was a devastating blow. For some reason, just before Circle, I was rinsing the filter whilst sat in the canoe, don't ask me why I was doing it there! During the cleaning process I managed to ping the metal disc out of its rubber casing and watched it describe a graceful, arcing parabular, glinting in the early morning sunlight, as it went over the side of the canoe, and gently fluttered down through the silt-ladened river, winking at me sarcastically in the diminishing sunrays as it sunk. Utterly bereft, I was close to abandoning my journey. The gift of the paper coffee filters by the store owner in Circle was just one example of my undeserved serendipitous luck. All I had to do now was keep them dry for the next 1100 miles.

Morning coffee on a still Yukon River

JOURNAL 1 JULY 2019: The wind continued to blow last night with a little drizzle and this morning turned from S to SW but with the breeze and white caps on the water I couldn't relax or navigate properly so sensibly, reluctantly, I've put ashore and will have a coffee and read and wait and see what the wind does. This may do me some good as it messes with all the timings and speed calculations in my head which means I'll have to throw those out and try again to go with the flow – mentally and physically! I'm in a strange mood at the mo, I think it's got a fair bit to do with talking to Sophie, I suddenly got home sick which messes with my state of mind for dealing with what's ahead. Oh well, nothing I can do about that I've just got to accept that I'll probably feel like that every time we talk. It's important we talk, Sophie has been so supportive and strong in letting me come and attempt this.

The Sat-Phone calls home were vital but proved more emotional than I think either of us had expected. My initial idea was that I would be able to make quick, fairly regular, calls home to let Sophie know where I was using the shared copies of the maps we both had. The Sat-Phone went everywhere with me, my only real form of communication and, in effect, my insurance policy for the paddle. Mind you, I had taken the precaution of procuring some actual travel insurance and was amazed that I could so easily purchase some very basic insurance to cover my particular trip. Every insurance policy that I looked at had, amazingly, within their basic range of schedules, coverage for the sort of canoeing and camping I was planning. Provided the river was not more than a Grade 3, so "fairly big waves and stoppers... continuous rapids...with obvious routes" (it was not) I was covered by a very minimal, cheap, travel insurance for Canada and the USA regardless of exactly where I was going to be, or for how long. I'm glad I didn't have to use that insurance cover.

Given its importance, to keep the Sat-Phone safe, I kept it in a waterproof, indestructible 'Peli' box; a hard plastic box with internal foam compartments for added protection and a secure locking system. This was the case that doubled up as part of my pillow when in the tent. I had emergency numbers for the Royal Canadian Mounted Police, Alaskan Police and a long-distance emergency co-ordination centre for Alaska, pre-programmed into the phone in case I got into trouble. I was fastidious in making sure the phone was charged at all times. As well as being my insurance policy, I also naïvely believed that the quick odd call home would be enough to reassure Sophie that I was OK. Funny old thing, that didn't quite work as planned!

My first call home from the river was picked up by George, my youngest, as Sophie was out, and George being George we had a very quick chat in which I told him all was well and furnished him with my location using a corresponding map page. My second call, a few days later, was a different matter. Sophie answered and was clearly upset having missed my first call and not being able to work out from the mapping where I was. We chatted and I tried to put her mind at ease as best I could but realised that I was getting emotional too. I had, naïvely, only purchased as many call minutes as I'd thought would be needed for a quick chat once a week and enough for any potential emergency calls; another of my witless sops to the costs involved during my planning. I quickly realised I'd been a bit tight and inconsiderate.

Sophie and I were used to chatting periodically via satellite, usually no more than ten minutes a week, from around the globe, but this was different: I was no longer part of a well-resourced organisation, I was on my own and I owed Sophie an awful lot more reassurance. We agreed to talk at 9pm UK time (so midday for me) every Sunday and Thursday and Sophie looked into buying some more minutes for the phone. I felt very emotional when I hung up after that first call. I came to the conclusion that the sudden switch from my, required, 'Yukon mindset' to 'home-mode' had caught me off-guard and every time we were to talk, I would effectively be stepping from my all-encompassing Yukon focus into the comfort of home in the gentle rolling hills of Devon. I hadn't expected this but needed to accept that it would probably happen after every call: the calls were vital, I just had to make sure I was ready and prepared for them.

With the extra minutes secured, I made sure to carve out the time for proper calls home and that I was in a secure position when I did, so they became easier as we went along. After my first few weather-related strandings, I had the cunning idea of asking Sophie if she could find me a forecast for my projected locations, which with her usual energy and efficiency she duly provided. Bizarrely, when these forecasts didn't match the conditions I faced on the river I found myself resenting her for her mis-information; not her fault at all. We concluded that I didn't really need any forecasts as there was little I could do about the weather anyway – it would be what it would be and I would just have to deal with whatever came along.

So far so good: I had cracked the first, relatively mellow, 250 miles of this trip. The only really serious mishap thus far, besides a few close misses with trees and rocks in the river, was losing my coffee filter. When I set off from Dawson City I felt as though I were stepping into the unknown, but in reality, other than crossing into another country the river between Dawson and Circle was very similar to that south of Dawson. If anything, once in Alaska, the Yukon is more accessible and attractive to visitors. Beyond Circle this was going to change, there would be just the one other road reaching the river, at Yukon Crossing, throughout the next 1180 miles all the way to the Bering Sea and from now on I would be reliant on my own homemade mapping. Once again, and despite enjoying this first section of the river and with my planning thus far seemingly holding up, I had the feeling that yet again I would be paddling into the unknown.

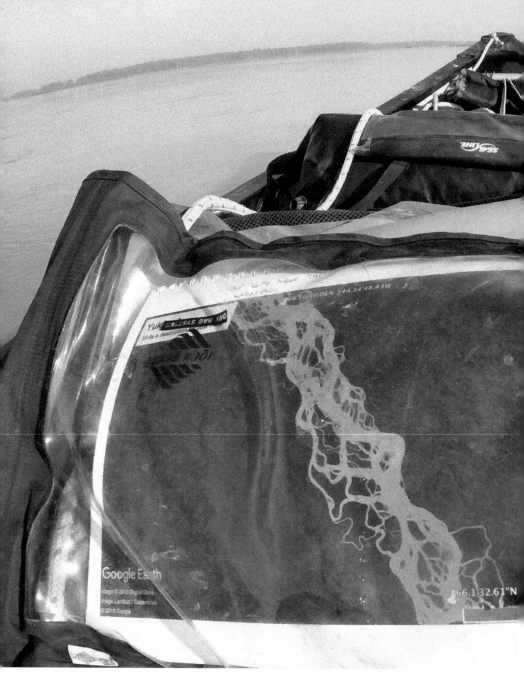

Following my homemade mapping through the Flats

The Flats

North of Circle the Yukon River slackens as it enters the appropriately named 'Flats'. It continues to head north for a further 70 miles, crossing the Arctic Circle for a brief moment, before turning west for another 160 miles, after which it picks up a pace as it passes the Fort Hamlin Hills. The Flats are a designated wildlife refuge, the third largest in the US, and encompass over 11 million acres of wetland, bogs (known locally as 'muskegs') and islands. It is an area of extremes. Temperatures can vary from 35°C in the summer, to -57°C in the winter and it is also prone to storms. Up to 2000 lightning strikes were recorded in a single day, sparking the highest incidence of naturally occurring wildland fires in Alaska. On entering the Flats, the Yukon River fractures into a 20-mile-wide lattice work of river and sloughs snaking their way around thousands of islands and mudbanks. Whilst the Flats are bounded by mountain ranges to the east and north, the land immediately around the river is level with no discernible hills, mountains or landmarks defining the surroundings above the spruce-lined banks.

At home in the UK over the preceding winter I spent long hours poring over satellite images on Google Earth, following the long, milky-tea coloured braids of the Yukon as it passed through the unfrozen taiga. Studying the one-dimensional images of the camouflage-patterned muskegs, forests, hills and oxbow lakes, I compared the detail on the imagery with the black and white sketch maps in Dan Maclean's guide. With hindsight and now blessed with greater knowledge, I could have followed Dan's maps and they might have been sufficient, but from the comfort of my kitchen back in Devon, I was presented with a forbidding and unknown wilderness and I wanted the safety of greater detail to work from.

Studying the course of the Yukon, the Flats looked like a nightmare to navigate. I started my mapping by trying to capture roughly 10km of river per A4 page from the online satellite images, as per the published river guides. This was workable for the first four or five pages but was time consuming and I soon got bored. I worked out that I'd need somewhere between 130-140 pages to complete my own mapping in this way, which would possibly take longer than it would to complete the paddle! So, I started matching the scale on each page to the amount of detail I thought I would need, anywhere between 10km to 80km on an A4 page.

For the Flats, I worked on producing the smallest scale possible to aid my navigation. Onto these sheets I added the information from Dan Maclean's guide that I thought would be useful, mainly parts of the river to avoid such as the whirlpool! Throughout the paddle, at the start of each day, I would compare my satellite images with Dan's descriptions, primarily to confirm my route and prepare myself for the day ahead, but also because Dan gives the miles covered in his book. This was both a good thing but also, at times, very demoralising information. In addition, I pinned a latitude and longitude waypoint on what looked like prominent physical features near the start and end of the river on each map page.

Whilst making my mapping I naturally thought my GPS would be vital, not only for general navigation but to enable me to pinpoint my precise location, and so relate my position to the waypoints I'd created. I thought this would be essential in helping me find my way through the Flats, but in reality, I didn't really need the GPS for such precise navigation. As it turned out, I was able to manage with just visual reckoning, matching the river and surroundings to the aerial images. Initially, I did use the GPS to try to sit exactly on every waypoint pin: it was gratifying if rather surreal to be able to place my boat over points on the Yukon that I had selected as I sat at my kitchen counter many months earlier.

However, I quickly realised that it was impractical and occasionally downright uncomfortable trying to sit on each and every virtual pin; no pun intended! More often than not, whilst these waypoints were placed on easily recognisable features – heads or tails of islands or the confluence of rivers and sloughs – they were not always great locations to be paddling on the actual river and would take me away from the course of the main flow or into eddies I didn't want to be caught in. So, very quickly I got used to taking the satisfaction that I could spot the waypoints I had created as I passed them, without needing to see the digits on my GPS screen match exactly the latitude and longitude figures printed on my maps.

I also found that placing the GPS in easy view on the canoe cross-strut just in front of where I sat to monitor my speed was a ridiculous, pointless and soul-destroying thing to do. I would find myself mentally working out how long my entire trip would take if I maintained a certain speed, for a certain duration, per hour, per day. It was crazy and would have driven me mad if I had continued. Whichever way I looked at it, my minute-by-minute, hour-by-hour calculations still brought me to the conclusion that, even if I should finish, my journey was going to take me somewhere between 35-45 days. So, before long my GPS was consigned to reference backup work, for confirmation rather than day-to-day navigation and calculation.

In hindsight, I should have spent longer on my mapping and stuck to producing the smaller scale images. Little did I know at the time that the mud banks below the surface would, on certain parts of the river, plague me and my progress, and that these were far more discernible (and therefore avoidable) in the close-up images. I took two copies of my mapping, both professionally printed locally and ring-bound on waterproof rip-stop paper, and left the original home-printed paper copy at home with Sophie. The idea was that she would be able to follow my progress and during our satellite phone calls I could let her know quickly and easily which page I was on and therefore where I was on the river. The concept worked to a fashion, albeit it took a couple of phone calls for us to get synchronised, but I guess I've always struggled letting Sophie know what page I'm on! Of the two allegedly indestructible versions I took with me – one for daily reference and the other as a backup – neither managed to get waterlogged or ripped, but the one I had out in front of me whilst paddling through the Flats melted thanks to the attention of the Yukon mid-summer sun.

Personally, I came to think of the Flats in terms of a layman's version of Dante's Inferno, as described in his Divine Comedy, not because of the atypically hellish heat and fires which I encountered, but it's likeness – in my mind at least – to Dante's outer rings of hell, or perhaps more fittingly the fabled River Archeon on the shores of Purgatory. Maybe an unfair association on my part and not how the Native Peoples would view their home, but as I worked my way through the featureless landscape, negotiating the myriad islands and sloughs on the slow running river, through hot and often windy days that halted my progress, it did seem a form of purgatory.

In the ten days that it took me to negotiate the Flats, I quickly realised that having a routine was pointless. The river was steady and slow but the weather was capricious, mostly combinations of severe heat (many a day the thermometer attached to my GPS read in the mid- to high-30s) and strong winds that would whip up the back of the river, making it impossible for me to continue. I would shelter ashore when the wind was up, often needing to build covered frames to block the heat of the sun and provide shelter from the wind-blown sand, but then try to seize any and every opportunity to put in the miles on the river whenever the conditions allowed. This lack of routine and feeling of 'being done to' only added to the sense of surreal otherworldliness of the Flats.

Despite my experiential negativity toward the Flats, the area did hold a

Eerie smoke-filled morning in the Flats

number of intriguing and arresting experiences as well as insights into the nature of life on the Yukon River. Predominant amongst these were the ingenious contraptions that it would also be easy to imagine Dante may have witnessed on his journey through the inferno: machines of torture, lumbering, unceasing racks of pain, if not for the damned in this instance, then certainly for the poor salmon of the Yukon. Fishwheels.

As I had already decided that I wasn't going to be doing any fishing on my paddle, I hadn't given the fish or fishing on the Yukon that much thought until my planning was already well underway. Previously, when I kayaked to Dawson, I was asked if I intended to do any fishing during my trip and whether I therefore wanted a licence. The guy from Up North Adventures seemed positively disappointed when I said I wasn't interested. To my mind, I was there to paddle and not faff about with a rod and line from boat or bank and, importantly, to me at least, I didn't want to be messing around with what I considered bear bait, even if I could catch one; a fish not a bear!

I was still very much of the same mind for this latest longer trip until just before New Year 2019. Sophie and I were wandering about the narrow, seasonally festive lanes of St Ives in Cornwall, perusing the contents of the small, eclectic, bespoke shops clustered in the narrow lanes, with no real intention of buying anything. I was just waiting for a civilised time to fall into a pub for a pint or two, when in a trendy, rather expensive, outdoor clothing shop my eyes fell upon a copy of Adam Weymouth's Kings of the Yukon. The book stood out for two main reasons: one, it had the word Yukon splashed across the cover in large bold font, and with my own planning already well underway this immediately grabbed my attention; and secondly, the cover had a drawing of an aerial view of a canoe floating on a river full of fish. Adam's book was, as I found out once I looked closer, about the salmon of the Yukon, particularly the Chinook salmon ('Chinook' in Canada, 'King' in Alaska). I bought the book and eagerly started to read it. It turned out that Adam had completed the trip I was planning and more, having started high up on McNeil Lake, which feeds into Lake Teslin, and paddling down through the Teslin and then onto the Yukon all the way to the sea.

I was fascinated by Adam's authoritative and informative account of the plight of the salmon, particularly the King salmon, and the subsistence living of the Native Peoples along the Yukon and Teslin Rivers. I read with fascinated interest about the use of fishwheels, but it was not until I saw the contraptions for myself that I got a sense of just how incongruous – and what cunningly efficient machines – they are. I saw my first fishwheel laid redundantly in some undergrowth near the landing point at Circle.

I had not seen any up until that point and believe they are probably banned upstream from Circle, in the Yukon–Charley Preserve. Which is not to say that there weren't any, just that I didn't see any. Even when redundant and laid in the grass it was easy enough to make out the contraption, the two great scoops that formed the wheel were laid on their sides looking like abandoned hockey goals lying back-to-back. Other than taking a quick, curious look at the abandoned wheel I didn't take much notice of it, or indeed visualise it upright and working, but it wasn't long after leaving Circle that I had that opportunity. I heard my first operational wheel before I saw it. I was, by then, attuned to the sounds and occasional random noises on the Yukon so when I heard a regular loud creaking of what could have been an oversized, slow-moving and very rusty bicycle, or probably more pertinent the sound of a windmill, it didn't take me much longer than usual to put two and two together.

As I rounded one of very many corners ahead on the Flats there it was, the source of the squeaking, my first fishwheel. It stood out like a proverbial sore thumb, not just because of the sounds coming from it, but also because it appeared to be orange in colour; it looked like bamboo, but I assumed it was freshly stripped spruce. It was moving in a manner so alien to the surroundings, with river water pouring from the upward moving scoop and glinting in the sun. I manoeuvred my boat so that I could drift close by and inspect the wheel properly whilst trying to film its motion as I approached and went past.

Just as I'd seen in the undergrowth at Circle, the wheel is in fact two great wicker scoops, set opposite each other, rotating around a central spindle supported on an A-frame and square base. It is held out in the river by outriggers and lashed to the bank strategically to keep it in place, and on the back of each scoop are a couple of planks working as paddles. When in the water, the paddles are pushed by the current and force the open mouth of the scoop downstream and into the oncoming salmon as they swim upriver. As the downstream scoop comes out of the water, dripping and ideally containing a salmon or two, the upstream scoop is just entering the water where the paddles are caught once more and the whole thing is forced around again in perpetual motion – truly ingenious.

But the really cunning bit is that fitted inside each scoop is a wooden slide that angles from high on the river side down toward the bank. As each scoop rotates upwards, any salmon that have been caught slide down the shoot and into a conveniently placed, sealed, water-filled tote. All the fishermen have to do is check their totes on a regular basis to see what's in them; brilliant! For the next 50 miles or so there were fishwheels dotted along the banks and I don't doubt there were many more in sloughs away from the main river. All along this stretch I saw skiffs shooting backward and forward their occupants inspecting their wheels. It was amazing how quickly a skiff would appear if you even looked like you were about to stop and check out a wheel.

Seeing the fishwheels I got to wondering, given the immense width of the river, the fact that the scoops were only about 2 metres wide, and that they were positioned only as far from the shore as necessary to allow them to spin unimpeded, how many fish they caught and why were the fish stupid enough to get caught with so much more river to swim in. But then, as if the river deliberately chose to answer my question, I took one of my very few wrong turns on the Flats. I inadvertently headed left at the point of an island and started heading up a large, long, slough having mistaken it for the main flow. I noticed my mistake pretty much straightaway as I drifted left and could see the main weight of water heading to the right of the point. There was no question of trying to paddle up against it and after a quick look at the map I concluded that I'd be better off man-handling my boat back around the point rather than taking a long detour through the slough. I paddled like mad to get to the island as quickly as I could and before the current took me too far into the slough. Once ashore I got out of the boat and whilst holding the bow and stern lines I floated the canoe back out on the water. I then angled it so that the current was pushing the bow out toward the slough whilst the stern was fixed and I could propel the boat forward along the shore against the flow.

Once the boat was at the right attitude and with the lines held firmly in one hand, I waded along the shore using my paddle in my other hand to steady myself and check for holes and obstacles. I only had a hundred metres or so to drag the boat and it was relatively straightforward. There was of course the obligatory dead spruce washed up on the point of the island, creating what the locals call a snag mound, but once I had negotiated this I was back on the right-hand side of the island and in the main flow. I decided to walk the boat up a little further to get away from the point and the snag mound before putting back in and it was here that I suddenly, and rather alarmingly, felt something knocking my ankles with some force.

Wading about calf deep as I was, I couldn't see my feet in the silty water and really couldn't work out what was happening. It was then as I was looking down, keeping a firm hold on the boat lines whilst leaning on my paddle and lifting each foot out of the water to inspect my ankles, that I saw my first salmon. There was a line of them, on the march, big, dark looking brutes, muscling their way blindly along the shallows, slapping my ankles out of their way in the process. I finally realised why the fishwheels could be so effective: these salmon were on a mission to get upstream, regardless of what might be in the way or out to catch them, and seemed to be using the shoreline as a handrail to guide them up through the silted water. I started to marvel at just how these amazing creatures managed this feat. Not only were they trying to make their way upriver, possibly through thousands of miles of melt water travelling downstream at about $6500m^3$ per second, but they also had to deal with the immense amount of silt contained in that water.

At the delta, the Yukon disgorges an average of 75 million tons of silt per year; at Dawson, where the river is narrow, this works out at about 60 tons passing per minute, all being washed down the river and over the advancing salmon. There were times on the river, both up beyond Dawson and on the lower reaches, where I could feel and hear the silt abrading the bottom of my boat. When I joined the Yukon from the Teslin at Hootalinqua in 2017, there was a clear delineation of the greener Teslin water and the grey-brown Yukon flowing out of the bottom of Lake Laberge. Seventy-five miles before Dawson as the White River fed into the Yukon, the demarcation was again clear to see, but this time it was from the white, ice melt and silt-ladened

White River which flows down from the glaciers around Mt St Elias to the south that added to the now lighter brown of the Yukon. It was here that I first really felt the particles washing under my boat. Further downstream after the Tanana River joins even more silt is added.

What effect must this have had on the salmon? They must have armoured scales! I could feel the sediment on my boat and I was travelling with the flow in my 'Tuff-Stuff' canoe, while the salmon were heading up through it. I've read that the silt can cause problems for the salmon, particularly by getting into their gills and also by covering the gravel beds of their traditional spawning grounds, but I had to wonder what it must do to their eyes as I'm not aware of salmon having a nictitating membrane. I imagined they must end up with polished eyes, perhaps a bit like Vin Diesel's title character in the Sci-Fi Riddick films, where he has his eyes polished (it's not real!) to help him see in the dark and therefore be able to take on and defeat various, ludicrous alien creatures. But I digress.

Redundant fishwheel at Circle

Fishwheel in operation

The author as shoreman salmon netting on the Exe estuary (copyright Adam Oseland)

Salmon Fishing

When I said I had no interest in faffing about fishing when my focus was to paddle the river, that was not entirely true. I do, actually, have a strong interest and connection to salmon fishing and have had the huge privilege of being one of the last few remaining traditional River Exe Salmon Fishermen. I had recently spent a few short seasons working as part of the crew of a small row-boat, 'Seine' netting (from the Old English SEGNE, or the Latin/Greek SAGENA for dragnet) sections of the Exe Estuary, just as our legendary octogenarian skipper and mentor Ken Pym had been doing for nigh on 70 years (give or take a couple out for national service) and as local people had been doing – in the same way, in the same location – since well before Roman times. Indeed, the Roman name for the city of Exeter, just upstream from the Exe Estuary, was 'Isca Dumnoniorum', Exe, along with Usk, Esk and many others, being derived from Isca the native Brittonic meaning 'river full of fish'.

So, whilst I wasn't concerned about catching salmon on the Yukon, having read Adam Weymouth's book I was still very interested to see how the First Nations' and Native Peoples' approach correlated with my own experience of what could be considered a native British approach. The first big distinction between the Yukon and the Exe is, as with many things North American, the scale. The Yukon River forms one of the longest salmon runs known anywhere in the world and boasts a number of Pacific salmon species including the King, Chum, Coho (silver), Pink (humpback) and Sockeye, which still migrate the length of the river in their hundreds of thousands, albeit these numbers have, as with most rivers, been falling over the last few decades. The River Exe on the other hand, whilst one of the longest runs in the UK, is less than 1/35 the length and size of the Yukon and is one of the spawning rivers for a single, but majestic, species the Atlantic salmon whose decline around the UK in recent years lead to a moratorium on all UK estuary and river Seine netting in 2019.

The differences in scale are immense and lead to the next obvious difference: along with the rest of the ecosystem of the Yukon Basin, the First Nations People have, for millennia, relied on the salmon for their lives and way of life, while people along the Exe no longer rely on the salmon for their living, although this has only been the case in the last few decades. The salmon netting that I experienced was for fun, a way for a few retirees to uphold a very ancient local tradition. When Ken started fishing as a lad back in the late 1940s, there were thirty plus boats fishing for salmon on the Exe. Once caught and landed the salmon were packed in ice and sent by train to London and many of the fishermen made their living from the salmon. Of course, the Exe fishermen of Topsham always had other odd jobs to help with the lean times, back then they usually fished from February through to November, but as Ken told me, for many of them if they couldn't catch they couldn't feed their families. Mind you, when Ken started his national service training at Wyvern Barracks, three miles down the road from his home in Topsham, not only did that interrupt his fishing, he found he was earning considerably less. There were still plenty of River Exe salmon about then.

For the Native Peoples of the Yukon their relationship with the salmon is, arguably, far more integral, more dependent – and also more spiritual. That is not to say that the connection did not exist on the River Exe, rather that the connection is now more distant. Each salmon species has its place in the First Nations and Native Peoples hierarchy of fish: the King (Chinook) salmon is top of the hierarchy and favoured for its rich, tasty meat; Chum (Dog) salmon, on the other hand, are much leaner and were caught to feed and sustain their dog teams, once so vital and the only practical form of transport through the long, frozen winter months; as John McPhee put it, once upon a time they were basically the equivalent of gasoline. During the fishing season, along the river, near the native fish camps, racks can be seen hanging with red strips of salmon flesh being air dried and preserved. It is difficult to exaggerate the importance of salmon, not just to the Native Peoples, but also for the entire ecosystem of the Yukon Basin. Arguably, without the salmon and the nutrition they provide throughout their life cycle, much of the native flora and fauna would not and could not survive.

For a far more detailed and insightful view of salmon, salmon fishing, and the impact fish numbers have had on the traditional subsistence lifestyle of the First Nations and Native Peoples along the River Yukon, I would recommend Adam Weymouth's Kings of the Yukon. For those of you looking for a deeper understanding of the scope and the 'spirituality' inherent within the interaction between the people, the wildlife and the environment of the North American Arctic, I'd thoroughly recommend Barry Lopez's Arctic Dreams. What follows is a brief account of how we fished on the Exe Estuary in Devon, so if you want to skip this bit and get back onto the Yukon give the next few pages a miss.

On the Exe Estuary, when I was privileged and lucky enough to be considered part of the 'A' team on boat 'E6' under Ken's skippership, I probably helped to reduce the average age of the boat to nearer sixty, albeit I'd just turned fifty myself. All of us were retired, except for Ken, for whom, whilst he no longer relied on it, salmon netting was just his way of life. E6 was a 6-metre, fibreglass, two-oared boat, designed to contain the precious Seine net. The Seine was 100 fathoms (180 metres/600 feet) in length, made of panels of 4.5 inch mesh netting stitched together. It was 4 metres deep and designed to hang horizontally in the water with a buoyed line on top (the head-line) and a lead-weighted line below (the foot-line). Both these lines, along the top and bottom of the net, came together beyond either end of the net via a 'pole-staff', a metre-long wooden pole with a spike beyond which there was a further 30 metres of single line. The idea of a Seine net is that it is used to create a purse in the river into which the fish, hopefully, are corralled and recovered alive, unlike a gillnet where the size of the mesh is designed to entrap the fish you're aiming to catch by their gills and recover them at a later point, usually once they had drowned.

The principle for deploying – or 'shooting' – the net was pretty straightforward, but not always as smooth as it could have been in practice. We would usually set off from the fisherman's 'causey' (slipway) at the bottom of Higher Shapter Street in Topsham two or three hours prior to low tide and paddle out to our chosen netting spot to start that day. At the desired moment, as the river was still ebbing, a member of the crew, the shoreman, would get out of the boat on the home bank and hang onto one end of the net by the line running from the pole-staff. The amount of line and position of the pole-staff (and therefore the position of the end of the net) was dependent on the height of the tide, depth of the water and the width of the river: the higher the water the more line was let out and vice versa as the tide dropped.

The boat would then be rowed directly across the river (between 50-

100 metres wide at this point), with two men on the oars and one paying out the net and usually, given his age and seniority, Ken in the bow giving instructions, although if we were shorthanded Ken was more than capable and embarrassingly proficient at working the net. Once the boat was on the far side of the river with the net stretched out between either bank – ideally in a straight line, but more often than not, given the wind and strength of the tidal flow, with a bit of bow in it – the net was allowed to drift momentarily with the tide. The boat pulled toward the far bank while the shoreman pulled in the opposite direction trying to keep the net taught across the river and walking, either calf deep in mud, or on slightly firmer footing, downstream parallel with the boat.

If there were any salmon making their way upstream at this exact point in time they would, hopefully, hold up in front of the net and drift back with it. On the surface, at a given point, the boat would then be rowed quickly and steadily along, and as close as possible to the far bank paying out more of the net. Just after half the entire length of net had been paid out, a point marked by a larger float known as the 'totter', the boat would turn and, as quickly as possible, head back over to the home bank, the aim being to reach it at exactly the point where their end of the net had finished paying out, thereby creating a 180-metre purse of netting in the river, with any salmon that may have been held up caught inside. The guys in the boat would then jump out, which despite their age they invariably managed in a pretty sprightly fashion, and two of them would haul the pole-staff at their end of the net up toward the shore and thrust the spike into the mud of the riverbank, securing their end of the net. Meanwhile, the shoreman would continue walking his end of the net down toward where the boat had landed and when 30-ish metres away – or in my case, when Ken started shouting – would also thrust his pole-staff into the foreshore.

The 'Haul' would then begin, the trick now being to let the tide do most of the work. The pull on the net from the weight of the tidal flow made it impossible to haul it in by hand when it was fully deployed, so the tide had to be allowed to swing the net downstream and toward the home bank where the weight was more manageable. My early attempts to prove myself and fight with the net and lines before the tide had done its work produced a few decent blisters and were met with Ken's amusement and advice. He suggested that I should be gentler and pull on the line as if I were pulling on my own 'todger'; I told him I was there to help catch salmon and not go blind!

The weight of the net on the pole-staff was not insignificant and with any real tidal movement it needed a knack rather than brute strength to hold it in place, the knack being to place the pole in the foreshore at an angle whereby the weight and pull on the lower, leaded line would help force it deep into the bank and provide more purchase. Often it required all of my 15 stones to hold it in this fashion and stop the net running away. As the net swung down river toward the home bank, the third man from the boat would make his way to the shoreman. If this was Ron, this usually involved a few dips in the mud – the water coming over his thigh length waders – which he still managed whilst rolling a fag. Once there were two men at either end of the net – one on the float-line and one on the lower leads – and as the weight of the net dictated, all four would start to haul in the net, hand over hand, whilst the two pairs moved steadily toward each other so that as the purse of the net in the river got smaller, the gap at the neck up on the shore started closing.

At this stage, everyone's eyes were on the net and the surface of the water therein, trying to ascertain if there were any fish in there. This is where Ken usually became pretty animated. I've had a reasonable bit of experience in leadership, but it was a real joy to work under Ken. He had the knowledge and experience to see precisely what was going on, and without having to consider anything as mundane, modern and boring as a dynamic risk assessment, he had us covered. He could see how the net was performing, what the tide was doing and who within the crew was struggling (and know the likely effect of all these variables) and, without being overtly caring, he protected us. That was until we were in the last few metres of recovering the net and particularly if Ken thought there was a salmon in the purse, which normally meant there was. Then he gave no quarter – the fish was to be caught and woe betide anyone that didn't do their job correctly. I occasionally had some difficulty with Ken's strong Devonian accent, but in the vinegar strokes of the haul, with signs of a salmon, this was not a problem: if he wasn't happy with your work and effort, he'd make himself very clear through the use of pure Anglo-Saxon invectives.

These final few metres were crucial – the men of the leads had to keep their lines as low as possible, in the mud, to stop the salmon from nosing under the net and escaping, while the float men had to keep their lines higher to stop the salmon making their way over the top. All the lines had to be brought in at the same time to maintain the integrity of the purse, the very back of which was known as the 'bunt', the place where the salmon would usually retreat to when finding themselves caught. The bunt then had to be dragged up out of the water intact to ensure there was nowhere for the fish to escape.

This was easier said than done as invariably the bunt would also contain a fair amount and weight of weed, not to mention the odd rock, shopping trolley, sunken dinghy and, allegedly (though fortunately not on my watch), a carcass. More often than not, if we had caught a salmon, it would be visible at this point but occasionally the net and the weed had to be searched to find them. Once found the salmon were quickly dispatched with a priest and respectfully placed in a clean part of the boat, always with their heads pointing toward the bow. The reverence with which the salmon were treated is, perhaps, another example of that atavistic relationship between hunter and prey, a relationship that mirrors the Yukon Natives' relationship with their surroundings. Regardless of this reverence, however, the salmon all had to be fitted with a plastic environment agency tag, weighed and logged. It was astounding how the exhilaration of catching a salmon made the haul feel easier and lighter, while several days of fishing without catching anything other than weed was hard work. There were days when we felt as if we were just sieving the river.

Once this was done, we had to shake out the net to remove any debris, then drag it back out into to water where it was easier to handle and, as the tide continued to drop, lift and lap all 180 metres systematically back into the stern of the boat ready to return to our starting point or another part of the estuary to begin the process all over again. We stopped fishing at low tide since trying to conduct the haul process in reverse on a flooding tide was an altogether different and dangerous prospect. Each haul took about 45 minutes, from shooting the net to having it loaded again ready to go (netted-in), and in reality the net was actually deployed on the river and therefore in a position to catch some salmon for probably no more than ten minutes of that time.

When I started with the crew, we used to manage three hauls before the tide turned, but over the last season, when Ken was often too ill to come out and take charge of us, we usually managed just two. What would he say!

Salmon netting on the Exe was a traditional, elemental style of fishing, but one that required hard-earnt know-how and skill to properly conduct. It gave me a very real and privileged sense of partaking in something deeply ingrained in the past and a sense of being at one with the river and my adopted hometown. But at the same time, in the 21st century, with salmon numbers waning, there was something slightly anachronistic about it. The three remaining salmon netting licenses for the Exe Estuary were subject to a ten-year moratorium from 2019, in truth they are unlikely to be picked up again after that. Another ancient tradition and way of life will have lost its place in the world.

I must admit I can, of course, see an element of logic behind this, particularly if it means maintaining (and, hopefully, increasing) the Exe salmon numbers, but I do still struggle to see anything particularly holistic in the Environment Agency's approach. It does appear to me that the Seine-boats were taken as 'low hanging fruit', an easy option, targeting the relatively low-income licence holders. If the Environment Agency is committed to protecting the salmon, then surely they should also be looking at a moratorium on all the other factors that would potentially impede the successful life cycle of our salmon.

Rod-and-line fishermen, for example, are still licensed to provoke salmon into taking their lures. Salmon stop eating when they enter the river to spawn, so the rod-and-line fishermen entice them to act against their instinct, bothering them with their lurid lures and flies. And surely, once caught on a hook, the energy the salmon wastes fighting against the line must reduce its chances of successfully spawning. Of course, all rod-and-line fishermen return their caught salmon to the river! I have no particular beef with the rod-and-line fishermen, but surely if salmon numbers are low enough to halt the netting, then, as I say, all possible means of easing the salmons progress should be adopted.

Then there is the management and protection of the spawning grounds, the agricultural run-off into the river and the development of new flood defences, all of which impact on the salmon's run. And when the poor exhausted salmon that do spawn, followed by the young that do manage to hatch attempt to make it back down the river toward the open ocean, they have to run the gauntlet of the Exe Estuary, which even without the netting remains a designated, protected Bass hatchery, and as such has (in salmon terms) an unfair number of predators. Finally, the coup de grace, once out at sea, large trawlers with nets tens of kilometres long hoover the salmon up indiscriminately.

So, I do still wonder how effective is the removal of three Seine licences for small boats with nets that are each in the water for less than 1% of the time the salmon are in the river; that's without taking into account the actual possibility factor of catching which, in theory, reduces the potential catch to well under that. These are people who could also act as environmental canaries on the river, able to report on general stock numbers from the salmon taken and the bycatch. There are numerous cases highlighting the divergence between technology and native knowledge, particularly when the technology is immature.

Adam Weymouth cites the case of the 1977 US National Marine Fisheries Service moratorium placed on the Yup'ik Eskimo's subsistence harvest of bowhead whales without consultation. The Yup'ik elders insisted that the Fisheries Service had grossly underestimated the actual whale population; the Fisheries Service insisted it had not. However, as the Fisheries Service whale survey technology improved it was shown that the bowhead population was in fact sufficient to support the Yup'ik subsistence needs; it took twenty years and millions of dollars for the technology to catch up with and prove that the native fishermen were right all along. Now, I am not saying that the scientists or the environment agencies are not acting in the best interests of the salmon (and I'm not saying that the traditional salmon netting on the Exe is entirely appropriate today), it's rather that, as with many organisations all alleging to be working toward common goals but coming at them from different angles, they often fail to recognise each other's contribution and can become antagonistic toward each other rather than working together. As a result, they end up with sub-optimal solutions and fail to act in the very best interest of their aims, often losing something more fundamental to the process along the way.

The rod-and-line fishermen along the river Exe have spent many years buying out the Seine licences in the belief that the netting has been reducing their sport without any real evidence; they want to protect the salmon for their entertainment, but at what price? By all means let us protect the salmon, but let's do so holistically with all interested parties involved, and without any bias toward the salmon being seen as sport and a source of licence income, rather than an integral part of life on the Exe.

I still miss the allocated ten weeks of muddy, hard work out on the estuary each summer in return for the odd precious salmon, albeit that the first year of the moratorium was the year I was able to make the journey in this story. I will miss participating in the living history of my adopted hometown, just as I will miss the gentle banter amongst those involved when out on the boat and listening to the daily 'guestimations' as to when exactly the tide would turn, the most crucial timing by which to judge when to cast the final haul and therefore the hauls preceding that. This conversation was usually predicated by the question, 'what time u givin 'e?', or, 'wez 'e to today?', followed by various interjections of calculations involving factors including the tide-table, the time when 'e' turned yesterday, the projected height of the tide that day, the amount of rainwater coming down the river and, if one-eyed Ed was involved, the additional effects of barometric pressures and longitudinal wave systems off the Azores. Needless to say, Ken was usually spot on.

I also enjoyed Ken's quiet and sometimes bawdy tales of the 'old Topsham' and occasionally of his national service, but I will particularly miss the silence, when we would sit waiting for the 'off', on those balmy, ever-so-still, early summer mornings. We would sit soaking up the silence on the mirrored surface of the estuary and occasionally, if there were any breeze and it was in the right direction, were gently serenaded by the Band of Her Majesty's Royal Marines practising at the Commando Training Centre further down the estuary. Of course, the regimental quick march of the Royal Marines, Life on the Ocean Wave, was my favourite and seemed very apt.

I visited Ken on my return from the Yukon in 2019 and sat with him for a while in his small room in White Street. He was riddled with cancer and had been given months to live, but he was still so lively, interested and full of fun. I took him some pictures I had taken of the fishwheels and we sat and discussed the people, the fishing and the fish I had seen on the Yukon. He looked smaller and older sat on his sofa than he ever did perched, flat capped, at the prow of 'E6', but his eyes were still very much alive, and I could see, as I described the Yukon to him, the excited yearning for the river and the glint for the salmon that only a lifelong fisherman and someone so connected to their environment could really know and hold. Ken died in the summer of 2020.

I didn't witness any Seine netting of the sort we practised on the Exe whilst on the Yukon, but I note that John McPhee talks about Seining being used by the Native Peoples on other rivers and the tributaries of the Yukon, notably the Kobuk and Koyukuk Rivers in northwest Alaska. This would make sense, with a group of locals working smaller such rivers in a similar manner to us on the Exe. Trying to haul a Seine net through the waters of the Yukon, given the sheer amount and weight of water along with the debris being washed downstream, would have been very difficult if not impossible, not to mention dangerous.

Other than the fishwheels, the form of fishing that I witnessed most often on the Yukon was gillnetting. Along the Yukon from Circle to the sea, and particularly near the settlements and fish camps, there were fluorescent marker buoys dotted sporadically along the banks of the river. Once again, the concept with these nets seemed easy enough, even if not as ingenious or elaborate as the fishwheels. One end of a 10-metre net was fastened to the bank with the opposite end thrown out about 3 metres into the river downstream, weighted at the bottom and held afloat by the buoy. This effectively formed a flat sided V-shaped funnel between the shore and the net which the salmon heading upstream and hugging the bank would swim into.

Being a gillnet and with the salmon muscling their way upstream through the silt, the salmon would try to push through the net and become ensnared by their gills and drown. As with the fishwheels, these nets were deployed and left out for later (and I assume regular) inspection. I thought it interesting that given the width of the Yukon, both forms of fishing I witnessed only fished the first few metres from the shore, but again I think

The Skipper, Ken Pym, looking for salmon in the net
(copyright Adam Oseland)

this was to do with trying to manage the sheer volume of the river. I am not entirely sure if there were preferred locations for these nets, or if there was a technique for knowing where best to place them – presumably where the salmon were – but I did also see a few gillnets spread out in areas of slacker water between islands and covering the mouths of sloughs.

It was at one of these nets across the mouth of a slough somewhere between Tanana and Ruby that I met a small, incongruous Alaskan Native family group – father, mother and daughter – inspecting their gillnet. Unlike the majority of the fishermen I'd seen, this group were particularly well dressed in what looked more like recreational sailing gear and were working form a boat more akin to a pleasure cruiser than the usual aluminium skiffs. It was the rather attractive tall, slim, dark-haired daughter that was providing the muscle and hauling in the net whilst the father gave instructions and the mother looked on. The daughter was hauling in a heavy net full of decent looking fish and I was close by so asked if I could film them in an attempt to record some footage to show the guys from the boat back home, albeit with my camera skills this was touch and go.

The daughter said she was happy with this, but I heard the old man grumbling that they were there to fish and not be recorded for the National Geographic. That made me smile: clearly all fishing boat skippers specialise in a similar form of cantankerous sarcasm. Just then the daughter hauled up a beautiful, shimmering, silver salmon about a metre in length. I asked what type it was. 'King,' said the old man. 'Ah, Chinook,' said I. 'No, King,' said he; I liked him. After a few short minutes of cack-handed back-paddling trying to stay next to them whilst holding my GoPro camera, I gave up, thanked them for their patience and went on my way. They passed me a few minutes later heading for the plushest looking fish camp that I saw along the whole of the river, neatly set on its own island. I had a little bit of salmon fishing envy.

A little later, out on the river one afternoon just short of Nulato, I became conscious of a skiff approaching me from behind. They usually gave me a clear berth. I looked over my shoulder and could see that this one was coming toward me, so I stopped paddling and prepared to greet them. The aluminium skiff that pulled alongside my small craft was skipped by Rick, a squat, strong but amiable-looking Alaskan Native, probably in his early forties. Onboard with Rick was his son Robert – probably in his twenties and with a strong family resemblance – who in turn was holding his son, a real toddler, wrapped up and sound asleep in his arms. Their boat wasn't big, but its gunwale was well above mine, and I held onto Rick's boat with both arms trying both to keep myself steady and maintain a gap between the two craft, whilst talking up at the guys on the skiff.

After our introductions, Rick asked how I was doing and where I was off too. Like most of the people I met on the river, he seemed genuinely interested in my trip, and particularly amused by the fact I was from England. For some reason the term English seemed to resonate with the locals more easily than British and it appeared from some of my conversations that there was a couple of other 'Londoners' out paddling ahead of me somewhere as well. He appeared quietly impressed with my plan, probably weighing up my chances of making it, and helpfully suggested that I still had a very long way to go. He then asked if I'd like a salmon, and before I had the chance to answer honestly that, no, I didn't really, I had a 9-10lb Chum salmon in the canoe between my feet. It was another of my wonderfully English moments: despite my recent isolation, I was still unable to say 'no' for fear of confusing Rick with my random excuses and also for appearing rude or dismissive toward his kind gesture.

Aware that the Native Peoples used to feed Chum salmon to their dogs I said thank you as enthusiastically as I could. Rick and Robert smiled, waved and powered off ahead toward Nulato a couple of miles downstream on the right-hand bank leaving me bobbing in their wake and wondering how on earth I was possibly going to deal with this unexpected gift. I like salmon and normally would have no problem gutting and cooking such a beautiful fish. I considered building a fire to cook it whole but finding enough firewood on some of the sandbanks on that part of the river wasn't always easy, so I thought about cutting it into small chunks to boil in my pint-sized Jet Boil. I quickly dismissed both ideas, as, predominantly, I was working out how to minimise any contamination or lingering fishy smells on me, the boat and my kit. In the end, just before landing on a sandbar, and to my great embarrassment, I slipped the fish quietly and reverentially over the side of the canoe and into the river giving it a short burial at sea ceremony, an attempt to assuage my guilt at wasting my offering. I then washed my hands and the boat thoroughly before stepping ashore.

That night I was camped almost opposite the settlement of Nulato, where Rick had headed off toward in his skiff, and subsequently spent the night paranoid that he might decide to pop out to kindly check that I was OK and enjoying his generous and hard-caught gift. Fortunately, he didn't. In the following days I paddled past a few, dead, floating Chum salmon of about the same size as the one I had ditched and in my isolated mania wondered if, perhaps, this was the spirit of my wasted fish coming back to haunt me. It's amazing what your mind can do to you when left to its own devices in a place such as this.

Gifted chum salmon on board before Nulato

Aside from the actual act of fishing, one notable similarity that struck me came from John McPhee's account of the Native Peoples working the Kobuk River in northeast Alaska: he notes that they had a sense of place and had their own shared names for almost every part of the river. On the Exe, for the fishermen, and the initiated, this sense of place was, perhaps, the same. Within a small stretch of river, particular places were known by their own specific names such as the 'Black-Ore Hard', the 'Range', the 'Clock', 'Ting Tong', or the 'Cupboard', which, so I was told, is where the river deposited its more gruesome debris. I'm sure there were many more, that I did not pick up on, all with their own history and specific, river-related stories attached, many of which, along perhaps with more of Topsham's sense of 'place', and therefore our connection to that place, will now, sadly, soon be consigned to the distant past, if not lost altogether.

"It has been said that place names are linguistic fossils."

Christopher Hadley, Hollow Places.

As another philosophical tangent, I find I am drawn to this concept of 'place' seen as an ancient human connection. In the introduction to his book Off the Map, Alastair Bonnett sets out a thesis arguing that in much of the modern western world, 'place' has now been demoted or displaced to the position of being viewed as parochial. This is the result, he says rather strongly, of the combined "universalist pretensions of monotheistic religion, the Enlightenment and modern abstract visions of global oneness", a rather contrary set of 'pretensions' that have, of late, come under attack from almost every quarter. He further suggests that in the modern world, 'place' has been replaced by the more acceptable concept 'space' which evokes mobility and the absence of restrictions; promising empty landscapes filled with promise. An interesting dichotomy if you believe that enlightenment and global oneness hinder mobility and access to landscapes filled with promise, or that monotheistic religions do not promote restriction and inertia.

Perhaps this does point to a key difference between my experiences on the Rivers Exe and Yukon. In Bonnet's terms, the Yukon still offers space;

it still promises empty landscapes filled with adventure. Mind you, when I found myself confronted by the awesome threatening space of the Yukon, I would invariably stick firmly to my perceived place. I would shun too much mobility in favour of security, whether that was in my 16-foot canoe, which I kept on a safe part (or place) on the spacious river or, when camped ashore, where I would undertake a search of the space I had stepped into, if I found no potential threat, I would render the space as my place.

So, whilst I yearned for the space – it was that essence of the Yukon that I had come to experience – I was also intimidated by it and as such I created daily places where I felt safe. The geographer, Yi-Fu Tuan proposed a slightly different view of space and place which better echoes my experience on the Yukon. He suggested that "The ideas 'space' and 'place' require each other for definition. From the security and stability of place we are aware of the openness, freedom, and threat of space, and vice versa. Furthermore, if we think of space as that which allows movement, then place is pause; each pause in movement makes it possible for a location to be transformed into place." However, for me 'place' did not necessarily just relate to a pause because, as stated, I was able to find 'place' within my little canoe whilst being borne seaward on the spacious river, as long as I felt I was safe and had a degree of control; so I would add that 'place' also requires an element of control.

I wonder if that fleeting sense of place I felt back in Devon on the Exe, that sense of connection with something older, something real, that I had experienced whilst salmon netting, that sense of partaking in history, has now, just recently, been assigned to the parochial, to the anachronistic, the passe, it is no longer there. The Exe Estuary is now perceived more as a 'space': a space of mobility and freedom where mobility and freedom now equate to the further fulfilment of modern, urban, utopian lives currently epitomised by stand-up paddle boarders, perhaps unaware that the utopia we seek can be translated from the Greek as 'no-place'. I have absolutely no issue with this use of and idea of space – it's what I choose to seek for recreation. But I wonder, perhaps, if we may be losing something deeper by inadvertently, in our rush to be mobile and free, overriding our connection to our sense of place, to history and the ability to pause and possibly wonder, even for just a while.

At that time, I found myself able to reflect, abstractly, on the hurly-burly of modern life. I recalled the observation attributed to the American children's TV entertainer, Fred Rogers (played by Tom Hanks in the 2019 film A Beautiful Day in the Neighborhood) when he mused, "It seems to me that some of us value information over wonder, and noise over silence. And I feel we need a lot more wonder and a lot more silence in our lives." The Yukon River gave me a profound sense of both wonder and silence.

The A Team (!) with the best day's netting of my time on the boat

Approaching Yukon Crossing

A River Highway

"If you are not close to the river you are lost."

Yupik Elder, Mary Anne Immamak of Emmonak, Alaska

As I paddled on those quieter days, I got to thinking about my relationship with the Yukon River and, more generally, what rivers actually mean to all of us. Once again, caught in the duality I was experiencing. At the pragmatic level, rivers are, of course, either a physical boundary, offering protection or demarcation, or otherwise a transportation medium, offering access, movement and freedom. They were, and still are, also life-giving, providing sustenance to those that have traditionally congregated along them, just as people do along the world's coastlines. Somewhere in the region of 40% of the world's population live within 60 miles of a coast (source: The Ocean Conference Factsheet, United Nations, New York, 5-9 June 2017) and the vast majority of those live in places where rivers run into the oceans.

Historically, rivers (as with coastlines) provided frontiers, barriers and boundaries and were – and arguably still are – therefore integral to our understanding of who we are and where we come from: 'what side of the river are you from?' Latterly, the relationship has started to change. We now recognise, less and less, the physical boundaries provided by rivers, although it could be argued that the recent rise in devolutionary desires may see us hiding behind wet walls again. Alternatively, perhaps this modern interest in devolution is a last gasp grab by smaller communities and nations to hang onto a sense of security offered by 'place' as globalisation heads, otherwise, towards the mobility and a perceived lack of restriction within the global 'space', with terms such as 'global village' being used to make it sound cosy and quell the autonomists fears.

Either way, our rivers – particularly those that have been cleaned – are now seen as a space for recreation and sport which offer us the chance to exercise our bodies and, increasingly, to commune and reconnect with nature. For much, if not all, of human history, rivers have been spiritual places, the places of gods and deities, of worship – elemental elements in their own right. I find it interesting that as we appear to be moving away from the security and comfort offered by a sense of 'place' and more toward the freedom and mobility of 'space' we are still looking everywhere for new connections and security; we still have not, and I suspect cannot, really shake off or lose our atavistic being. Rivers have been fundamental to the development of the human psyche, and whether we appreciate them or not we are indelibly linked and drawn to them.

In her book To the River, Olivia Laing suggests that "rivers move through time as well as space" and in Rising Ground, Philip Marsden says, "All rivers are stories, connecting places, carrying history." These ideas of movement through stories, history, time and space are all germane to the Yukon River. To witness its history and movement, through time and space, you only need look at the Yukon from the air, or better still from the satellite images available online. You will see that, when not confined by rock gorges or mountains, the scars of the river's past litter the landscape: old sloughs, oxbow bends and thousands upon thousands of small lakes, all remnants of the Yukon's writhing path through both time and space. More pertinent, perhaps, is the fact that much of the water that currently forms the Yukon comes from the glaciers that surround the Yukon Basin. It consists of unlocked water and sediment captured thousands of years ago, predating much of the Yukon's modern history.

It is also a river that has captured and embraced an evocative ideal, spawned in fictional literature. It is an archetypical literary river, synonymous with recent North American history, of frontiers, wildness, courage, greed and human endeavour. For the First Nations and Native Peoples, this relationship predates the arrival of Herman Melville's "all-grasping western world…the money making animal"; their relationship is deeper, longer and far more spiritual, based largely on the fact that the Yukon is also a corridor of migration, bearing precious life, sustaining life, where otherwise it would not have been possible.

In his book Underland, Robert MacFarlane explores the idea of 'starless rivers', those rivers, real and literary, that run through classical culture and fire the human imagination, albeit MacFarlane explores rivers of the dead, such as the Lethe, the Styx and the Acheron. From my experience – with the exception of my very last night – the Yukon was, for me, a 'starless river'.

However, unlike MacFarlane's rivers of the underground, the mind and the dead, the Yukon is a river of life, even if for the majority of its flowing, liquid, existence it runs under a starless, sun-dominated sky. The stars only reflect in its bubbling waters around the times of its annual persephonic incarceration and release.

When it is under the stars, the Yukon bides its time, locked in ice – and when released the Yukon brings life to the country. For my part, I longed for the stars. Twenty-four-hour daylight is all well and good but there is something nonsensically grounding about being able to see the light from the further reaches of space, from stars other than our own. In my own travels, I have always looked to the stars to give me a sense of place, to help me locate my place on this planet. Generally, this is as a reference relative to my home, usually in the northern hemisphere, seeking out Cassiopeia or Ursa Major, the Great Bear, to locate, or at least indicate the position of the unmoving Polar Star.

I thought it a rather circular concept that the culture that eulogised many of the archetypal rivers also gave the region I was paddling through – the Arctic – its modern name. Arctic is derived from the ancient Greek, 'Arkikos', meaning the country of the Great Bear, the country under Ursa Major; the constellation of Ursa Major is even represented on the Flag of Alaska. So here I was on this most fabled and evocative of rivers, unable to see the stars and unsure about wanting to encounter a great bear.

> **JOURNAL 4 JULY 2019:** I have seen one or two local skiffs going up and down the river, they appear to be bouncing around quite a bit and the occupants are well wrapped up, if I can, I try and get a friendly wave from them.

Back to reality. The Yukon is, of course, more than just an ideal, an archetype enshrined in literature and imagination: the fact that it is most definitely still a working river is abundantly evident. The run of skiffs ferrying fishermen, hunters, families, or just out for a spin, is rather like the run-of-the-mill road traffic between isolated communities in any remote part of the world. A mix of commerce, communication, community, casual (and occasionally downright dangerous) commuting. Most of the skiffs were flat-bottomed, indestructible (well almost), aluminium boxes with one or two huge (mostly about 140-horsepower) outboards roaring on the back. Many of these would have been part funded by the locals from their Alaskan Permanent Fund dividends, a fund established using revenues paid to the state by the oil and natural gas producers. All Alaskan residents receive an annual cash dividend from the permanent fund – in 2019, the annual dividend was $1,625.80 per resident.

These skiffs could be powered up onto the shore and simply tied off or anchored, rather like cowboys in the old western films riding their horses into town up to the salon before nonchalantly jumping off, throwing the reins over a convenient banister and going about their business. The cockpits were, variously, a simple console with a small wheel and accelerator lever; some had windshields, many didn't, and the pilots could normally be seen with hats pulled down, goggles on and hoodies wrapped tight. Those with windshields were often homemade wooden and Perspex affairs; a few had cabins built to shelter their families, most of whom were again wrapped up against the elements, huddled down and bouncing about, as the skiffs powered upstream at speed against the current.

For the Native Peoples and locals, the Yukon provides their highway, their country lanes, and within them there were clear traffic routes. Most of these ran through the sheltered water at the edges of the river, where I was usually paddling, or they negotiated the winding maze of sloughs with the seemingly reckless ease of those with local knowledge. From my perspective, the majority of skiff pilots were respectful of my intrusion and would give me room, a wave and the odd shout of encouragement, at least that's what I think they were shouting – a few were just scary!

Another key form of transportation noisily – and for the most part welcomingly – evident along the Yukon were the aircraft. In the areas without road access (pretty much all of the Yukon Basin), aircraft are the go-to form of transportation for speedier trips and, of course, emergencies. The US Government built a comprehensive network of airfields across Alaska during WWII to support the defence of the state against the threat of Japanese invasion from the west. The little-known Japanese landings on the Alaskan Aleutian Islands were the only enemy invasion of US soil during that war. As a result, nearly all the settlements along the Yukon have an airfield of some sort, and, as I was told in a bar in Anchorage, here having a pilot's licence is the norm rather than the exception. The saying was that if you want to go anywhere in Alaska you need to fly, or at least it used to be the case.

The toing and froing of the aircraft across and along the river did, at times, help reinforce my navigation, particularly when nearing some of the larger settlements. Near the settlement of Beaver, after a particularly turgid day of paddling, it was great to see four US Airforce A10 'Warthogs' fly low and loudly overhead. I found it weirdly comforting. Although ageing, the Warthogs remain super-agile fighter jets; with their twin engines mounted on the rear fuselage just ahead of the tail fins, they invoked some great personal memories. I hadn't seen any of these aircraft since the mid-1980s when they used to stage dogfights across the sky above northern Norway during our regular winter military exercises.

There was also, from time to time, the familiar and distinctive bass thrumming of Huey helicopters. These seemed prevalent near the forest fires, so I assumed they were used in the firefighting. My memories of these aircraft are less favourable as I'd sworn I would never get in one again, at least not one piloted by the Bruneian Airforce. Someone had told the Bruneian pilots that the Huey double-bladed rotors were capable of cutting through foliage, of what thickness I don't know, but being flown through the jungle rather than over it was not a pleasant experience and constituted one of the very few occasions where I opted to walk out of the jungle rather than fly when offered.

My own experience of flying whilst in Alaska was a very windy and bumpy Cessna 207 flight out of Emmonak at the end of my paddle. I only narrowly avoided using the sick bag before landing 35 minutes later at St Mary's. At the risk of being inappropriate, I was pleasantly surprised to realise that the gorgeous young blonde in the high-vis vest that loaded me and two locals onto the plane at Emmonak was our pilot. Given her no-nonsense approach to the whole business and her calm, professional adeptness at taking off sideways in the wind that was still howling in from the Bering Sea, I felt entirely at ease – the greenness that developed in my gills was the result of my own weak constitution.

In that short time aloft, we followed the course of my last two days of paddling, taking off to the south over the Kwiguk Pass, then turning left back up the course of the Yukon. Despite the buffeting and the haze of rain, I could clearly make out my route, the Tunurokpak Channel, the big bend after St Mary's and just before turning into land, the location of my penultimate, rather idyllic, campsite. It made the efforts of my last 48hrs on the Yukon seem rather paltry when viewed so briefly from the air and I realised why aircraft were so important.

Back on the river, supporting the lives of those that live along the Yukon – and doing the heavy lifting – was the 'pusher' tug The Tanana. For the technical geeks, The Tanana is a 336-tonne vessel measuring some 30m x 11m, with a 2-metre hull depth, powered by two Luger 6170 diesel engines, turning two 1.2m x 0.9m, five-bladed, fixed-pitch propellors providing 1400 horsepower; so a big powerful craft. The Yukon has been worked by larger craft for well over a century, most iconically by the rear-paddle steamers that serviced the Gold Rushes, both downstream from Whitehorse as well as upstream from the Bering Sea. The evidence of this herculean trade is still clear along parts of the river, from the wrecked steamers and the woodyards or coalmines that fuelled them, many of which remain only in name having been reclaimed by time, the river and vegetation. It was also clear from the size of some of the newer wharfs that I saw in Dawson, Eagle and Circle that the desire and ability to receive larger vessels is still there.

Despite knowing about The Tanana, I was still surprised to meet her for the first time. I'd made an early start in the Flats trying to use the occasionally calmer conditions at that hour and was on the water for 2:30am paddling above the Arctic Circle in the still, misty, dimpsy light, just west of Fort Yukon. As soon as I was on the water, I was aware of the humming of a heavy engine somewhere ahead through the maze of the Flats. In the limp air and through the multitude of channels that surrounded me, it was difficult to discern exactly where the thrumming was coming from – all I knew was that it was getting louder.

After about half an hour I rounded a bend to be confronted by the huge bulk of The Tanana pulled up on my left bank facing toward me. The floodlights from atop the three-storey high superstructure, illuminating the gloom and filtering through the mist, were focused on the two barges side by side in front of the tug. There was a crew of about 4 or 5 guys busily working on the tug, some attaching hawsers to brigade the barges, some operating cranes and heavy machinery loading the barges, each of which had a deck area the size of a tennis court. These barges were loaded with machinery, 4x4 vehicles and various containers. I received a single half-hearted wave from a crew member working on the back of the tug and could see what looked like the skipper high up on the bridge, lit by an Anglepoise lamp, looking down and over the work below with an intercom phone held to his cheek.

I had no idea why it was there. Well, actually, it was obvious why it was there, what I couldn't grasp was where it might be going and just how far up and down the river it worked; I was going to find that out on a few more occasions over the coming weeks. All I knew at that time was that it was startling and incongruous to see this behemoth throbbing, clanking and lighting up the otherwise subdued Flats. As I made my way downstream, the noise of the tug faded behind me and I entered a bank of smoke from a forest fire. The whole experience put me in mind of the scene from Apocalypse Now where, after a river trip, Martin Sheen finally reaches Colonel Kurtz's (Marlon Brando's) base deep in the steamy swamps of Cambodia. Had I paddled into yet another archetypal river reference? Possibly, the un-specified river and the story of the journey in the film was based on Joseph Conrad's masterpiece, Heart of Darkness, set on yet another evocative river, The Congo.

I met The Tanana on three more occasions. The first time was when it passed by one night as I was camping on the sheltered side of an island north of the 'Big Eddy' thirty miles west of Ruby. I recognised the sound of the tug someway off but didn't see it as it passed heading upstream in the main channel on the other side of the island. I did, however, see its wash coming around the end of the island and hurriedly rushed down to my boat to pull it up away from the waterline. The second time, she was again chugging upstream, this time whilst I was sat by my boat with a fire going having been forced ashore on the spot that the black bear had been occupying just seconds earlier. That time the skipper gave me a cheery wave from high up on his bridge, probably wondering what I was doing and completely unaware of my unease at that time.

The final time we met, I actually paddled past her as she was coming toward me upstream, driving her barges before her, in a reasonably wide section of the river. She must have passed me on a few other occasions, unnoticed, heading downstream in order to be, again heading upstream past me, but I don't recall seeing or hearing her doing so. Faced with the tug nosing her way up against the current I could see the considerable wash being forced up by the snub nose of the leading barge and the ridge of water trailing diagonally away from the craft toward the bank. I moved over to the edge of the river, on the left, giving me some clearance from the tug but also getting ready to turn into the wake once the tug had passed in order to try and breach the wake head-on. I couldn't work out how high the wake was from my position in the canoe, but there was going to be no hiding from it.

As the tug passed, seemingly oblivious to my presence, I turned into the wake which was now effectively a wall of water a metre high, glinting in the sun, moving at some speed; this was going to be fun. I was confident enough that if I hit the wake nose on and could keep my line I would be able to paddle over it and any following ridges. What I didn't account for, or expect, was the refraction from the shore which sent more waves heading back onto the river, slightly lower than their parents in height and perfectly perpendicular in direction. I was faced with a series of waves coming at me, with a limited interval, from opposing right-angles. The previously calm river before the tug was now a neat, symmetrical, crisscrossed pattern of waves. It was one of the few times I got to employ my limited sea kayaking skills, as I used the top of each ridge of water to help turn the canoe through 90^0 to face the next set. It took over twenty minutes before the river surface returned to its usual gentle roll and I was ready for a cup of tea.

I had expected to see some forest fires and one of those apocalyptical thoughts that I had entertained during my planning was what if I got caught in a major fire and had to paddle through a flaming inferno? Those bloody trees again: if they weren't trying to drown me or crush me, they'd set themselves on fire to get to me. Perhaps I needed a break? Of course, it was extremely unlikely to happen (or at least I thought it was) and thankfully it did not, but throughout my paddle there were a number of fires burning

Distant forest fires in the Flats

around me and across the Yukon Basin.

The first fire I became aware of was one in which I mistakenly took the distant smoke to be an approaching storm. It was another ridiculously hot evening somewhere in the Flats and the sun had again been ripping apart any cloud foolish enough to get between it and me. I was gratefully relieved, having set up camp and contemplating another sweltering night, when a bank of what I believed to be cloud did eventually manage to screen some of the sun's intensity. In my journal, I commented on the hope that this would bring some rain in which I could strip naked and dance around in. There was no rain, so I maintained my modesty and had a more comfortable night's sleep. It was only in the morning when I awoke and found a fine layer of ash covering my tent and the surrounding area that I realised that what I had seen that previous evening had, in fact, been smoke from a huge distant fire. I then spent the first of many days, particularly in the Flats, paddling through lingering smoke. The Yukon, in the Flats, in the wee small hours, can be an eerie enough place without having special effects thrown in as well.

Later, I passed a few actual fires blazing on the hillsides around me. It was frightening to see the ferocity with which some of them burnt: it was almost as if some of the trees were erupting spontaneously and more than once I saw flames appear to jump from one tree to another. Along with this, I could see the crackle and fizz of the spruce needles as they popped into the air like exploding ammunition, above which a thick plume of smoke rose vertically before being dragged off by the breeze. These were relatively small fires but still impressively violent and destructive.

In numerous spots along the river where recent fires had burnt, the gap in the trees was marked by an incongruously beautiful carpet of red. Wherever the fires had destroyed the spruce and willow, it had given birth to the appropriately but unimaginatively named fireweed (Chamaenerion angustifolium), the floral emblem of the Canadian Yukon Territory, a plant that mockingly, posthumously, mirrors the destructive force that gave it birth. Alaskan folklore states that when fireweed blooms winter will only be six weeks away; perhaps a grain of truth in there, if fireweed blooms in late July or August after most of the lightning strikes and the fires, then winter will start in mid to late September, which is about right. As it transpired, July 2019 when I was on the Yukon was the hottest on record in Anchorage and South-Central Alaska, with 10,000 – yes 10,000 – lightning strikes recorded throughout the state that month. Having witnessed some smaller fires close up, I could only imagine, with reverential awe, the horror that lay under some of the vast smoke plumes I saw, thankfully from some distance. Perhaps, my apocalyptical visions back home may have been realised had one of those infernos chosen to straddle the river as I paddled through it.

I was now, finally, heading west, actually toward the Bering Sea. I had been travelling in a mostly northerly direction until reaching Fort Yukon, halfway through the Flats, and until then had been struggling with the counter-intuitive concept of heading up north whilst paddling downstream. In fact – and another of my asides which I think is interesting: many, many years ago, about 5.3 million to be precise, the Yukon used to flow southwards and drain in the Gulf of Alaska. A combination of the uplift of the St Elias Mountains to the south and the formation of the Tintina Trench to the east in the late Miocene and early Pliocene eras, followed by a shift in the regional glaciation, diverted the upper Yukon drainage northwards to flow into and overtake the then Kwikhpak River Basin, forming what is now the Yukon Basin. To this day, the Yukon is still referred to by some of the First Nations as Kwikhpak.

The river now felt like it had more of a sense of purpose, more than it had in the Flats for sure, and this pick-up had reinvigorated my own sense of achievement and determination. I approached the next phase of my paddle, not with the slightly trepidatious sense of stepping into the unknown as I had done previously, but with a tangible feeling of excitement and adventure. The river was now getting bigger, it was now carving its way through the hills of central Alaska and I could now occasionally glimpse distant snow-capped mountains giving me a sense of the space that I was in and which I had missed in the Flats.

Small fires along the river just after leaving the Flats

Entering a smoke-filled canyon before Tanana

Yukon Crossing
to Tanana

It was early July, and I was looking forward to reaching Yukon Crossing, partly because it would mean that I was definitely beyond the purgatory that was the Flats which I'd left at the Fort Hamlin Hills where there was a slight pick-up in the momentum of the river and, at last, some very welcome mountains and wider, open scenery. It would also mark a noteworthy point in my journey, 500-miles down, and I would hopefully be able to have a cooked meal and a shower.

The day before Yukon Crossing, I was having a lazy morning by my tent after a final night of paddling to get out of the Flats during which I was blessed with the sighting of another lynx. I had spotted this one from the boat as it watched me pass, stretched out along the bough of a lower spruce branch looking for all the world like the Cheshire Cat himself. It had been completely nonplussed by my presence, and I'd half expected to see him slowly vanish into the background leaving nothing but a grin hanging in the tree. I was contemplating the lynx in the morning sunshine as I packed away my stuff, when I saw another canoe approaching from upstream. It contained the first paddlers I'd seen on the water since Circle nine days earlier.

In the canoe were Mike and Vreni, a Swiss couple who had put in back in Beaver Creek just after Fort Yukon and had spent a few weeks paddling down to get picked up at the Crossing. Mike really looked the part, dark hair and beard, lean, wiry, in a checked shirt with a large bowie knife on his belt. Poor Vreni looked a little tired and remained sat in their canoe while Mike waded ashore to say hello. In their canoe they had their kit, along with a pile of firewood, lashed down under a tarpaulin, they had clearly been in for the authentic outdoor, backwoodsman, experience. They were a lovely couple and we chatted, ankle deep in the water, by the riverside, sharing experiences, for about half an hour before Mike jumped back in their canoe and they continued on their way. I passed them later that afternoon as they were setting up camp on an island, Mike erecting a screen using his tarpaulin to shade Vreni who was sat outside their tent preparing a meal. The sun still had considerable power. They must have leapfrogged me early the next morning as they were ashore just before the Yukon River Bridge emptying their boat and cleaning their kit the next time I saw them.

I had deliberately chosen to reach the bridge just before midday so that I could ring home and let Sophie know exactly where I was. The bridge, high above the river, was visible from about six miles away along a straight stretch of the river and I had spent an hour or more that morning paddling without it appearing to get closer. I was glad to get there. I said hello to Mike and Vreni from my boat and we agreed to meet for a coffee up at the diner above the bridge once we'd sorted ourselves out. I canoed under the bridge and pulled up on the concrete slipway downstream.

The Yukon River Bridge, the Yukon Crossing, is the only bridge crossing of the Yukon in Alaska. Officially known as the E. L. Patton Bridge, it is a 700m long girder bridge that stands 30 metres above the river and carries a 9-metre-wide wooden decked road – part of the Dalton Highway – as well as the Trans-Alaska Pipeline. The bridge was built in the mid-'70s to carry the pipeline connecting the Prudhoe Bay Oil Field on the Arctic Sea coast with Port Valdez on Alaska's southwestern coast. When opened, it was one of the world's largest pipeline systems: 800 miles in length, with a diameter of 1.2 metres, it was capable of transporting two million barrels a day, although it actually pumps a fraction of that nowadays. The sheer audacity of the project – the engineering obstacles that were surmounted and the environmental and legal challenges that were overcome – bear testament to the desire to exploit natural resources regardless of how remote or who may actually own them. Whatever your perspective, it is an impressive feat and stands as a monument to modern Alaskan determination.

The slipway was relatively busy with people manoeuvring and loading their skiffs, cruisers and RIBs onto trailers, no doubt ready to head home to Fairbanks after a weekend's fishing and camping on the Yukon. I hadn't noticed quite so many boats on the river over the preceding few days, but they must have been out there somewhere, unless they all headed downstream from the bridge. But it is a big river. I sat in the shade of the bridge and rang Sophie at home, and we had a good, positive chat. I think we had both got back into the swing of those truncated, long-distance, conversations and I had got better at being able to switch between my Yukon-focused mindset and talking about life back in Devon, although I think that perhaps being nearer people and a little bit of civilisation made it easier as well. I dug out some clean clothes, picked up my now empty water carrier and walked up the slipway onto the open expanse of the diner car park next to the Dalton Highway.

The car park was busy with pick-ups manoeuvring boat trailers, coaches, and a couple of huge Kenworth articulated trucks. It was hot, dusty and noisy and I was pleased to get into the subdued, air-conditioned diner. The Yukon River Camp looks more like a provincial airport terminus than a diner, a low single-story wood-clad building, with a huge white butane cylinder outside. Inside is the restaurant, a souvenir shop and outback staff accommodation, rooms and showers. My timing was perfect: there were only a couple of other people in the diner so I could get straight to the counter and order a cheeseburger and coffee – as always all I could drink – and ask about a shower. The waitress, a handsome, middle-aged woman, was uber-efficient with an air of having seen it all before and was unfazed by my appearance and random babbling. She quickly had me sat down with a large mug of filter coffee, my burger ordered (what type of cheese, straight or curly fries, etc, etc.) and provided me directions and instructions for the shower.

On my Formica table beside the usual selection of condiments was a homemade plastic-covered A4 folder with 'Yukon River Camp – A Bear Story' on the cover. As I waited for my burger, my skin tingling from the sensation of being indoors in air-conditioning, I picked it up and read, with alarming interest, the bear story. In short, a few winters previously when the Camp was in hibernation and therefore uninhabited, there was a report that the building had been broken into. When this report was investigated, it became apparent that the culprit was a bear and that it was probably still somewhere inside. It was decided that the bear should be removed, and two guys went in to find it, not really knowing what they might find. Working by torchlight – as there was no power available at that time of year – it was clear the place had been ransacked and the bear had been in there searching about for food and bedding, but it was now nowhere to be seen. It was only when one of the guys searched through the back of the building that he came face-to-face with a huge, angry male grizzly bear in a dark narrow corridor. With nowhere to run, the guy had to resort to shooting the bear several times – never a guarantee to stop a large grizzly. The book was complete with pictures of the state of the diner and the bear that broke in. I thought

I might have lost my appetite, but then my burger arrived, and I was more worried that my stomach might have shrunk.

The burger was most welcome, giving the one at the Carmacks campsite 750 miles upstream and two years previously a run for its money. As I carefully ate it, I watched coachload after coachload of tourists, predominantly Asian, descend on the diner. They would walk in, look around the souvenir shop, maybe buy something, check out the pictures on the walls and then just as quickly depart, usually with a pre-prepared takeaway lunch box. There must have been at least three coachloads and up to a hundred tourists making the circuit as I sat there. They were stopping off on a day trip from Fairbanks up the Dalton Highway to cross the Arctic Circle, now 60 miles to the north. Intrigued as I was with people-watching, I finished my burger – just – and headed off for my shower which was situated off one of those long low corridors at the back of the diner. I thought briefly about meeting a grumpy grizzly in the dark corridor and shuddered to myself.

The tiled shower was luxurious, complete with soft, fresh towels; it felt odd to be so clean. Whilst in the shower, the waitress had kindly filled up my water container, which was waiting for me as I reappeared in the restaurant. I thanked her and headed out into the glare of the parking lot and back down to the river. I was conscious that Mike and Vreni had not turned up at the diner but didn't really give it much thought what with all the entertainment in there, but tucked under my canoe seat I found a little hand-written note explaining that they'd been picked up earlier than expected and wishing me 'good luck and safe lines'. It was a really nice thing to do, a small simple gesture that meant so much in the circumstance. I did drop them a line confirming that I had made it, once I finished my trip, as they requested.

Replenished and clean, I got back onto the river and set off in the knowledge that from now on, for the next 800 miles, all the way to the sea, there were no more roads that reached or crossed the Yukon River. In the next 12 hours I must have drunk most of the water I'd picked up, a raging thirst as a result of the burger and fries back at the Crossing.

It took just a couple of days to reach Tanana from Yukon Crossing and I enjoyed this part of the river. We were back in the hills and the river was now bound by steep-sided, spruce-covered banks. A slight aside: when talking about this trip (and others for that matter) I constantly find myself referring to myself, I, as 'we', I'm not entirely sure why. I think it might have something to do with either the bond you build with your inanimate travelling companions, in this case my boat and paddle, or with a mild type of schizophrenia induced by being alone in such a place. As such I've left it in the text, if for no other reason than to give my boat and paddle the credit they're due!

The Yukon before Tanana is constrained by the steeper banks of the Ray Mountains to the north and the Yukon–Tanana Uplands to the southeast and therefore unable to wander at will as it did in the Flats. It now had to focus its energy on the path prescribed for it and as such, when the weather allowed, the paddling felt easier. The spruce-lined hills rolling down to the river cast shapes, some of which looked unerringly like the heads of enormous sleeping lizards, or dragons, their chins resting on the water's edge. The drab green foliage of the spruce needles produced a texture that could be seen as fine scales; fallen, bleached trees on the shore looked like exposed fangs; and, occasionally, random small clearings on the hillsides added the impression of eyes.

OK, so again I'd been on my own on the water for some time, but I found it easy to believe in these shapes and could appreciate why so many distinct landmasses back home in the UK are still known as 'worms' or 'orms', a derivation of the Viking term for a dragon. My sense of the unreal on this stretch of river was further heightened by the fact that I spent a couple of days paddling through a haze of forest fire smoke, not enough to be choking or particularly cloying, but enough to make me and all my kit smell of smoke, and thankfully, also dissipate some of the sun's intensity.

Tanana marked the halfway point of my trip, both an encouraging and disheartening concept, and I was hoping to celebrate and commiserate with a spot of retail therapy. I had no idea what I wanted to buy, but I knew from Dan Maclean's guide that there was a decent sized store there, and I thought that after a few days in the smoke with dragons a change of scenery and another touch of 'normality' might be good for me. Sadly, I arrived in town after 5pm and the store was already closed. I wandered about aimlessly for a bit and had a chat with a couple from Anchorage who had come down the Tanana River in their motorboat from Fairbanks, before buying a lukewarm can of coke from the liquor store which was still open.

I purposely and uncharacteristically resisted the temptation to buy a cold six-pack of beer, still focused on my mission, and headed back to my boat. Back in the canoe, which I had landed upstream from the town, and now passing the point where the store was, the couple I met were sat on a bench overlooking the river, a six-pack of beer on the bench between them, opening a cold can each. Their entreaty to come and join them for a beer was very hard to resist, but I kept going and left Tanana feeling particularly self-righteous and very sad.

At Tanana the Yukon is joined by, appropriately, the Tanana River, a 584-mile tributary of the Yukon with access to and from the city of Fairbanks, from where my cold beer tormentors had come. Clearly much of the hazy, lingering, smoke that had been blotting the sun and through which I had been paddling over the previous few days had come from fires further south along the Tanana. The burnt, river-borne, remnants of the forest were spiralling out of the Tanana and into the flow of the Yukon. The river became littered with a fine coating of burnt and still smoldering flotsam, including a thick black slick of charred spruce needles. Along with the blackened needles were a few larger remains of burnt and charred trees, and marooned on one of these charcoal arks that drifted too close to me and my boat, was a colony of ever so grateful flies that quickly and, without so much as asking for permission to come aboard, joined me in an act of what I can only refer to as pest piracy!

They weren't large flies, and I can't honestly say that I could tell you their proper scientific name, but they knew what they were doing and to me they quickly became known as the ears, eyes and nose flies – or 'bastards' for short! It was these orifices that they seemed to favour for their piratical incursion. Their modus operandi was particularly annoying: somehow, they knew that it was advantageous, for them, to remain behind me where I couldn't see them and then to attack my ears, eyes and nose from behind. Having these flies get in behind my sunglasses was a nuisance, to put it mildly. Whenever the wind picked up, they would sink down into the shelter of the canoe while I concentrated and worked on keeping my line, then as soon as the wind dropped and I had a chance to relax, they popped up again to attack my facial cavities.

Plagued by flies and mosquitoes somewhere between Tanana and Galena

Despite my best efforts they remained with me for several days. I had hoped that if I pulled over, I could move away from the boat, and they would follow me giving me the opportunity to outflank them and at a suitably windy moment get back into the boat and onto the water whilst they were still disorientated ashore. No such luck. They would stick with me – and on me – until I was about four metres away from the boat and then head back to its sanctuary and wait for me to rejoin them. I tried lighting a fire next to the boat in the hope that the smoke from the fire would drive them off, but clearly, given their origins on the Tanana River, they were veteran smokers and clung determinedly to the depths of my boat. I can only imagine what the few locals must have thought as they whizzed past in the skiffs and saw the strange, grey-bearded, old bloke sat next to his boat shielding his eyes from the smoke of a small fire on a clear sunny day!

Mind you I'm grateful that no one was about to witness the more than one occasion where I accidentally sprayed myself in the face with my 'Woodsman' high-strength DEET mosquito repellant. I discovered that it was important to wear my glasses when chasing any particular individual bug with the spray either in the boat or in my tent. This was not in order to see the bug more clearly, but to be able to see which way the nozzle on the can was actually pointing and therefore avoid squirting it in my eye. It really hurt, just as much the second and third times I did it as it did the first!

It occurred to me that perhaps these flies were attracted to me personally. I'd had a shower three days previously at Yukon Crossing but hadn't given my paddling T-shirts and shorts a dhobi for a while and to be honest they probably were a little 'fresh', so after my second day of bug occupation I found a creak where I could give my kit a good wash. It was, in all honesty, probably about time that I sorted out this bit of my personal admin and whilst I felt a little cleaner and sanctimonious, the flies couldn't give a damn what I smelt like and stuck with me. They finally left me after a few more days of torture during a particular wet and stormy spell just before Ruby – every cloud has a silver lining.

The horseflies, which I encountered throughout my paddle, were also particularly sneaky: they appeared to work in pairs and would head out to the boat even if I were in the middle of the river. It must have been the vivid and unnatural red of the canoe, as it appeared to attract all sorts of bugs from across the water. The horseflies had a knack for working out when I was focusing on the river and concentrating on my paddling, and also knew which bits of exposed flesh were the hardest for me to see and therefore most difficult for me to prevent them getting at.

The particular modus operandi for these critters involved one of them ducking down into the footwell of the boat to start prospecting for exposed flesh around my calves, clearly aware that I would at that moment be negotiating a tricky piece of water and therefore not wanting to be looking at my feet. Meanwhile, its mate would sneak up behind me and work at getting its teeth into either tricep. This way, when paddling in shorts and a T-shirt, I was particularly vulnerable to horsefly attacks and whilst I don't think I'm much of a wimp and I knew their bites wouldn't do much damage, they did hurt and usually had the effect of making me swear loudly to no one in particular. It was a real treat to occasionally catch one of them with a satisfying, squelching, bloody slap.

My sometime saviours from these attacks were the dragonflies, creatures that I came to marvel at and respect immensely. It was not just their iridescent beauty, aerial agility and bionic vision, but also their ability to pick horseflies out of mid-air with barely a flicker or noticeable change in direction and attitude. At times it felt like having my own on-call quadro-winged attack helicopters stationed above each shoulder ready to pick off the pesky flies.

Not only did these magnificent creatures offer me a little respite from the horseflies but they also provided another visible link to the prehistory of the Yukon – primordial creatures that have barely evolved since well before the time of the mammoths. I remember at one point rounding a bend on the river to come upon a vast mudbank littered with the desiccated carcasses of hundreds of washed-up trees and hovering above and within these were dragonflies as far as the eye could see. Whilst I don't know for sure, it was a sight that I was convinced was prehistoric, and half expected to feel the shadow of some large leather-winged creature pass overhead or see some terrible lizard lumbering across the mudbank.

Another stunning day on the river

Reading

"One glance at a book and you hear the voice of another person, perhaps someone dead for thousands of years. To read is to voyage through time."

Carl Sagan, Cosmos

Regrettably, I'm relatively new to reading; I certainly didn't get into reading in my youth and was completely uninspired at school, preferring 'doing' rather than reading. It has taken me a long, long time to be convinced that reading is a constructive activity and not something you do to fill in time. It was only through studying for my Open University degree in my late thirties that I really took to reading, although I still find myself having to justify a couple of hours spent reading when there are always so many 'things' that I could or should be doing otherwise. Six weeks on the Yukon was, in theory, going to offer plenty of space to stop, and time when there would be nothing else to do but sit and wait for the conditions to change, so plenty of time to read, guilt free.

With this in mind, I took a random selection of books with me, all downloaded onto my iPad, and all of which (imaginatively on my part) contained 'Alaska' somewhere in their title. I flicked through a few of them but quickly settled on John Muir's Travels in Alaska as well as James A. Michener's Alaska. On my previous trip I took just the one book, a paperback copy of Jack London's To Build a Fire and other stories. The London short stories were wonderful: I looked forward to the time by the fire or in the tent when I could stop and read them. Heading toward Dawson City, at the confluence of the Yukon and Klondike Rivers, London's stories were compelling and I just loved the way he captures, or creates, the evocative life, characters and brutality of the country in the Gold Rush era.

As a youngster, of the limited books I did pick up (or listened to on audiotape, my preferred medium), I remember London's classic work Call of The Wild and recall the impression it left on me. Likewise, more recently, I had read some of the works of Robert Service, not just his Yukon poems but also his haunting WWI prose. As with London, Service seems to capture the evocative atmosphere of the Yukon and Klondike at the turn of the nineteenth century. That's not to say that I knew, or now know, what the atmosphere of the Yukon was like back then, but there remains something real and raw within their poems and stories. I am sure London's accounts of the nobility of the early incarnation of the Royal Canadian Mounted Police and Service's Spell of the Yukon have influenced many a young person's dreams of adventure. It's hard to believe that Jack London actually only spent one winter in the Yukon territory and that despite, in 1913, being considered the highest-paid, best-known and most popular writer in the world, he subsequently took to excessive drinking and died of kidney failure and of a possible self-induced drug overdose at home on his farm in California, aged just forty.

I started Muir's Travels in Alaska first and enjoyed his account of his visits to the Pacific southwest of Alaska in the late 1800s. I particularly enjoyed his dated, but nevertheless straightforward and highly lyrical style. His clear knowledge and love of the mountains, the glaciers, wider nature and the people was captivating; he is positively modern in his appreciation and attitude, but I still found myself skimming the last few chapters looking for his interactions with the Native Peoples and the accounts of their lifestyle whilst skipping over the mountains and glaciers that he so loved. I then picked up James A. Michener's Alaska which is a whole different ball game.

I found that for this longer journey, moving from Jack London's Klondike across the border and into Alaska, I required a much larger story and Michener's Alaska, as with many of his other works, is an epic to match that crossing. The size and sweep of it captures much of the land, people and history. It took me a little while to get into it, but once I'd got used to the idea of woolly mammoths having personalities and conscious thoughts, and that throughout the book Michener uses vignettes involving characters – human or otherwise, good or bad – that are imbued with similar traits (the matriarchal mammoth protecting her young, the Russian Orthodox priest protecting his church, or Tammy 'Bigears' Ting fighting for the freedom of her native people against corporate exploitation), his story started to flow and get under my skin. There is no denying that if you want a good grasp of the history and influences that have shaped Alaska then Michener covers it all with some historical authenticity and captivating storytelling. I suspect, having previously read Muir's travels, that Michener had read it too as much of his late 1800s chapters reminded me of Muir.

As I read Michener's Alaska during my trip, I didn't immediately make the connection with the truly epic televised version of another of his expansive works Centennial, a similarly framed story but this time spanning the prehistory through to the 1970s of northeast Colorado. Centennial was televised in the UK in the late '70s and I particularly remember watching the first few episodes covering the early explorers and exploits of the fur trappers on the rivers in their canoes, such as the French–Canadian character Pasquinel, replete with his distinctive red woollen toque, which had such a profound effect on my desire to explore North America. There seemed, to me, once I had made the connection, a circularity in my reading Michener's work whilst on the Yukon having been so wonderfully, juvenilely, influenced by his storytelling in my youth.

On my return home and as I have endeavoured to articulate my adventure for posterity, I looked for inspiration and ideas in published works and took to reading and re-reading a number of books by established authors. Some of these related directly to the Yukon, Alaska and the North American Subarctic; some were out-and-out classic travelogues; and a few, most of which I had already read, were works relating to nature and the natural world, books that I thoroughly enjoy and have gravitated to over the years. Within this final category, writers whom I reread in the hope that I could learn from their descriptive and lyrical prose included firstly Roger Deakin, amongst whose wonderful works was Waterlog, his delightful telling of his mission to wild-swim throughout the UK. In it, Deakin's passion for nature and his acute, lyrical style shine. This book has been an inspiration to me – I have even attempted to swim in some of the spots he visits in his book and one day must try to complete them all.

Reading Deakin led me to Robert MacFarlane who must, currently, be the pre-eminent nature writer in the UK. MacFarlane has written a number of beautifully executed books on the natural world and if I could ever, at any point, get anywhere vaguely near his competence in writing and descriptive prose I would be very happy, not to say extremely surprised. I think, however, that one of MacFarlane's greatest gifts, beyond his writing, is his ability to signpost other writers and point out other beautifully written works on nature. Two of these that stand out for me are J. A. Baker's Peregrine and Nan Shepard's The Living Mountain, books that simply ooze with the writers' intense passion for, and knowledge of, their subject, coupled with a poetic style that belies their hard-earnt and long-forged craft, something that as a committed half-hearted fanatic I can only partly aspire to.

Of the second category – the travel writers – I was pointed toward Eric Newby by my sister-in-law and cannot thank her enough. The first of his books that I read was A Short Walk in the Hindu Kush and I was immediately hooked by Newby's style from the start. His entertaining, descriptive and self-deprecating way of writing about a particular place and arduous times make it easy for you to follow him on his adventure. I quickly followed the Hindu Kush with Love and War in the Apennines, Round Ireland in Low Gear and most recently his photographic journal What the Traveller Saw; there are many more I still need to read.

From Newby, I flowed into Wilfred Thesiger, mainly because Newby mentions him in awe in A Short Walk, after meeting him on his way back down the Panjshir Valley following his attempt on Mir Samir. I have had the dubious honour of visiting the Panjshir Valley and I can therefore, personally, testify to the awesome beauty, the resonant potential for hostility and the sheer inaccessibility of the place; and by way of 'black-catting' Roger Deakin's swimming exploits – and to the surprise of my companions at the time – I can say that I have swum wild, naked, in the Panjshir river; its clarity was irresistible, but by heck it was cold! In their time, Newby and Thesiger would not have had to pick their way around the scattered, burnt-out hulks of Soviet-era tanks and personnel carriers that now litter the valley bottom near its entrance. No modern armed force – and there have been a few that have tried – has successfully subdued this remote valley and its fiercely independent people.

I see Thesiger as a writer of his age, a remnant of post-colonial masochistic muscularity in the same vein as T. E. Lawrence, both hardcore when it comes to spartan immersive travel. His books, particularly the tales of him crossing the Arabian Empty Quarter in the company of Bedouin tribesman, Arabian Sands, are epic. Again, like Newby, Thesiger seems able to write in a way that makes you feel included in his adventures, for good and bad.

The last of the travel writers I need to mention is Patrick Leigh Fermor, another author signposted by McFarlane, and his three-part telling of his walk from Rotterdam to Constantinople in the 1930s, which included, in the first of the trilogy, A Gift of Time, crossing Germany and Austria as the shadow of Nazism was growing. Whilst Leigh Fermor's world and background were so different to mine, I thoroughly appreciated the way in which he is able to build a seemingly natural narrative from his journals, recorded on his walk but only written as a book many decades later. I was particularly interested by the fact that the story of his walk tails off toward the end and in the final part of his trilogy, The Broken Road, completed much later in his life, there is no conclusive mention of his reaching Istanbul, or of how he felt after completing his journey. I suspect that, just as I have experienced, the journal notes acted as a companion, a way of capturing the journey as it unfolds, and whilst pertinent and real during the journey itself, the need to capture the events diminishes as the end hoves into view. It is only, perhaps, in hindsight, when gifted with time and space, that the need to describe the end of a journey (which in itself is really just the start of another journey), to summarise that intersection, and, if required, to reflect and provide completion, becomes necessary or apparent.

The final category of authors and books that I have subsequently engaged with are those again dealing with the Yukon itself, Alaska and the North American Arctic, but this time (unlike London and Service) coming from a more modern, non-fictional angle. Key among these have been John McPhee, Barry Lopez and Adam Weymouth. McPhee, who I have mentioned already, in his description of the Alaskan social-political dynamic of the mid-1970s so beautifully captures the machinations of the people of the town of Eagle and surrounding area along the Yukon River as they try to come to terms with the development of the Alaskan state in the wake of the discovery and exploitation of oil on the Arctic coast. His Coming into the Country is a classic of the genre, and I was delighted to note that a number of McPhee's observations and thoughts about life along the Yukon chimed with my experiences and still resonate some 45 years later.

Another writer I discovered after my trip is Barry Lopez and notably his book Artic Dreams, an evocative, even spiritual, book that explores the inter-relationships of the people, the animals, the history of exploration and exploitation, and the environment along the North American Arctic coast. Finally, I need to mention again Adam Weymouth and his work Kings of the Yukon, which I had the joy of reading through the later stages of the planning for my own trip in 2019. Weymouth's writing helped me prepare better for many aspects of my adventure as well as opening my mind to some of the more transient experiences I would have.

All these writers set a standard for writing about their travels and the natural world, and it is the passion for their travels, the world around them and the people they meet, whether they liked them or not, that for me, shines through.

"Mud unto mud! Death eddies near!
Not here the appointed End, not here!
But somewhere, beyond Space and Time,
Is wetter water, slimier slime!"

Rupert Brooke

This section of the Yukon beyond Tanana, bounded by the hills, had less sandbanks and the available islands they created were further apart. This meant that I needed to look more carefully at my mapping and plan ahead each day when looking at potential boltholes, pull-out spots and camping locations. Throughout my paddle, the mudbanks and sandbars were my preferred camping spots, in fact they constituted the majority of my stopover locations.

They were invariably exposed and windswept with no shelter from the elements or the heat of the all-day sun, but they offered a degree of safety being situated in the middle of the river or, if connected to the shore, offering a good field of view against unwelcome visitors. Camping in the trees on the shore was always a slightly more unnerving experience: regardless of the area being clear of any sign of bears, or even when having a raging fire going, you always have one ear twisted toward the forest and would constantly, unconsciously and consciously, scan the close surrounding trees for any sound of movement.

*Another muddy day on the river – note the padding on
the seat to help ease my aching back*

The sandbanks were a little more relaxing to camp on, but I developed a love-hate relationship with them. I loved the drier, slightly higher bars, the ones that had a few bleached spruce carcasses lying about on them, the ones where I could pull up ashore without having to wade through sucking mud before finding a firmer, drier base to camp. But more often than not the edges of these islands would just be slimy, sticky, silt as if the bars themselves were merely a continuum of the silt flowing in the river. As the silt builds up and the island forms, the material consistency transforms from liquid to solid over the space of several hundred metres and a few inches in height. Landing the canoe on the soggy, more liquid, edges of a bar was a pain, dragging the ladened boat ashore through sucking mud before making several trips back and forth to set up camp on the firmer sand further ashore and then reversing the process again when setting off was sapping, physically and mentally. I took to carrying a few selected straight driftwood branches in my boat to act as rollers for the canoe and to rest it on to keep it from sinking into the silt. A drier bar, preferably with a stranded tree that I could shelter behind and some driftwood that I could use to build a fire, was a welcome luxury.

Pulling up and camping on the bars was draining enough but negotiating them in the river was a wretched experience. Being able to see your route ahead but finding a slightly submerged, hidden mudbank barring the way and then having to paddle perpendicular to your desired route for hundreds of metres, and then back again onto your route, usually in slack water, with very little assistance from the current was soul destroying. This was particularly the case on some of the big sweeping bends in the meandering river beyond Tanana. A course along the inside bank following the tree line could be long enough, but when you have to prescribe a large arc, way out into the river, to avoid a mudbank as well, it hurt.

I could have followed the outside of the bends and possibly used the faster flow more effectively but some of these were so vast they would have added kilometres to the distance around the bend and as the river got bigger these became more dangerous with swirling eddies and dangling trees out to catch you. In hindsight, much of the paddle on this part of the river was made up of these daily – if not hourly – competing choices between the conditions, the route, possible pull-out spots and safety.

Whilst I may not have been overly joyed to be picking my way through these mudbanks, it transpired that the inhabitants of the banks and were even less happy to see me. In the sheltered channels between the bars, beavers would follow me from behind and dive slapping and splashing their tails, telling me I was not welcome and to sling my proverbial hook. They could get particularly vociferous if I dared camp anywhere they were not happy with. On more than one occasion I took my precious wooden paddle to bed with me when faced with belligerent beavers beating their tails and tutting on the river: I was worried that they might decide to gnaw chunks out of my paddle to spite me as I slept.

On the open river, gulls and Arctic terns would strafe the boat, screeching at me to clear off. It amused me to see the, understandably, inhospitable nature of these birds. The gulls were by far the more aggressive and boisterous, truly 'nature's bagpipes' as Roger Deakin calls them. They would actually try to shit on me, circling round before coming in for a 'pooing run' from behind. They were never really close and offered no real danger, but I took great delight in occasionally scaring them by pretending that I didn't know they were coming and then suddenly sticking my paddle vertically up in the air above my head in front of them.

They were probably two or three metres above where I could reach with my extended paddle, but the effect was hysterical. More than once I watched a strafing gull try to stop in mid-air when confronted with my paddle blade, trying to fly backwards, their feathers flaring on their backs like the airbrakes of a fighter jet coming into land on an aircraft carrier. Having scared the shit out of them – literally – the gulls would then adopt that cat-like nonchalance, that attitude cats take after they have been surprised or inadvertently slip off something. The gulls would fly off, smoothing their feathers and then gad about or land on a nearby shore pretending nothing had happened; nothing to see here, carry on as you were! Those small victories, even if over a gull, were good for morale.

The Arctic terns, on the other hand, were far more graceful and clinical in the defence of their domain, less thuggish than the larger gulls. They would come close but were never as intent as the gulls. I would sit and marvel at their agility in flight, their fragile-looking calligraphic V-shaped wings manoeuvring effortlessly in the wind (so easily distinguishable from the flattened 'W' of the gull's silhouette), their monastic black caps and dagger-sharp stiletto red beaks ready to pierce the river. Whilst smaller, they were adept at seeing off any gulls that were getting too close to their patch.

Perhaps even more impressive is the thought of the journey that these delicate-looking birds make. Up here near the Arctic Circle in July they were protecting their newly hatched offspring, but in a few weeks they would be heading south, not for temperate grounds to overwinter, no these remarkable creatures would be travelling 12,000 miles or more to summer in Antarctica, where food is bountiful and they feel safe in the isolation. Barry Lopez suggests that this remarkable migration effectively means that Arctic terns experience fewer hours of darkness than any other creature on earth.

The story of the Arctic tern's migration is just one of many associated with the Yukon River. We have already mentioned the tens of thousands of salmon that pour up the river each year, but others such as the caribou, the creatures that probably first lured man to the Yukon, still cover vast distances across the continent. Many species of whale migrate past the Yukon–Kuskokwim Delta annually and occasionally some of them follow the salmon up the river; and, according to Lopez, it is estimated that some 24 million migratory waterfowl use the delta between May and September each year feeding on the nutrient-rich waters. This is why I came to see the Yukon as a corridor of life, an avenue of migration or, as Lopez refers to such regions, a 'corridor of breath':

> *"Watching the animals come and go, and feeling*
> *the land swell up to meet them and then feeling it*
> *grow still at their departure, I came to think of the*
> *migrations as breath, as the land breathing. In spring*
> *a great inhalation of light and animals. The long-*
> *bated breath of summer. And the exhalation that*
> *propelled them all south in the fall."*

Barry Lopez, Arctic Dreams

Passing the birds flocking on the sandbanks and knowing that underneath me thousands of fish were fighting their way upstream as I casually paddled down, enjoying the still warm sun, I could feel the long-bated breath of the Yukon summer but knew that it would very soon be exhaling.

The few times when I could slip past the gulls and terns unmolested was when there were bald eagles present. Bald eagles get their name from their colouring rather than the fact they're bald – they're not bald. Their magnificently striking, white-feathered heads and tail plumage, book-ending their menacingly black bodies, would at one point have been referred to as piebald, a term now more commonly used to refer to black and white patterned horses, but shortened for use with these eagles. When sat on a sandbar, either on a washed-up tree carcass or on the sand itself, the gulls and terns would mob these majestic statue-like raptors, which in turn, generally, took absolutely no notice of their tormentors.

Occasionally, when an eagle would appear to lose patience, it would slowly and deliberately unfold the expanse of its huge wings, casting a shadow across the sand, sending the slighter birds scattering, before beating downwards and within several beats be cruising low across the river, threatening yellow talons trailing suggestively under the bulk of its flight. The eagles rarely moved far, just taking up a new sentry position a short distance away. I saw quite a few bald eagles stood by the river; I didn't see any soaring high above, but then, I didn't spend much time looking up, as I focused on the river ahead. I have a small regret in that I didn't get to see any peregrine falcons on my trip. I read that these were probably the only bird that could bother the eagles, not in size or strength but in pure agility and lethality in flight and could keep an eagle pinned down and agitated if they chose. I would have loved to have seen one of these deadly dive-bombers in action. If you are interested in these birds I would recommend a read of J. A. Baker's classic book Peregrine for some of the most amazingly lyrical descriptions of their nature on the English, Essex coastline.

*Looking back at some mountains on the
southern stretch of the Yukon after Koyukuk*

Smaller Creatures

*"Nothing can compare to the joy inspired by even
a brief encounter with a scarce and beautiful wild
animal in its natural element...it's not about what I
have seen, it's about forging a momentary connection
with the wild, and finding a place in the world for
my own wild heart."*

Neil Ansell, The Last Wilderness

In such an expansive, wild and at times inhospitable place, frozen as it is for the majority of the year, it is easy to focus on the pesky flies and mosquitoes, the majestic birds and the archetypical larger beasts, the moose, bear and wolf, and even the thought of a mighty mammoth, all of which are, or were, evolved to live in the harsh conditions. I was conscious that I was privileged to be on the river at this time of year when it is open and the conditions are more accepting of outsiders and adventurers. I was also conscious that I was in a big country, on a big river, under a big sky with big animals also making the most of the available accessible resources while they could. So, imagine my surprise the first time I saw a shrew out on the water and then my sheer incredulity at stumbling across a tiny frog on an exposed mudflat.

The first shrew I saw was in the Flats, swimming out toward the middle of the river. At first, I thought it was just a small piece of flotsam, it was spinning about in the various vortices and eddies thrown up by the tumbling water, but as I got closer, I could see its elongated, whiskered nose held aloft, its tail steering and its tiny, splayed claws working ten to the dozen. It looked surprisingly buoyant with the majority of its body out of the water and its brown fur looked remarkably dry, not at all waterlogged.

Although it was over a hundred metres from the nearest dry land it appeared to have a sense of determination rather than desperation about it. It looked like it knew what it was doing and where it was going, even if I didn't credit it with much of a chance of survival. Maybe I was wrong. Later at Yukon Crossing when being served my cheeseburger, I mentioned my sighting to the waitress, she responded nonchalantly signalling that this was a regular occurrence for those accustomed to the river and with, typical Alaskan frankness said, 'yeah, the salmon love 'em'. I sighted a couple of other shrews gaily gadding about on the river over the weeks after that but didn't see any salmon taking an interest. And then, just to confirm that this wasn't a random occurrence limited to the river, I found one in the canoe one morning.

I had started the trip by emptying my canoe every time I camped. As per the advised best practice, I'd take the camping stores ashore away from the boat and turn the boat over on the rest of the kit to protect it from both the weather and any interested critters. That palaver didn't last long: it was a pain, and the idea of taking reasonably dry and clean kit bags out of the canoe to lay them in damp mud under the canoe seemed counterintuitive. Instead, I took to tying a camouflaged basher – a waterproof tarpaulin – securely over the canoe. By stretching and securing it diagonally between bow and stern and wrapping the sides under the hull, it covered most of the boat. This set-up worked pretty well in all but the heaviest downpours when invariably it would be overwhelmed by the sheer weight of water and collapse inundating the canoe and testing the waterproof qualities of my packing.

The shrew must have climbed up the folds in the basher that were tucked under the boat in order to get up and inside. As I was re-loading my kit ready to set off, I suddenly caught a glimpse of something scuttling from beneath one dry bag to another. I quickly found out what it was and initially toyed with the idea of just leaving it in the boat and taking it with me as a companion, but equally quickly realised that this would be cruel, and the chances were I'd end up inadvertently squashing the poor beastie. Besides, I really wasn't that desperate for the company and probably would have spent more time looking for the shrew than watching the water ahead. So, I spent longer than I'd have wished chasing the little bugger around the bottom my boat before I finally caught it in my bailing scoop. Once in the scoop, and despite all of its previous efforts to evade getting caught, it didn't want to get out and I had to resort to some rather forceful jerks to persuade the shrew to let go and get deposited on the mud. At which point it promptly ran back toward the boat.

Trying to dislodge the stowaway shrew from my bailer

Having made so much effort to save it from getting squashed in my boat I didn't then want to crush it under the canoe as I manoeuvred it out into the water. So, I spent a few more minutes on my hands and knees in soggy mud trying to fish it out. At one point, in order to evade me, it ran out into the water and swam around the bow of the canoe into the river and then promptly turned about and headed in and under the boat on the other side from me. I eventually caught it again and took it for a walk along the shore away from the canoe before releasing it, hoping it would find a different source of cover. There was no other cover, so I guiltily left it scampering along the sand and made my way back to the canoe and put in. I looked over my shoulder as I left, half expecting to see a gull or some other opportunist predator suddenly appear and make off with my little shrew. I saw nothing and could only hope that this remarkable wee thing survived.

My only other sighting of shrews (or were they mice?) was on the night later in July between Kaltag and Anvik when I'd found myself forced ashore by the wind just yards from where I had bumped into a black bear on the bank. I subsequently spent the night awake next to my boat on the water's edge with a fire going in order to ward off any large furry critters as well as for my own comfort. It was difficult to work out in the then half-light of the Alaskan night and with the shadows cast by the flames but there were certainly, from time to time, smaller, more welcome, critters flitting around by the fire. I noted in my journal that it put me in mind of a short stint in the Omani desert in the early 2000s, where I would, as is my morning ritual, percolate a pot of coffee on a small solid fuel stove. Pretty much every morning I would be joined by a couple of gerbils who would happily, it appeared, come and sit by the stove to warm themselves after the cold desert nights. I enjoyed their company. I also remember my surprise at seeing a lemming poke its head above the snow one winter up on the Hardangervidda in central Norway.

So, I could just about get my head around the idea of small rodents living in this environment – after all, it is creatures such as these that allegedly survived our planet's last mass extinction event – but I really wasn't expecting or prepared to find a frog living up here. The frog, when I met it, was sat at the water's edge, next to where I'd landed on another large expanse of flat exposed mud. It was late July, so I was well over toward the west of Alaska, the days were still long and the temperature warm when the sun was out. It must have only been 3cm in length, perfectly formed and perfectly camouflaged against the wet, buff-coloured, mud on which it sat, which is why I nearly stepped on it. It looked so small and so fragile that I marvelled at the seeming incongruity of its situation. It didn't seem overly bothered by me and only moved as I leant in closer to try and take a picture, at which point, just like the shrew, it instinctively headed for the cover of my canoe. But unlike the shrew, which scurried frantically for any cover it could find, the frog merely hopped languidly on its way. I thought it might have headed for the river but, again, whilst that may have seemed appropriate for a frog, the idea that something so small could survive in the mass of tumbling murky water seemed impossible. How could this cold-blooded amphibian survive or even exist in such an implacably hostile environment?

The Frog (look closely at the very left edge of the picture, not the lump of mud!)

I subsequently investigated the frog, just to be sure I wasn't imagining it even though I have the photos to prove it was there. It was a wood frog, which are present over much of North America and, in fact, have an impressive in-built freeze tolerance. Apparently, they can produce both urea and glucose which act as a cryoprotectant and limits the amount of ice that can form in their cells when they are dormant through the long winters. As I set off, I gently lifted and pushed the canoe back into the water leaving the frog blinking on the bank. Again, I set off with a pang of guilt half expecting to see some form of predator, a raptor or gull, swoop down and take the little creature I had left exposed and alone on the expanse of mud. The truth is that both the shrew and frog, as small as they were, were probably both better suited to live and survive along the banks of the Yukon than I was with all of my new-fangled kit and technology.

It was always rewarding, and I felt humbled whenever I met the amazing wildlife in its own environment, no matter how small the animal or fleeting the encounter. At home we are too disposed toward the concept of animals as 'entertainment', either as pets when they provide companionship, or, more pertinently, when alive in captivity or on our television screens. Our modern inattentiveness demands that animals must be doing something to interest us. How often do you hear people complain that the animals in our zoos and parks did 'nothing'? Even more remarkable are the lengths camera crews now go to in order to capture animal behaviour that is new or unique for our safe, comfortable, technicolour entertainment.

Seeing these animals in their own backyard, being the visitor to their homes, produced an almost spiritual connection, although there was always the hope that they would do something interesting for me (though preferably not to me) and that I might capture some footage to show off at home, but mostly when confronted by a bear, moose, lynx, eagle, shrew or frog – and more often than not the landscape, river or sky as well – I found myself just staring silently in awe. Feeling again that atavistic connection, that sense of sharing the place and space with something bigger. Of course, always mixed with that sense of wonder were the ever-present thoughts and concerns about the here-and-now: where is the river taking me as I sit here gawping; has the wind changed direction again; what else might be lurking watching me watching its prey; is this creature as curious as I am or is it hungry? As ever, the ability to dwell in the spiritual was tempered by the practical.

So, whilst living in someone else's backyard and regardless of the majesty of my surroundings, I still had to find somewhere safe to stop and sleep. I generally had a reasonable choice as to where I stopped.

On the upper reaches of the river, the printed river guides showed where the previously used locations were and these spots were particularly welcome as they usually had a few hand-built mod-cons provided by previous occupants: a rudimentary table, log seats, drying racks and fire pits. These may sound basic but when you're out in the bush and after a day on the water they are welcome luxuries. Having something as simple as a shaped log to sit on rather than the ground or being able to stand up at a make-shift table rather than squatting whilst preparing your supper, is a comfort indeed. Which is why on this trip having more room in a canoe versus a kayak, taking a camping chair had been an easy decision.

More often than not, the decision as to where to pull over and camp came down to a matter of, or combination of, fatigue and weather. It was amazing how many seemingly idyllic camping locations I could pass during the day (or sometimes the night), only to be confronted by a less than ideal spot by the time I could paddle no further or the weather had picked up to an extent where I was forced to stop.

Regardless of where I pulled over, or when or for what reason, the first thing I had to do, and nearly always did do (and this was probably where my military background and any limited residual discipline did kick in), was to conduct a 'clearance patrol'. Before stepping out of the boat I would buckle up my clasp-belt complete with the aerosol can of 'bear spray' in its holster, safety catch removed, in easy reach of my left hand, and a cheap rather pointless sheath knife on my right. If entirely honest, I had little faith in the utility of either (more so, perhaps, in the bear spray), but if I ever had to get that knife out to defend myself, I was probably already buggered. The knife was another sop to making me feel better out in the bush but without spending too much on it.

Back in Whitehorse when I was perusing the comprehensive display of axes and machetes in the locked glass cabinet in the Canadian Tire store, I was of the mind that I should really have some such thing for emergencies and for cutting firewood. But then I saw the cost of them and plumped for the basic, small, cheap knife. Alongside the axes and machetes were catapults, longbows, crossbows, pistols and rifles, the selection of which was only beaten by Hougen's Sportslodge, the specialist hunting store in central Whitehorse.

I must confess that I wasted quite a bit of time in Whitehorse wandering around Hougen's checking out the hardware and from my former professional standpoint the selection both awed and scared me; the thought of bears seemed less of a concern compared to the idea that there were people wandering around out there with this sort of firepower! I say my time perusing the weapons in Hougen's was wasted because from the outset of my planning I had made the conscious and deliberate decision that I did not want to carry a rifle. I wasn't going to be shooting anything to eat, so it really would have been a case of wanting to defend myself against a bear that may have induced me to carry a weapon. That just seemed a little unfair on the bears. I think I was more interested and excited by the idea of trying to use my experience, wits and discipline rather than testing my snap-shooting skills, whilst paddling the Yukon. I subsequently found the following quote which I think best captures my approach to both weapons and my experience as a whole.

"One must follow the role of an uninvited visitor - an intruder - rather than that of an aggressive hunter, and one should go unarmed to insure this attitude."

Andy Russell, Grizzly Country

In addition to my utility belt, I'd take my paddle on patrol with me in the hope that should I meet anything untoward, the addition of a large wooden or plastic stick would make me appear bigger and therefore less appealing or edible, whilst counterintuitively trying to adopt a stance that was neither showing fear nor being threatening. The final piece of equipment in my less than formidable personal armoury was a rechargeable air horn, which came equipped with its own small bike pump for recharging. I liked this bit of kit and would often use it to announce my presence whenever I stopped somewhere I was a little unsure of, in the hope it would warn off any large animals and therefore reduce the chances of a surprise response. Despite looking for reassurance, I often felt bizarrely guilty about using the horn, about disturbing the environment with such a loud unnatural sound. I did, however, use the air horn a couple of times whilst in the tent, when I thought I could hear noises outside – a cowardly way of warning off imaginary beasts.

So, armed like some weird Yukon version of Don Quixote, I'd conduct my patrols and in accordance with the advice in all the guidebooks look for sign of recent bear activity, conscious that recent could also mean current. I applied this routine rigidly – well almost – which brought back some old memories. It wasn't long ago during a paddle around the Isle of Arran, off West Scotland, that having pulled up after a difficult day's kayaking, I got a telling off from my kayaking buddy, Ian – the mate I would have taken along to throw at bears! As usual, I was busying myself making camp and sorting my kit whilst Ian, in accordance with his routine whilst kayaking and in life in general, was busily downing the first of many a can of ale – important ballast lining the keel on many a good kayak trip – and smoking a fag whilst scratching his arse and offering me less than helpful advice.

I suggested he might want to sort his kit out as well. Ian's response was typically and welcomingly blunt, 'Mate', he said, 'you may have had a long and relatively lofty career in Her Majesty's Royal Marines but as far as I'm aware as I sit here after a long, hard day's kayaking, and now trying to enjoy my well-deserved fag and first beer, there are no enemy forces lined up over the horizon ready to attack us, so how about you chill the fuck out!'

He was, not that I'd ever tell him of course, correct, but I still sorted my kit out before getting stuck into a welcome beer! Whilst my lingering ingrained tactical discipline may not be appropriate in all situations, I'm glad remnants of it were still there as it made it easier for me to keep on top of things over a six-week period on my own.

Once inside the tent I would lay out my roll-mat, sleeping bag and a stuff-sack containing my night gear and clean, fresh clothes. Along with these

I'd take the bear spray and air horn, some water, my various entertainment devices and, always by my side, the Sat-Phone. I had room to arrange my damp, smelly canoeing clothes either side of the roll-mat and would use the Sat-Phone's hard plastic case to support my inflatable pillow. In all honesty, I liked being in my tent: even if it did only consist of a couple of layers of thin fabric it still gave me a certain fatalistic sense of sanctuary. I slept well most nights once the temperatures started dropping, and once I had finally managed to settle all of my various, age- and lifestyle-related aches and pains.

The tent itself was tested to its fullest in mid-July, just before Ruby, when I spent a couple of nights sheltering from successive storms – the ones that got rid of the flies, one of which was particularly gnarly. As I lay there with the wind trying to flatten the tent walls against me and the rain looking to sneak into any and all of the openings, thunder and lightning danced about outside. There was no way I could sleep, so at what seemed like the peak of the storm, I tried the old trick of counting the seconds, trying to note the directional difference between the lightening that was illuminating my tent with such a ferocious intensity and the heart-stopping claps of thunder that came right on top of the light.

At one point I thought I could ascertain a gap between the flash and crash but, just as I started to think that perhaps the end was nigh – for the storm not for me – another bolt and clap exploded, and then another. I reckoned there must have been three or more different storms stomping on my tent at that moment! That would be stomping on me, lying in my tent, on an exposed island on the Yukon River, possessing the only pieces of metal, including my cobalt-chrome right knee, for miles around. What could possibly go wrong! I pulled up my sleeping bag, used the eye mask to block out the flashing light, and waited for the storms to pass whilst having flashbacks, literally, to previous experiences of feeling so vulnerable in the face of nature's inherent power.

Many years ago, during a training exercise in the stunning primeval primary jungles of Brunei in northern Borneo, I remember a particularly nerve-gangling night. As part of a small team conducting a long-range patrol exercise we had stopped for a night, doing our utmost to be as tactical and professional as possible. We were in our hammocks, strung between the forest trees, when a tropical storm struck. I had witnessed many tropical storms off the coast of Brunei, mostly from the luxury of a dry veranda, and usually sipping a G&T. I would sit and marvel at the forks of electric violence as they ripped open the dark tropical sky over the South China Sea.

This particular storm, however, had decided to come inland and was close – very close – to where we were resting. I remember being abruptly woken and nearly thrown from my hammock by sheer static energy and the painful brightness of a strike of lightening, then laying in my hammock, white knuckled, listening to the creaking and cracking of vast hardwood fibres rupturing somewhere in the dark, accompanied by the rush of acres of tree-top foliage crashing into one another high up in the canopy. One of the nearby, giant, buttressed Sal trees had begun to fall.

Whilst trying to ascertain where and in which direction the destruction was coming from, there was another muffled thud which sent more tremors through the canopy and even heavier litter falling to the forest floor. I breathed a sigh of relief believing the fall had stopped, listening helplessly in the utter blackness. Then over the noise of my thumping heart there was another, new sound of ripping tissues and further massive movement somewhere close by out in the dark, and then another; the gods were playing dominoes around us with sixty-metre-tall hardwood trees.

There was absolutely nothing we could do. Getting out of our hammocks and trying to run away would have been pointless. It's too dark in the jungle at night to have any chance of getting anywhere and we had no idea from the surrounding cacophony which way to go. We just had to sit it out. It seemed to take an eternity for the sounds of breaking and falling to cease – I can't remember whether there was a final crash. The lightning storm continued but seemed to be retreating northwards back toward the sea. The wildlife, which is never quiet in the jungle, was in uproar, but eventually the noise subsided, and debris stopped falling around us. It was at this point when, from within our small group of highly trained, professional men of action, there came a shaky voice in the dark: 'Anyone fancy a cup of tea?'

Prompt replies followed of 'too right' and 'yes please' as blinkered torches started to prick the blackness. I remember that nothing was said over tea of what had happened; no one really wanted to discuss it just then, so the conversation weaved around how we'd been working pretty hard and deserved a break from the tactical rigour and silence of the training. Tea finished, and everyone slightly reassured, we went back to our hammocks. At first light we could see close by to the north the tangle of wood, the incongruous sight of huge trees not standing vertical and proud but horizontal and askew, highlighted by the light penetrating the newly formed gap in the canopy. We quickly moved away in the opposite direction, another chapter in the continuing saga of my fear of dead and dying trees in the bush.

Wearing my utility belt and with fog horn at hand

Bigger Critters

One night in late July, about fifty miles north of Anvik, and in the middle of a 48-hour period where I had only managed to cover fifteen miles or so, I heard something obviously large and close by moving about outside the tent. On tentatively peering out, I saw a magnificent, and slightly scary, bull moose striding by my site. It was on its way past and offering me no real threat but, in hindsight, I probably felt he was too close for comfort, so rather than look on in awe and admiration, I thought I would give him a blast of the air horn to hurry him on his way.

Unfortunately, I had neglected to pump up, to pressurise, the horn so I gave him a less than impressive blast. In response, he promptly stopped, swung his massive antlered head around and looked back over his shoulder straight at me. It was at this point, under his steely gaze, that it dawned on me that my half-hearted blast of the horn could have sounded like the seductive sort of call an amorous female moose might make, and I wondered if my cosy buff, moose-coloured tent might look, to a short-sighted bull, like an attractive mate crouching obligingly for the suitor she was calling. Fortunately, despite my best efforts, I was clearly not this bull's type, and after a snotty snort of derision he continued nonchalantly on his way, leaving me a little shaken and questioning the practicality of my horn – and thankful for the lack of his!

Back in 2017 on the Teslin River, early in my first trip, I was busily lugging my kit back and forth between my kayak and campsite when I suddenly became aware of a very inquisitive lynx sat on its haunches a few feet away, watching me intently. Probably 3 or 4 times the size of a domestic cat, it was magnificent: immaculate speckled white fur on its chest against the lightly stripped brown flanks; big yellow eyes; whiskers twitching; and, most prominently, tuffs of long black hair above each roving ear. We held the briefest of eye contact, at which I blinked first. I don't know how long it had been watching me and I wasn't sure if it was considering how best to take me down.

'They' say that your average household moggy spends a fair amount of its time watching its owner and working out how it could best eat them; I don't know how 'they' worked that out, but given the fact that this lynx was on a tactically well-chosen patch of ground, slightly above me, I reckoned, despite his size, if he pounced he may have had a good chance. I picked up my double-bladed paddle and dropped my voice an octave or two before continuing with my routine, pretending I was unconcerned whilst occasionally singing out loud and twirling my paddle about like a demented majorette. The lynx continued watching me for a short while longer before obviously getting bored and slinking away into the trees unobserved. I was left with more of a sense of wonder than of concern: it was an impressive beast in its own environment, and I felt privileged to have met it, but still very conscious of my position as the uninvited traveller.

On that particular paddle, camping along the shore among the trees, I would surround my tent with a picket fence of para-cord with bear bells attached. Bear bells are hollow metallic balls about the size of a golf ball containing a small metal ball-bearing and when shaken ring just as any other bell. However, bear bells also have a strap with a small magnet at one end which when placed against the metal bell casing holds the ball-bearing in place and stops the bell ringing. The bells can then be worn silently on a pack or belt until needed when the magnet can be released allowing the bell to ring, hopefully forewarning bears of your presence.

Normally I'd set the fence about a metre high or, as I thought without any real evidence, bear height. That night I took the precaution of lowering my picket-line slightly just in case the lynx had concluded from his earlier recce that it would be worth paying me another visit; it didn't! The only critters that routinely set off my picket alarm on the first trip were the bastard squirrels. On more than one occasion, once alert to the sound of the bells being knocked, I waited in the tent for the sounds of heavy breathing and padding paws to be followed by the ripping of thin fabric, with my bear spray clutched and cocked in a white knuckled fist. All that would invariably happen was the follow-on sound of the chattering of some excited squirrels as they headed off back up their trees no doubt delighted by the fact that they'd made me nearly shit myself. As I say, bastards!

"Doyonh ghahol!" A man who had caught a
wolverine would announce loudly as he came into the
village, "The great one, the chief of animals, arrives!"

Richard K. Nelson, Make Prayers to the Raven

It took me a little while to distinguish between the couple of wolverines that I saw and the few porcupines. They fascinated me. I only saw either creature later in my paddle, so further west in Alaska and in the latter half of July, on those stretches where I took to paddling overnight when the conditions on the river were more favourable. As such, and despite my efforts to get closer, I only really saw chromatic silhouettes rather than detailed views of these bizarre creatures as they rummaged along the shoreline. Very often my sightings of these animals were in conjunction with or very near a bear sighting, although I didn't spot a wolverine and porcupine together. Neither animal once stopped to check me out, despite an occasional shout in a vain attempt to get their attention – they seemed too engrossed with the smells in front of them, moving quickly and seemingly oblivious to my presence.

The porcupines were relatively easy to recognise, with their pointed noses and the fan of lighter-coloured spines flaring on their behinds. The wolverines were slightly bigger but had a less distinctive shape. Occasionally, if there was a breeze blowing up the fur on their short bristly tails, when viewed from the rear, it took me a while to distinguish the wolverines from the porcupines; but once my eye was in, I could see that their bodies were too long, hunched between four short powerful, big-pawed, pillar-like legs. Both animals were invariably picking their way along the debris on the shore, always with their noses panning back and forth, leading the way. I had read with interest some of the Alaskan Native beliefs regarding these creatures: according to the native Distant Time stories, bears and porcupines are cousins, proof of this being their occasional sharing a den.

In fact, porcupines are actually large rodents and recent research has shown that, despite the atrocious winter conditions, they don't hibernate like bears, they actually remain active, surviving on tree bark, insulated by the coarse hair and often resting in trees to keep off the snow and ice below. They are widely considered as pests for the damage they can do to trees and the injuries their spines can cause nosey dogs, but conflictingly many still regard them as benignly cute, with their rodent features and waddling walk.

Wolverines, on the other hand, have a quite unique reputation for ferocity, particularly when cornered: very few other animals, including the bears, would bother a wolverine unless absolutely necessary. Additionally, for some of the Native Peoples, the spirit of the wolverine is one, if not the most potent, of the spirits within their hierarchical constructs, above that of the bear and wolf. And yet here it was, a rather scruffy, non-descript, short, antisocial-looking creature that appeared oblivious to the world around it. For all its renown and its physical and spiritual power, there was just something rather ordinary looking about the wolverines that I saw. I wondered if it could be this rather understated, unbothered, nonchalant nature, coupled with the potential for such aggression that gives these little 'hard-cases' their reputation? I didn't get close enough to either animal to experience any sort of interaction to prove either way their ferocity or cuteness, and just as with all of the other creatures I saw – especially bears – I felt blessed and humbled to see them.

As it happened, I was blessed to sight many bears and fortunate enough not to have any enter my camp. One of my first sightings was of a family of four grizzlies in the Flats, about 20 miles downstream from Fort Yukon. I was paddling into the early morning sun and saw what I thought were the shapes of some fishermen crouching by the shore on the left bank, as if hauling in a net. Once again, my brain had equated something it saw with previous experiences and concluded that this must be what I was seeing. As I got closer with the sun still in my eyes the 'fishermen', still crouching, began to move away from the river and into the willows. It was only as they were about to disappear into the brush at the top of the bank that I got a proper view of their silhouettes and realised that in fact they were not fishermen but bears.

As I passed the spot where they had been, I spun the canoe about and tried to get another glimpse. With the sun now behind me I could clearly see an inquisitive brown and black nose peeking out from the willows. I tried to hold my position but was slowly slipping downstream as one of the bears reappeared and headed back down toward the water, followed in short succession by two more. I was no more the 30 metres away when the first bear came out and, as the others joined it, I could clearly make out their shaggy golden coats and the distinctive ruffs on the back of their necks. They were definitely grizzlies. They appeared oblivious to me and had clearly decided that I was not a threat. The fourth bear was slightly more tentative but, as I slipped backwards still further away, it also reappeared. They all looked to be about the same size, but I assumed it must have been a mother and her three larger cubs, the mother probably being the more hesitant of the group.

Most of my other bear sightings were in the late afternoons or evenings and consisted of me floating past the bear on the shore anywhere between 10 and 50 metres away. I had a particularly close encounter – well, as close as I was happy with – with another grizzly. It was a big bugger, rummaging around on the water's edge as I passed. It could obviously smell something and could probably see the red of my canoe, but bears being notoriously short-sighted I don't think it was sure what I was. Then, with its nose twitching and mouth agape, trying to sniff me out, it reared up on its hind legs to get a better look: it was bloody massive! It stayed like this as I passed, its usually hunched trunk now stretched fully, uncannily human-like in the vertical, exposing the true enormity of the bear, a size that is not always fully apparent in their hunched lollop when on all fours. Its hub-cap sized paws were held out searchingly – jazz paws – as it wavered hopefully at full stretch, before falling back onto all fours to watch me go.

The majority of my sightings like this ended with the bear making its way back for cover in the trees or shrubs away from the river, but not this one: it watched me go. For the next hour or so, as I paddled, I kept looking over my shoulder at the river behind me, half expecting to see the huge shaggy head of the grizzly, powering through the water after me.

"Alaska has long been a magnet for dreamers and misfits, people who think the unsullied enormity of the Last Frontier will patch all holes in their lives. The bush is an unforgiving place, however, that cares nothing for hope or longing."

Jon Krakauer, Into the Wild

As I mentioned in my planning considerations, second on the list of my safety concerns, after log jams and fallen trees, and above bears, was me and my ability to look after myself – my own personal admin. As anyone that knew me from my military days would testify, my personal admin was one of the least strong of my qualities, amongst an array of less than dazzling attributes. I did, however, have a degree of confidence in my ability to live and survive in the 'bush' and I ensured throughout my planning and packing that all the potential weak links – fire-lighting, water-making, cooker and shelter – were backed up with spares and repairs.

Maybe it would have been more authentic to live off the land and the river, but I know from experience just how random and time consuming that can be. Had I been fulfilling my youthful ambition to be dropped off in the middle of the boreal forest to walk out, as opposed to paddling through it, my approach would have had to be different. Whilst the surrounding environment may have remained the same, being assisted by, and travelling on, a body of open water in a weight-bearing craft into which I could relatively easily load forty days of supplies – and which, when the conditions were right, could travel at at least 3mph – as opposed to physically carrying everything I would need for such a period whilst being immersed the woods, would have realistically necessitated the need for a weapon, to both sustain and defend myself.

Over the years I have caught and eaten any number of poor unsuspecting creatures: spit-roasted resus monkey; flame-grilled snake kebabs; sour-tasting ants; enough raw fish to put me off sushi for life; and, sadly, a rather pathetic little river turtle which I felt very guilty about eating – in hindsight it might have been the last of its species, but, in my defence, I was hungry. As Crocodile Dundee famously said about eating a lizard in the bush, 'you can eat it but it tastes like shit'.

I once had the real privilege of joining some Dayak tribesman in the Kelibat Highlands of Sarawak. When out one day, they heard a barking deer somewhere in the trees and were able to call it to them, mimicking its bark by using a blade of grass between their thumb and forefinger, just as we did to imitate owl hoots as kids. As they called, I stood behind the tribesman with the rather ancient, but well-cared-for shotgun, the best place to be I thought. I could not, for the life of me, see the deer until after the shot rang out and the tribesman ran over to it. They dismembered the small deer on a bed of palm leaves in reverential silence, with an efficiency akin to a swarm of soldier ants, before wrapping every artfully butchered piece in the leaves – including the stomach contents – placing them in the wicker baskets on their backs and continuing on our way. We spent a very pleasant evening camped at the top of a 50-metre waterfall complete with its own plunge pool and a view over the Indonesian border; for supper we had barbequed barking deer complete with stomach-content soup.

Drinking the watery, green-flecked soup reminded me of the stories of the 'Telemark Heroes', the guys parachuted into Norway during WWII to sabotage the Nazi production of 'heavy-water' – a key component in their nuclear weapons programme – being manufactured near the town of Rjukan. The first team dropped were unable to complete their mission, and whilst many were caught and executed, a small band lived out the Norwegian winter high up on the Hardangervidda (the high plateau in central Norway) hiding from the occupying Nazi forces. Short of rations, they hunted and ate reindeer for sustenance and supped on the reindeer stomach contents to stave off scurvy. They ate lichen as well but knowing that reindeer have the ability to digest and extract vitamin C from the lichens and mosses they find in the snow, the men took the vitamin C they needed from the deer's digested stomach contents.

The use of lichens for survival also appears in the harrowing accounts of Sir John Franklin and his search for the Northwest Passage. Franklin made two unsuccessful expeditions along the north Canadian Arctic coast between 1818 and 1827, prior to his final ill-fated voyage of 1843 taking HMS Erebus and the Topsham-built HMS Terror in search of the illusive Passage. In his accounts of his first expeditions, Twelve Years in the Arctic, Franklin details how his team would employ native hunters to go ahead to find food to cache for them so that they could effectively cover the ground required without carrying everything they would otherwise need over the months they would spend mapping the Artic coast. However, the hunters were often unsuccessful, and at times he and his men were reduced to eating rock lichens – or 'tripe de rouche' as the Canadian voyagers called it – and, when in real trouble, boiling their boots and belts to make them 'edible' in order to survive. Whilst not explicit in his account, it also appears that some of his party succumbed to eating each other to survive: at least one man was summarily executed for cannibalism. I wonder what Franklin would have thought of Amundsen's appearance in Eagle, 62 years after he was last seen, to announce that he had finally successfully discovered a route through the Passage?

It would have been interesting for me to have attempted to live off the land but trying to do so and still being able to cover the distance required in a reasonable time and without introducing any more risks than strictly necessary would not have been workable. For me, I felt that focusing on my aim and keeping everything simple and straightforward in support of that goal – rations, water, power, communications and personal care – was key. Distractions, such as fishing, hunting and trying to prove my bush skills, were not for me on this trip. I didn't have the time or the inclination to immerse myself in the landscape and therefore quite simply had no real desire or need to hunt. I did have a small survival kit in my 1st line kit, just in case, but knew that if I had to employ the contents of that and dredge up any residual associated skills, it would have meant that something somewhere in my approach and behaviour had gone horribly wrong.

Before I left home my sons had been taking the micky, as usual, out of my planned lunacy and had suggested that I should 'watch and learn' from the film Into the Wild. The film was based on the book of the same name by Jon Krakauer and tells the story of Christopher McCandless, a young man in his early 20s, who in 1992 gave all of his savings to charity, abandoned his possessions, hitchhiked to Alaska and walked alone into the bush north of Mount McKinley (now called Denali, the Alaskan Native name). His decomposed body was found four months later by a hunter. I was aware of the film, although I'd not seen it, but I read the book on my return from the Bering Sea and was enthralled by Krakauer's biopsy of McCandless's life, motivation and approach to his ill-conceived and fated adventure.

I was particularly taken by Krabauer's handling of the suggestion that McCandless had not shown enough humility in his approach to the wilderness. Kraubauer makes his point by using the example of Sir John Franklin and his ill-fated expeditions to compare and contrast McCandless' approach and proposed arrogance. He points out that for Franklin the wilderness was an antagonist that would inevitably submit to force, good breeding and Victorian discipline, whilst he says that McCandless went too far in the other direction and tried to live entirely off the land without bothering beforehand to master the necessary skills.

In both cases, Kraubauer suggests neither protagonist attempted to learn how to properly rely on the country for sustenance but points out that McCandless did manage to last for sixteen weeks on no more than his "wits and ten pounds of rice." I note he doesn't comment on just how awful those last few weeks, days and hours must have been for McCandless, just as they undoubtedly were for Franklin and his crew before their demise. Kraubauer also suggests, in defence of McCandless, that it is not unusual for young men to be drawn in the pursuit of an idea that may be seen as reckless by their elders but says nothing about older men drawn to the pursuit of an idea that may equally be seen as reckless by their family and peers!

> **Journal 28 June 2019:** I think I might have overdone it slightly today, my arms, wrists and shoulders are a little sore. I was hoping for an early night with the help of some painkillers and a small whisky to put everything at ease, but I'll have to wait for the temperature to drop, there's no point in waiting for the sun to set it won't!

It would be very easy to ask, again, was it really wise, and respectful, for a late-middle-aged man with a physical history of bodily breaks, tears, replacements and compressions to take on such a journey, particularly on his own? My answer to this, of course, would be 'yes', with the proviso that I had properly and conscientiously considered and weighed my limitations and abilities in my planning. I was, relatively confident that I had done these things, and along with this consciousness of my physical condition comes the more mature man's outlook on pace, discomfort and risk. I knew from experience how to pace myself: if I found myself working at more than 50-60% of my capacity for any extended length of time, without a short-term goal like to reach a bank or negotiate some rapids, then I was probably working too hard. I knew how to look after myself in the bush and was fairly sure I could complete the distance, I just had to nurse my body through it as well.

To support my decrepitude, I took a range of painkillers and anti-inflammatory drugs, the majority of which I knew I would have to use throughout the paddle. It was just a case of what strength I would need and when. I was conscious of a recent, self-inflicted shoulder impingement, the result of a reckless attempt at a warmup on the way to take on my eldest son and some of his mates in a sea swim off the north Cornish coast. I don't know why I decided a bit of vigorous milling would do any good – it didn't, it just caught my bicep long-tendon at the shoulder and sent shooting pains down my right arm, something it has been doing intermittently and without warning ever since. I was never really one for warming up before any exercise or sport: in my short and less than illustrious rugby career I think I had more injuries from pre-match warmups than from actual games. A pint of Guinness was my idea of a warmup.

Combined with a couple of compressed vertebrae in my neck, I knew that I would inevitably, from time to time, be in quite a bit of pain when my bicep tendon became impinged and my neck tightened up. The kayaking on my first trip was certainly more painful than canoeing, the action of pushing a double-ended paddle at shoulder height going right into the point of the pain. In the canoe, I could control the movement more effectively and manage the effect on my neck and shoulder. It was at night when I really struggled. Whilst awake, I subconsciously controlled my posture and therefore could manage the impingement, but as soon as I was in my sleeping bag and started nodding off, my muscles would relax, my shoulders would roll forward, the nerve would get pinched and the pain would shoot down my arm. When this happened, invariably my neck would also tense up and the damaged vertebrae would add to the impingement, leading to a chain reaction of spasming nerves and muscles.

My only effective management system for this was knowing that it would happen, combined with a nightly round of pillow, neck, shoulder and arm adjustment, in an attempt to find the least painful position for that night, topped off with a healthy supply of painkillers. At home, my usual solution is to knock back a bottle or more of red wine and take a few painkillers prior to bed (not recommended), the combination knocking me out, allowing me to sleep and my neck and shoulder to relax; I usually wake up and just have to manage the pain in my head, my neck and shoulder feeling much better. Here on the Yukon my ill-advised remedy was not an option: the booze wasn't available and I was reluctant to use the painkillers overly, for fear of not then being fully conscious or functional should I be visited by something untoward in the night.

However, it was the onset of a back spasm at the end of the third week that really caught me by surprise and made me seriously think about my ability to keep going. It started, or at least I first noticed it, one morning as I was pulling out some tent pegs. They weren't firmly embedded but the action of bending to pull them out started twinging my lower right back. After a careful sit down in my camping chair with a coffee, some more painkillers and a short period of contemplation, I knew I had to get on and I found I could continue packing my kit away as long as I took it slowly. I had to kneel down on one knee, keeping my back straight, to pick stuff up and to roll away my sleeping bag, roll-mat and tent.

With everything carefully stowed I had great difficulty in lifting the stern of the boat in order to push it out through the sticking mud until it was buoyant enough to manoeuvre and launch, preferably with me in it. Once sat in the canoe – and thankfully with the support of the back rest on my canoe seat – I was extremely relieved to find that I could paddle, albeit gently on my right side. The spasms continued for a few more days and I gradually adjusted my approach and routine in setting up camp and tried to regulate the pain with the drugs I had, conscious that I maybe couldn't really complete my trip in such a state.

The situation came to a head one morning whilst I was taking comfort break. Heading off for a poo, away from the perceived security of my tent and into the trees or higher up onto a sandbar, was always a rather unnerving experience. Despite checking the area and taking my bear spray with me, this was the one point each day when I felt most exposed. So, having wandered away from my camp with shovel and biodegradable paper in hand, my feeling of exposure was blown sky high when a particularly nasty spasm shot through my lower right back. Fortunately, I'd finished what I was doing; unfortunately, it was the action of trying to straighten up that caused the spasm.

My trousers were still at half-mast when it hit. I couldn't stand up, all I could do was roll onto the sand and lie on my side and try to find a position that would relieve the pain. I had to ignore the flies buzzing about my undercarriage and hope that the horse flies wouldn't take advantage of my predicament. After a few minutes, as the initial spasm eased, I was able to pull my trousers up which made me feel slightly less exposed although I still couldn't get up and had to lie in the foetal position for what seemed like an age while contemplating my woe. Eventually, I eased my way up onto my feet, carefully made my way back to the tent and gingerly sat myself down in my chair. Although I could move, the shock of what had happened was slowly sinking in. How could I carry on? Would I have to pull out at the next settlement?

I sat in my chair for a while, popped a few more painkillers, nursed my still hot fresh coffee and studied my mapping with a view to finding the next suitable place to maybe finish my adventure. It looked as if it would be a couple of days away and, in my current state, it was going to be an interesting paddle. As I mused over my predicament, a cunning plan came to mind – perhaps I could fabricate a girdle. I knew I had couple of seat pads that I had fashioned out of an old roll-mat and brought along just in case they were needed. They were stowed at the bottom of my 3rd line bag – if I could fashion these, one to support my back and one around my stomach, then perhaps with a belt holding them in place, I could protect and support my back.

I gingerly fished the mats out of the bottom of my large kitbag and tried them for size – it could possibly work. Having tried to hold them in place with just the one belt, I quickly realised that I'd probably need another belt or some masking tape to properly secure the mats and spread the support. My other belt and the tape were also at the bottom of my 3rd line bag and having already put that back in the boat I didn't want to drag it out and delve in there again just then. That morning I set off sat on the two roll-mat cushions thinking that I'd fabricate my girdle later in the day. By mid-morning my back was feeling better; by the end of the day I'd put the girdle idea on the back burner and decided that the extra cushioning on the canoe seat was the way ahead. So, when I did eventually retrieve the masking tape from the bottom of my kitbag, I simply taped the mats to the seat rather than to me. I remained careful and conscientious and, thankfully, did not have any more major issues with my back; I could yet get to the sea!

The problems with my back made me even more conscious than I may

Sterilising drinking water by the river
beyond Galena

already have been that sitting in the canoe for 8-12 hours a day was possibly creating a few physical, as well as mental, imbalances. So, I endeavoured to start, where I could, doing 30-50 standing squats whenever I got out of the boat in an effort to try to keep up some leg strength over the remaining course of the journey. On a couple of occasions, predominantly when I'd been paddling overnight and was therefore a little cold and stiff come the

early hours, I gave myself some Swedish PT sessions on the sandbanks in an effort to warm up and get the blood flowing. I hoped that at that time of the morning they'd be no one about to mistake my 'arm stretching, up and to the side, with side stepping and heel raises', as a distress call – you'd have to have experienced Swedish PT to understand that one, and no, it's not a euphemism!

A quiet evening writing by the tent

Quieter Days

By no means was every day on this stretch taken up in battling long stretches of wind and rain-swept river, or in negotiating mudbanks and eddies. Just as many days, if not more, were filled with sunshine, light breezes, mirror-like water and mellow skies. It was on these days, where there was not much else to focus on or think about, that I was able to really enjoy just pottering along and could, for a while, try to properly assimilate my place in the scenery and surroundings. These were the days when I really got to think about my true size, my being and my situation.

I have heard it said that our landscape is seven-eighths sky and on the Yukon this certainly held true – the sky is enormous. Of course, this should hold true regardless of where we are on our planet but, for most of us, most of the time, we are surrounded by walls and buildings, trees or mountains and therefore to see the sky we need to look up. Out on the Yukon I rarely looked up, the sky was in front of me, behind me and either side of me – I didn't need to look up to find it. Bizarrely, after a while, unless there was some unusual activity – interesting clouds, birds or aeroplanes – I took the blue seven-eighths of my visual landscape for granted and focused solely on the remaining lower eighth which consisted of the consistently milky brown of the river and the mixed pastel greens of the spruce-lined banks and surrounding hills.

The only real injection of colour that broke up this drab yet compelling scene came from the muted yellows of the sandbars and geological colours of the bluffs and rock formations. These rock formations provided the occasional welcome splashes of spotlighted oxide-red, gold, silver or blue, that if caught by the sun reflected wonderfully on the river's surface. Why is it that almost any aspect of nature when reflected in an expanse of water appears magnified and enhanced? Is it that we are attracted to symmetry, and the symmetrical duplication of a view enhances its appeal?

The Professor of Psychology, writer and thinker on the human condition Steven Pinker suggests that we have an in-built receptiveness to the patterns in nature: "the brain's response may be a receptiveness to the counter-entropic pattern that can spring forth from nature". More poetically in To the River, Olivia Laing captures the way in which water within the landscape can enhance this open door, "A river passing through a landscape catches the world and gives it back redouble; a shifting, glinting world more mysterious than the one we customarily inhabit".

That certainly held true on the Yukon, even if it was easy to become nonchalantly blasé about the vista when immersed in it hour-by-hour, day-by-day over a prolonged period of time, and when focusing more on trying to achieve an aim than enjoy the surroundings. But there it was again, the duality of my experience, and Burke's idea of the sublime. There really was no getting away from the profound beauty of the place, not the sort of beauty that relies solely on the symmetry of reflection, or natural patterns and occasional vivid colours, but a beauty of character that is so deep it connects with and woos a primordial understanding and longing, perhaps like a long-lost love whose face you may not remember but whose effect on your being is irreducibly etched on your soul.

Or was it our atavistic connection with liminal places, those places that exist on the margins between one world and another, as if you can remember an Eden, or Elysium, and what they meant, regardless of whether you had been there or believe it ever existed? Or was it again a sense enhanced by the knowledge that behind this beauty lies an implacable hostility which makes you grasp and savour any moment of relative comfort and peace?

"Le Claire, finding me a good listener, told many stories of his adventurous life with Indians, bears and wolves, snow and hunger, and of his many camps in the Canadian woods, hidden like nests and dens of wild animals; stories that have a singular interest to everybody, for they awaken inherited memories of the lang, lang, syne when we were all wild."

John Muir, Travels in Alaska

I could feel the lure of Robert Service's 'spell', the draw of the uncluttered, undiluted, ancient connection that the Yukon still offers. I, myself, was born and raised on the banks of the River Lee, 14 miles north of its confluence with the Thames near Blackwall east of the City of London. Throughout my childhood I, was aware of, if not particularly conscious or interested in, the millennia of human history that surrounded my daily existence. The evidence of early Neolithic occupation in the form of 'midden-like' deposits found in amongst the gravel pits scattered along the course of the Lee formed my childhood playground. This evidence would have been left by people that found their way along the Lee after following the Rhine and then the Thames, when the Thames was a tributary of the Rhine and before the North Sea covered Doggerland disconnecting the European continent; people that would have entered my native homeland at about the same time the now Native Peoples of North America entered Alaska, circa 10,000 years BC.

But unlike Alaska, the Lee Valley and much of the UK became overlain by the thousands of years of human history that followed. The Roman settlements, causeways and roads, which I crossed everyday going to school, the route of the Roman Ermine Street; the alleged site of Boudicca's final battle in Epping Forest; King Harold's final resting place at Waltham Abbey; the Eleanor Cross, one of twelve crosses erected by Edward I in the late 1200s to commemorate the route of the return to London from Lincoln of the body of his wife Eleanor of Castile, to name but a few. Now I live in the West Country, in a Saxon town built on Roman remains, a shipbuilding, seafaring and salmon fishing town that provided ships and men to fight the Spanish Armada and, later, Sir John Franklin's HMS Terror, there is no getting away from the last two to three thousand years of my native history.

So, perhaps, when permeated by so many tangible layers of human historical development, surely the primordial connection – that direct link with our ancient ancestors, those hunter-gathers who lived and behaved in the same manner for millennia and whose brains we still use – surely this connection, for us, has been blurred and distorted. On the Yukon, the distortion – the veneer over our fundamental ancestry – is so much thinner. It's only a couple of hundred years at most since the Native Peoples lived entirely without 'modern' intervention as hunter-gatherers in a manner that was so readily relatable to our shared ancient ancestors, without any historical obfuscation. This may be why, for Europeans in 'coming to the country', that the will-o'-the-wisp of a couple of thousands of years of historical programming is lifted, leaving you feeling like some kind of spell has been cast or, perhaps, lifted; a feeling that is further enhanced by the knowledge that out in the country there are still some of those animals – wolves, bears, moose, lynx and beaver – that would have been familiar to our own Neolithic selves and whose presence and proximity makes us question our modernistic hubris.

Of course, sadly, the opposite may be true for the Native Peoples, who having lived with this direct connection to the land, animals and their past for those millennia have so recently had that severed without the benefit of any historical and cultural programming to help to come to terms with that separation. It is, perhaps, therefore easy to understand why so many of the Native Peoples are struggling to orientate themselves within a world they have so recently been introduced to.

Looking back through my journal, it is evident that my paddle wasn't just a battle against the elements with me trying to manage my mid-life aches and pains, although I remain acutely conscious that it's easier to remember the bad times than perhaps it is to recollect the beautifully inspirational moments, of which there were also plenty. But that leaves the majority of the journey, the frequent long, more sedate paddles and the easy, comfortable stopovers, to get lost amongst the chaff.

I made a note in my journal early on saying that I needed to find a way to collect and capture my thoughts as I paddled. It was easy enough to write something once I'd stopped, checked my surroundings, erected the tent and eaten, and therefore felt safe and comfortable enough in my perceived place to collect my thoughts. Looking back, I cannot remember one single occasion where I took out my notebook to write or capture anything whilst actually out on the river. In an effort to try and capture these thoughts, in the back of my journal I started writing down some of these ideas and observations, the sort of things that I hoped would be more existential than the mundane notes detailing my daily distance, the wind direction, and the type of curry I had for dinner. Now, reading back, I note that my first journal entry under the imaginative heading Thoughts while floating along reads, 'I must clean these glasses', followed by, 'why can't I think of anything now the notebook is open?'

The few other entries under this heading miss my own point entirely and comment on the physical, the sights, sounds and smells I experienced. That said, some of these entries have bought back great memories, such as the sound made by a huge flock of ducks that flew over me at low level one morning whilst paddling. They came at me from behind, in formation, just a few feet above my head, a hundred at least. They came with the soft roaring of a building wave and as they passed overhead, I could smell them and hear their strenuous breathing and the air moving through their primary feathers.

I also found a comment on the positive effect my music had on soaking up the hours as I paddled, but I still don't feel as if, in my journal, I managed to capture the majesty of my surroundings, the sheer wonder of my situation or the subliminal sense of peace I felt. I remember that these thoughts came to me as I paddled, on those passages when I had time to think and reflect, but just as quickly and easily as they entered my head, by the time I sat down to retrieve them they had vanished from view, a possible by-product of the otherwise positive mindfulness of paddling.

As I sit here now and think looking back at my journal, those memories and profound feelings are still there, hiding at the back of my head, their noses peeking out like wary bears in the willows along the shoreline of my mind. As I write, we are all currently working our way through the global COVID pandemic; for me and my small personal battle with the restrictions, having plumped for a life of travel and adventure, being locked down has proven particularly difficult, but in those times where I now need to adopt a little piece of soothing mindfulness, I find my go-to places for comfort are either those still evenings sat on the banks of the Yukon with a whisky in hand, or, actually, out on the river paddling steadily and contentedly for hours on end.

In his wonderful book A Time of Gifts Patrick Leigh Fermor recounts how he helped while away the hours as an 18-year-old walking from Rotterdam to Constantinople (Istanbul) in the early 1930s. To help pass the time, the young Patrick recited the poetry and prose he had learnt and remembered from his upbringing – I still love a book where I need a thesaurus to catch many of the illusions and references! Patrick was able to quote by heart and recite classical poems and Latin verse, words set in his brain when it "took impressions like wax...and lasts like marble".

Sadly, and embarrassingly, the songs and verses that imprinted themselves on my tiny brain at a time when it was still malleable, impressionable and, arguably, at its most creative are filthy inappropriate rugby songs, learnt in late '70s and early '80s as a youngster playing club rugby in North London. So, when it came to those quiet hours of contemplative paddling, not for me lines from the Iliad or Shakespearian sonnets, the verses that sprang most easily to my mind and lips were disappointingly and embarrassingly crude. The most used of these that I remember was, for those that may know it, "My sister Belinda she pissed outta the window". The reason, I think, I kept finding myself singing this particularly delightful ditty was because of its supposed Mexican refrain, apologies all round to modern sensitivities here, which starts with the words, "Aye, aye, aye, aye, si, si, Senora, my sister Belinda...", inevitably after a few hours paddling I would at some point moan 'Aye', as in 'Aye, that hurts', out loud and then without realising it I'd head off into the rest of the song and be singing about my non-existent Mexican sister, her filthy habit and my damaged sombrero!

Regardless of the puerile rugby songs, the music on my mobile phone was important to me on my trip. Many years ago as a child, I remember watching a TV interview with the former soldier and politician Enoch Powell. I don't know why I was watching it, it was a long time ago and I don't want to discuss his politics here, but there was just the one thing which struck me at the time and that I remember from that interview: when asked by the interviewer what sort of music he listened too, Powell's response was that he didn't listen to music as he believed that all forms of music encouraged emotions that were not real. I remember thinking at the time that it was an odd and rather sad thing to say and I still do.

I'm on Voltaire's side on this one: he is quoted as saying "Music is the pathway to the heart". Music – listening to it, that is – has been an important part of my life and it still is. I have always found that music has the ability to produce positive emotions. I'm sure some may disagree, but my experience of listening to music has always been helpful, even those late-night whiskies with Van Morrison. Paddling the Yukon, alone, certainly bought up quite a few emotions, emotions that I may otherwise not have had to manage, but for me, they formed part of the whole, real, experience and, at times, my playlists helped with this.

Along with the music on my phone I took an electronic tablet that held my books (taking them physically would have taken up far too much space), a couple of downloaded films and a range of card games, all helpful for those stuck-in-the-tent moments. I also took a mini speaker which I could pair with these devices so I could crank up the volume from time to time, and when the conditions were right out on the water, I could play the music from my phone and sing along. It really did help while away many an hour and stopped me thinking too much or repeating silly rugby songs, as long as I could keep these devices clean, dry and charged which I did using a power storage pack connected to a solar panel. It seemed wonderfully incongruous to be producing electricity from the sun in a land that otherwise receives so little stimulus or comfort from our elemental star.

In another sop to my age and so that I could actually use these devices, I took with me three pairs of cheap, plastic, off-the-shelf, glasses. Typically, within the first week, I could only find two of them, of which one pair had a lens missing and the other had only one arm. The missing lens was not a real problem as it was the left lens which is my better eye. I remember, a few years ago, in the days when I was still trying to be presentable and persuasive as a charity fundraiser engaging with so-called 'high-worth' donors, it was pointed out to me that I'd managed a meeting with just the one lens in my best prescription glasses. I hadn't noticed and the lens had probably been missing for a number of days if not weeks; I got the support we were after. And just to show that there is always a 'silver lining', the other pair of glasses – the ones with just one arm – proved themselves indispensable for reading in the tent when laid down and propped up. I could read with my head on my hand or pillow without knocking my glasses off; mind you I could only read like that on my right side.

The music also offered some comfort in camp: once I'd conducted my 'clearance patrol' and set everything up, having some music playing relatively loudly seemed a great way of letting any wildlife know I was there before they inadvertently stumbled across me. In theory, my noise pollution was doing the wildlife a favour, although I doubt anything or anyone that may have heard me singing along would have agreed. I had over 2500 songs on my phone, most of which are sorted into various playlists, so I could set the type and tempo of music I wanted to listen to at any particular time.

Occasionally, when I got bored with listening to my Van Morrison compilations, for fun I would let the music shuffle through all the songs and pretty much anything could come up whilst I was paddling. Christmas songs were not unusual: Bing Crosby singing White Christmas was surreal; Noddy Holder screaming "It's Christmas" made me self-conscious. The classical music could be pretty motivational: albeit with only limited power from my speaker it didn't really make its mark on the Yukon, Albinoni's Adagio in G was still haunting. The Australian singer Kevin Bloody Wilson was just crude and very wrong, akin to singing rugby songs, but fun to sing along to!

Looking out of the tent greeted by the rising sun near St Marys

Contemplating the river south of Anvik

Beyond
Koyukuk

Beyond Ruby and the nights of thunder and lightning, I passed through the Kokrine Hills and was running low on drinking water. When seeking suitable water sources along the river, I would either refer to my mapping or look ahead at the landscape to try and spot likely defiles or folds in the surrounding hills that would possibly hold a water-filled creek. If possible, I would then try to position myself on the river to be able to pull over as the creek disgorged its clear water into the Yukon and top up my collapsible bucket.

As I entered the Kokrine Hills, I spotted one such promising defile on the hillside some way ahead. I had to negotiate a couple of islands to get to the spot along the bank where the defile, and hopefully a water-filled creek, would meet the Yukon. Once I had rounded the right-hand edge of the final island, I could see the exact spot. Just like most of these creeks there was a camp of some sort, usually empty or abandoned, set up to take advantage of the water supply. As I approached this camp, I could see it was slightly different from the majority I'd seen: the skiffs were more neatly lined up and there was no fishing paraphernalia or barking dogs along the shoreline. As I pulled in at the upstream end of the waterfront, I could see, further back from the river, the well-ordered wooden barrack buildings with what looked like a sports field or parade ground in the centre.

In front of me, and between me and the buildings separated by a neat picket fence, was a pool of crystal-clear, inviting water, fed by a manicured bubbling creek; I wanted to jump in. I could not see anyone about in the camp, so I started making my way toward the buildings, stopping on the bridge across the creek to gaze longingly into the crystalline stream. I had every intention of finding someone to ask if I could have a bucket full of their delicious-looking water. It was then that I caught the sound of singing coming from one of the bigger huts.

Up until this point it hadn't dawned on me what this place was: it wasn't marked on my mapping, but it looked incongruous and felt just odd. Then it suddenly clicked. Adam Weymouth had mentioned it in his Kings of the Yukon – this must be the Kokrine Hills Bible Camp. OK, so, I'm not a religious person, although the usual attempts were made to indoctrinate me in my youth, but there was just something about this place that gave me the heebie-jeebies. To my mind, it didn't fit, it didn't seem to belong, the rationale for its existence felt at odds with the environment.

I changed my mind about finding someone to ask, quickly grabbed a bucket of water from their stream, jumped back in my boat and headed off downstream before the occupants came running out waving crosses, pitchforks or burning torches. It was only as I scuttled away that, further along the waterfront, I could see the huge white letters spelling out 'Kokrine Hills Bible Camp'. Yes, I am sure they were all very lovely people who wouldn't harm a soul – try to save one maybe but not harm it – and would have been more than happy to let me pinch some of their water; and, yes, I know my behaviour was as nonsensical as my feelings about the place, but that's how it happened.

I reached the town of Galena on the right-hand, northern bank of the Yukon just after midday on 14th July. I had deliberately timed my arrival, stopping short the evening before, in order to make a scheduled Sat-Phone call home, but also, taking my lead from Dan Maclean's guide, I was hoping to have another shower, maybe do some laundry and possibly pick up a few more supplies. Given the hold-ups I had experienced to date, I could no longer be sure that my forty days of food would suffice, so I was looking to pick up a few days' more.

I initially landed alongside what was already marked on my satellite imagery as the 'Galena City Hall'. These words were accompanied by two icons, which were already in place: one a large yellow building next to the words 'Galena City Hall' below which there was a smaller, white, classical, columned façade. I had concluded that, given this title and the icons on the mapping, this would constitute the town centre and that the airfield, which was clearly shown on the imagery slightly further downstream, would be on the periphery. Once again, I was wrong.

At the point where the City Hall was marked on the mapping there was – and I assume still is – a very impressive new, two-storey wooden building on stilts. The building stood out for some way upriver as I paddled toward it that morning. There was no obvious landing point adjacent to the building, which in itself should have raised some questions in my mind. But having concluded this would be the centre of town, and having had to search for such in both Eagle and Circle previously, I wasn't going to let that small point stand in my way. To reach the building, I had to scramble up the bank and across a patch of cleared forest, the clearing allowing the view of the building from the river and vice a versa.

As I tentatively approached the building, being careful not to twist an ankle negotiating the debris left from the recent clearance, there was the obligatory dog barking somewhere, which given the lack of a path on my approach route made me feel as if I were sneaking up on the place and therefore less than welcome. I reached what was effectively the back of the wedge-shaped building and realised, on closer inspection, that the building was a residence of some sort, with curtained windows lining the back walls. I worked my way around to the front to find an array of pick-up trucks parked neatly in designated lots and found the entrance, above which were the words 'Galena Native Elders Residence'. This was not the City Hall but in fact a rather grand retirement home.

I stepped back from the building and onto the road that ran alongside. I looked up and down the dusty graded road and saw absolutely no signs of movement, life and further development so concluded this was a rather impressive, if randomly isolated, old-people's home. Again, it put me in mind of Jack London's short story The Law of Life: I've found no other evidence to suggest that the First Nations used to leave those that could no longer keep up with the tribe or family to fend for themselves and accept their inevitable fate at the hands of the cold or wolves, but it was touching to think that these days, most probably another dividend of the oil, that their elderly are housed in such auspicious circumstances.

There was also another good reason why this building was new and on stilts, being as close to the river as it is. In May 2013, Galena suffered a catastrophic freak flood when the spring break-up on the Yukon caused an ice jam some 20 miles downstream, backing up the river and affecting nearly all the homes in the city. In the parts of town closest to the river, houses were submerged up to their roofs and most of the residents had to be evacuated. I returned to the river and my boat, again picking my way carefully across the felled trees, and paddled a mile downstream to pull in on a more productive-looking slipway.

Galena is, in fact, one of the bigger settlements on the Yukon River. Established in 1918 on the site of a former Alaskan Native fish camp, it was the supply point for the nearby lead ore mines from which the place takes its name. It also boasts one of the larger airfields along the river, another artefact of WWII, although now the military have left and it is managed by the city. Galena is also the halfway point of the Yukon 800, an annual summer speedboat race beginning in Fairbanks and taking place along the Tanana and Yukon Rivers. In addition, on even years in the winter, the Iditarod Trail Sled Dog Race passes through the town.

For me, personally, Galena was a bit of a disappointment and the only anomaly in Dan Maclean's otherwise excellent guide. Sadly, once I'd found the shop and adjoining liquor store next to the petrol station right by the western end of the airfield, I was told that the showers and laundry were no longer in use. I asked about filling up with water and was told that the water point was three miles out of the other end of town, probably back nearer the elders' residence I'd just came from, and no one seemed particularly forthcoming with offering me any at the store.

I didn't fancy what was potentially a two-hour walk back to where I'd been to fill up with water. In the end I begrudgingly bought a couple of plastic gallon demi-johns of distilled water from the store, noting that the water was more expensive than the gasoline being sold opposite. I also bought a few more days of supplies which, given the limited stock in the store, constituted a rather eclectic assortment of rations. I picked up some more sachets of freeze-dried meals, including a beef and dark chocolate chilli concoction which I still have, along with a tin of peaches in syrup and, excitingly, for me, a tin of Spam.

Now, my family would tell you that the Monty Python guys could have written their 'Spam' song about me. At home I can have Spam with pretty much anything and everything: I can happily eat it out of the tin, fried, in an omelette, in a sandwich covered with HP sauce or added to any veggie dishes they attempt to give me. Judging by their faces and contemptuous tuts whenever they catch me tucking in, this dietary habit appears to my millennial offspring like a sad throwback to the trenches or rationing. Bizarrely, toward the end of the trip when I did decide to treat myself and tuck into my newly acquired Spam, I found I could appreciate my family's concern: it was unpalatable, not because there was anything wrong with the tin I'd bought, but because my taste buds couldn't handle it. The Spam was too powerfully salty – I couldn't finish it out on the river! You'll be pleased to know that since getting home I have applied myself conscientiously to re-acquiring my taste for Spam, perhaps just to see that look of disgust on the faces of my family again.

Back on the river and now past Koyukuk, the river was wide and straight. It turned southwest down past the old Russian portage settlement of Kaltag, toward Anvik and down toward St Marys before turning west and hooking back up north into the Yukon–Kuskokwim Delta. According to Dan Mclean's guide, just beyond Koyukuk there is a point ominously named 'Last Chance'. I took a closer look at this in his description. Last Chance is in fact a liquor store and I found out that selling alcohol below this point on the river is illegal.

The river was now heading directly into the prevailing weather, and by this time I had become particularly paranoid about the ever-changing conditions, especially the wind. Having been forced off the river in the Flats where there were plenty of sloughs in which to seek shelter, and a myriad islands and mudbanks to choose to pull out on, now on this part of the river, with steeper treed banks and fewer islands spread out by miles rather than metres, I really had to start assessing the conditions before committing to the longer exposed paddles. I would undertake these at any time of the day or night to take advantage of favourable conditions in a concerted effort to cover some distance as long as my body would allow. The results were variable. I had many frustrating and disheartening days where I simply could not make the miles I wanted to, mixed – probably equally – with days or nights where I was able to spend long, long hours paddling long, long stretches of relatively nondescript river, always with a wary eye on the conditions and always in the hope of spotting some wildlife.

Occasionally on this stretch I was rewarded, once by seeing a mother otter with three cubs out on the river, the only otters I saw on my trip. It was a quieter afternoon, and I was content to be further out into the river than I had been recently, trying to catch some assistance from the current. I saw the otters some way ahead swimming out from the left bank and heading across in front of me. I've seen sea otters in the wild before, whilst kayaking off the west coast of Scotland and out of Tofino, Vancouver Island, so I quickly recognised the chevron wakes created by the lithe little bodies pushing through the water, their heads up with the occasional slithering curve of their backs and tails breaking the surface. The mother must have seen me, or at least my rather obvious red canoe, as she promptly stopped heading across the river and turned back the way she had come, initially leaving the cubs trailing behind, but then quickly stopping for them.

My initial reaction was to get as close as I could and try to take some pictures, but I could see that the mother was worried and that perhaps her cubs weren't yet as proficient or capable as she was. So, I chose a path further out into the river giving the otters what I thought was a respectable distance (besides, I don't think trying to chase otters singlehanded in a 16ft canoe would have been particularly fruitful). It seemed to work, and once she had her brood corralled, the mother swam parallel to me keeping herself between me and the youngsters. I knew I wouldn't be able to get any decent pictures with my cameras at that distance – maybe just a few ripples on the water – but as I still had a clear view of them from the boat, I kept up a steady pace to pass them and revelled in the privilege of, yet again, being able to see such beautiful creatures in their natural habitat. It is difficult to believe today that it was these animals and their precious pelts that attracted one of the first waves of European exploitation of the Yukon.

The mother otter seemed to read my mind and relaxed her pace, and as a result the three otter cubs began to gamble and tousle playfully alongside her. I spun around once I'd passed and watched the now placated otters continue their way across the expanse of the river, at once looking so small and vulnerable, but also so natural and determined. It was at that point it occurred to me how self-conscious I actually felt about being out there in my 16ft red canoe. I was, in reality, just a tiny speck compared with the river and country I was navigating, but when confronted by the otters I felt strangely intrusive, bolder, brighter and unnatural. As with most of the encounters I was privileged to experience, my perspective was momentarily changed: I felt much bigger sat in my canoe, in my world on the water, looking out.

My other sighting on this stretch, a few days after seeing the otters, was that of a mother moose and calf, again making a crossing of the river from left to right in front of me. I saw them approach the river out of the shrub line and enter the water from some distance, the size and shape of the mother so distinctive as she walked into the water with her calf following obediently and without hesitation behind. It looked as if I would meet them as they crossed, and I paddled downstream. The river must have been almost half a mile wide at this point and was flowing well. The pair, line-astern, with just their heads above the water, moved surprisingly swiftly across the river and whilst making good progress were also subject to the river's flow and were moving downstream at the same pace as me.

Once again, I decided that I didn't need to sit on top of these majestic animals to appreciate them in their own home, so I stopped paddling at a respectful distance to allow them to cross in front of me. They appeared to take no notice, if indeed they had seen me at all, and powered their way across the river, the calf seeming unfazed by the swim. Toward the right bank but still in the river the mother suddenly rose from the surface of the water: she had obviously met a submerged sandbank, and with her long legs was now walking, her belly clear of the river whilst her calf continued to swim. The calf, still subject to the river's flow, started to drift down below its mother who, without panic or any sign of concern, simply altered her course and walked down with the calf until they were both free of the sandbank and swimming again just metres from the far shore.

There is something noble about moose. It would be easy to look at them as rather stupid lumbering animals, but I think that would be to misinterpret their seemingly effortless and emotionless ease in their environment. John Muir said "bears move as if the country had belonged to them always" but I think this is equally applicable to moose. The majority of bears I sighted ran off when seeing me (thankfully); the moose paid me no attention except when I foolishly tried to bother them. They are perfectly adapted to their environment and therefore have little need to hurry or show signs of panic, particularly the bigger ones, although the young are predated by bears and wolves. Having accidentally skied into a moose in Norway I know from up close just how impressive they really are. It was stood sideways across the ski-track on a sharp bend at the bottom of a hill on a cross-country route, and I had neither the time nor the skill to stop before the tips of my skis were between its legs and my nose was inches from its smelly brown flank, my head level with its shoulder. Fortunately again for me, this particular moose, whilst less than impressed, was not perturbed by my sudden appearance and nonchalantly sauntered off, stepping on one of my skis and pushing it down into the pre-cut track as it went.

> JOURNAL 26 JULY 2019: The water was lumpy today but the wind was lighter, it was blowing from the west so, in places, had long stretches of river to fetch up waves in my face. Thankfully, when I turned the corner prior to Russian Mission these tailed off, so I had a good run past Russian Mission. I was thinking about adding a few more miles toward the end of the day but with the wind picking up again and after over 12 hours of paddling I decided to pull in on a decent looking sandbar. I've now got the tent up drying, with a little fire going and am much happier with the world. I can now look back and see two of the mountain ranges that I've passed today. I don't think I've travelled that far but when I look back it's quite impressive.

Beyond the wildlife on this part of the river I was also keen, but sadly unable, to spot any remaining Russian influences. It is this part of the Yukon that received, and still holds, remnants of the early Russian explorers and settlers. Spurred on by Vitus Bering's reports from his less than definitive first forays into the sea that now bears his name, they began hunting and trading in the rich furs and pelts (particularly the sea otter) as well as introducing the Native Peoples to their faith, Russian Orthodoxy. These early Russian traders and missionaries did not like the idea of negotiating the Yukon–Kuskokwim Delta – I could appreciate that concept – and preferred to reach the inner Yukon by portaging overland from the sea coast north of the delta at Unalakleet, over the Nulato Hills to the settlement of Kaltag, a distance of just 50 miles only passable in the winter. The settlement of Russian Mission, which sits at the start of the hook in the river as it turns west before heading up into the delta, still has a church with an onion dome, which I strained to see as I passed but to no avail. Interestingly 'Gussack', an Alaskan Native word for white people, is believed to be derived from the Russian 'Cossack'.

It took me just under a fortnight to cover the south-westerly stretch between Koyukuk and St Marys. As I passed Pilot Station the wind picked up again, and it became impossible for me make any further headway. With some small annoying waves being fetched up along the river from the west, I was pushed toward the left-hand shore. Nearing the shore, I stabbed the mud with my paddle and concluded, wrongly, that the mud was firm enough to step out and onto. It wasn't. I put my left foot out and down, holding onto the gunwales on either side, trying to stabilise the boat which was getting a battering from the wind and river on my right. I must have found a hole in the mud or there was something to do with the non-Newtonian viscosity of the mud that allowed it to give way under my weight but not the sharp stab of my paddle.

Either way, as soon as I applied my weight my leg disappeared into the mud above the knee leaving me straddling the gunwale which my under carriage hit with a slap that took away my breath and made my eyes water. I already knew that there was a nerve that directly connected my testicles with my eye muscles and tear ducts: my vasectomy was performed by a Royal Naval surgeon with whom I'd played rugby a few times, but I thought it rather ungentlemanly of him to bring up during surgery, under local anaesthetic, whilst he had my 'crown jewels' in his hand, a match in which I may or may not have given him a subtle and probably illegal 'dig'. He was clearly bearing a grudge – as well as a scalpel – and despite the anaesthetic, my eyes were twitching with each tug as he cut, twisted and tied my tubes down below.

Unlike moose that are adapted to wade through water and mud, I was now in the predicament of being half in and half out of my boat with my left leg firmly caught in the mud and the boat being pushed against and possibly over me from the right. After a few panicky seconds, whilst unsuccessfully fighting to manoeuvre the boat around me and stop it being flipped over on top of me by the swell, I reluctantly came to the conclusion that my only option was to roll out of the boat, lie on my back in the water and try to use the waves to push the rear end of the boat around or over me. All I then had to do was hang onto the canoe and not let it be blown away leaving me stuck. I held onto the boat's stern line and pulled up the hood of my cagoule before stepping out and bending backwards at the knee in preparation for my planned manoeuvre. In what must have been only a couple of uncomfortable seconds, in which the river managed to find its way in from my neck to my toes, I found myself on the other side of the boat.

By pulling on the boat from the windward side and gingerly twisting my stuck leg I was able to haul myself up and flop my body across the deck. I then used the wind and waves to help slowly free my left leg whilst trying to retain my shoe. A few moments later I found myself sat back in my boat, wet through, covered from head to foot in mud and being rocked steadily against the bank. I was pinned there and had to just sit and wait out the weather. Having stripped off, rinsed off as much mud as I could, wrung out my T-shirt and fleece and put them back on again under my cagoule, all I could do in response to this situation was rock gently back and forth and chuckle to myself, amazed at my own stupidity in not properly checking the consistency of the mud before stepping out and therefore having to keelhaul myself! I have always had a personal propensity for doing something stupid, normally in response (although never deliberate) to occasions when things seem to be going well in my life. It's as if I've got my own in-built self-destruct button, one that has sadly hurt a few people along the way, which I dearly regret, but one which I really needed to get a grip of now if I was going to finish my trip. Easier said than done!

It was at times like this that I found myself having another quick personal motivational chat. In all honesty, whilst my ability to complete the trip was subject to any manner of influences, my motivation and determination remained resolutely constant: I was confident I could do it if circumstances and the river allowed and I wanted test that ability. As mountaineer Mo Anthoine explains to his friend and biographer, Al Alvarez, in Feeding The Rat, "every now and then you need to flush out your system and do a bit of suffering...there's always a question mark about how you could perform... it can be quite a shock when you don't come up to expectations...that's why

Sitting out the wind with a mug of coffee

I like feeding the rat... The rat is you...when the rat's had a good meal you come away feeling terrific".

I think that in some way, perhaps, I was also looking to feed my rat; to use the fading skills, training and know-how I had picked up over the years and, hopefully, still had somewhere. Admittedly, my 'rat' is probably more akin to a hamster or guinea pig these days: a little more rotund and slower, but – arguably – a tad wiser. If only!

It had taken me three weeks since leaving Yukon Crossing to cross western Alaska, then turn south after Koyukuk, before reaching the hook in the river near St Mary's that would turn me north-westward and into the final stretch to the sea. Those weeks had involved many a long, uneventful paddle, predominantly through gently sloping spruce-lined hills, occasionally paddling through the now increasingly darker nights, interspersed with a few frustrating days sheltering ashore waiting for the river to allow me to continue. Taken as a whole, and ignoring the days stuck ashore, the flies, the wind, the rain, the thunder and the lightning, I think it's safe to say I enjoyed this section of my paddle.

The river was big and moving well, it demanded my respect, but in return it gave me passage and surrounded me with magnificent scenery: reflected bluf and views of distant white-capped mountain ranges by which I could gauge my progress. There were skies of overwhelming proportion and majesty; cloud formations that induced a state of mindfulness as they lazily processed above me; and others so vast that their seemingly limitless size, towering up into the troposphere, accentuated the ethereal beauty of the country. And animals – an embarrassingly complete gamut of subarctic, boreal forest wildlife, both great and small, that moved so nonchalantly past and around me as if I too were part of the river.

My experience through this section gave me the time and the space to really think about where I was and what I was doing there. The sense of my place within this space, which had been seeping into to me over the previous weeks, was now saturating my being and I was thankful, very thankful. However, I was approaching the section of the Yukon that had most concerned and worried me throughout my planning. It had been on my mind since the very start, but now, as I approached this piece of water, I no longer felt any of the trepidation I had experienced earlier in my paddle, that sense of constantly stepping into the unknown again.

Now, I felt a real sense of determination, as if what was ahead was the culmination of my journey – which of course it was – and that the paddle up until now had been preparing me for this. Indeed, I felt as if the Yukon itself had, in its own way, been preparing me physically and emotionally for these last few days. I could only pray that the river would let me travel just a little further and that, for my part, I wouldn't, as is normally my wont, cock things up!

*Evening paddle on sheltered stretch before
Russian Mission*

Reaching the Delta

"What one thinks of any region while travelling through, is the result of at least three things; what one knows, what one imagines and how one is disposed."

Barry Lopez, Artic Dreams

Throughout my paddle, the nature of the Yukon changed, and my approach had to adapt to match the river and the prevailing conditions.

First there was the relative civilisation and pleasant backwoods feel of the river as it crossed from Canada to Alaska and continued in the same fashion through the Yukon–Charley Preserve, with its winding, bluff-lined, almost (dare I say) welcoming river, where I could float and practise my techniques, rehearsing for the journey to come. Then there were the Flats, where the river slowed and fractured, offering no reference to the surrounding environment, where I had to focus on my navigation and paddle hard to make any distance, as and when I could actually get on the river. Just before Yukon Crossing, as the river picked up pace again, when the sloping tree-lined banks became steeper and mountains could be seen again in the distance, it was a joy to experience the increasing sense of power in the water and the enhanced sense of majesty in the surroundings. Once beyond Tanana, across past Galena to Koyukuk, and then down toward St Mary's, the river grew in size again, as more of the major Yukon Basin tributaries joined it.

From here onwards, trying to use the river's inherent meandering flow, or being able to flit about from shore to shore, was problematic. The Yukon was now wide – a mile at least in places – and the main current would invariably be out toward the middle of the river which meant, potentially, exposing myself to sudden changes in conditions. I started to seek the shelter of the bank, looking for boltholes as I went, eschewing any assistance from the current. Even when the current did come near to the bank, it needed to be treated with respect. Those early days of enjoying a hitch on the current around an outside bend were a bit like comparing a pleasant day's pony trekking to now taking part in a full calvary charge. Maybe I exaggerate – I've never taken part in a calvary charge – but hopefully you get the idea.

The current was so much stronger, the eddies were no longer annoying swirls that would grab the nose of your boat, they were now visibly deep whirlpools with lives, minds and attitudes of their own. Getting too near the bank on one of these currents was not advisable. On the wooded banks the eddies ripped the trees from the soil as they lined up like soldiers at Waterloo, one rank after another waiting to be felled, occasionally too close to my boat for comfort and adding to my very real fear of getting ensnared. Those trees that did not fall directly into the river remained rooted to the bank hanging horizontally over the water, their branches moving in the current like the tentacles of an anemone searching for its prey.

At times rows of these 'sweepers' gave the impression of the bank moving like a giant green millipede, its legs rippling beneath it along the river's surface. Then there was the sight of a huge circular gouge ripped out of the bank with whole bleached tree trunks stacked up as if some giant hand had picked them up and spun them down like spaghetti strands cast into boiling water, in that spinning motion used to get them all in the pan without breaking them. I assumed this must have happened just after the ice break-up in spring when the force of all the water that had been locked up in the basin throughout winter is first released. I was glad to be there in July but still abundantly aware of the power I was playing with.

> **JOURNAL 27 JULY 2019:** What a day, southerly wind but light and for part of today behind me. And the sun out intermittently as well. Not a long day but a good one as I negotiated 'Devil's Elbow' without any hold-ups. Started a bit slow, my mind and body are now at odds! Woke up at 5am to a look out and saw clear sky and calm water, my mind wanted to get up and get on the water, my body had to remind my mind that it didn't get into bed until near midnight and it still ached. So, I rolled over and woke up at 8, on the water for 9:15am.

There were times, particularly after Yukon Crossing, where I would make a point to remember to turn about and see where I had come from. To look back and see the mountain ranges or rocky outcrops through which I had paddled, usually spotlighted by the low sun as if emphasising their place on the stage, provided a visual affirmation of the progress that I'd only otherwise see on paper. It was much harder to see where you had come from in the winding gorges of the Yukon–Charley Preserve, or in the featureless purgatory of the Flats, and in those early days I was less inclined to look backward when I had so much to focus on in front of me. I was beginning to have a dawning sense of achievement, of progress and of relative inner peace, albeit the thought of the delta still held a degree of foreboding at the back of my mind.

Back in the Flats, hundreds of miles from the nearest ocean, the sky was a huge blue dome dominated by a searing 22-hour a day sun that would split in two any cloud foolish enough to enter its domain and vaporise the hapless whisp before your very eyes. Not that you could look at it – it was an unforgiving and brutal sky. Today, however, the sun held less power, and I was now running southwards, parallel with the Bering Sea 40 miles to the west across the Kaltag portage over the Nulato Hills.

The conditions put me in mind of one of my favourite passages from Waterlog where Roger Deakin refers to the end of an early autumn day so wonderfully evocatively as "Those evenings of long warm shadows when the sun's bowling under arm". It was late July on the Yukon and already it was possible to discern the coming end of the ever-so-short Alaskan summer. In Alaska the rate at which the amount of daylight changes is about 9.5 minutes per day (it's about 3 minutes per day in the UK), so just over an hour per week. This meant that after five weeks on the river, the amount of daylight had reduced from 23 hours a day to 18 hours, and I could feel the land starting to accelerate toward winter, to exhale Lopez's long-bated breath of summer. In just over a month, darkness would have parity.

Now, close to the sea and with more moisture in the air, the sky was full of small, dense altocumulus clouds looking like mishappen jelly babies floating on their backs, or on other days like cotton-wool rabbits. All of them spookily at exactly the same height and evenly spaced out across the now autumnal-looking sky. As evening approached, the less playful cumulonimbus reared up in the sky with weird, high, dark-bottomed, ominous shapes, some unerringly resembling huge 'Star Trek USS Enterprise' type spacecraft, complete with the round tubular, proton-tube-like protuberances. The jelly babies and rabbits skit happily across an invigorating azure sky all day before the more oppressive looming 'spacecraft' arrived in the late evening intent on causing trouble. Paddling under those awesome skies, whilst entertaining and mesmerising, also had the effect of accentuating my own real, conscious and subconscious, lack of size and remoteness out on the living river.

> JOURNAL 30 JULY 2019: I'm propped up in the tent now, so my writing will be worse than usual, with a lite drizzle outside. I eventually stopped at 10:30pm this evening after attempting to get a few more miles in today with the hope of maybe reaching Emmonak tomorrow. I still have 40 miles to go, so it might just be possible.

With about 60 miles to go and having passed Mountain Village on the right bank, I entered the bend that would take me into the last stretch of river heading north-westerly toward the turn into the Kwiguk Pass and Emmonak. Throughout my planning this last leg had filled me with dread. I think it was a combination of the worrying descriptions in the guides, the width of the river and the prevailing winds, added to the closeness to the Bering Sea. I had it in my head that this would be a battle against a large, exposed piece of water where I would have nowhere to hide.

There was a protected route, alongside the final leg, through the Tunurokpak Channel, a long, relatively straight slough that runs parallel to the river and which I had in mind to use, albeit this would only shelter me for the first third of the final straight. I would still have to rejoin the Yukon and face the final 30 miles of exposed water. The wind was from the southwest again and blowing at a bit of a lick. This meant that I had to battle my way into the expansive final right-hand bend that would then point my way northwards into the delta and to the sea. I had hoped that I could stick to the left bank and gain some assistance from any current that should have run faster around the outside of the bend (it looked less vicious than some I'd experienced) and then find some protection from the breeze by hugging the shore and hoping the bank itself, the vegetation and any trees there were, would shelter me as I headed for the sea.

As usual, and why was it still a surprise to me, I am surely the epitome of a hopeless optimist – perhaps a useful quality when paddling your own canoe through Alaska – the river didn't do as I expected, and the protection afforded by the bank was negligible. It must have been one of the least densely treed banks of my whole trip! The bend was littered with mud bars and any current in the river seemed to disappear, at least it did from the outside bank that I was on. I contemplated taking a shortcut between the bars: the ones nearest me were bare of vegetation but with a good covering of washed-up, sun-bleached, spruce trunks; beyond those and toward the middle of the bend the islands had a covering of short willow; and over towards the inside bank the islands were well populated with living spruce.

This, from my lowly position sat in my boat, allowed me to see my travel register against a background of overlapping and independently moving landscapes. Sadly, not all of them were moving as fast as I would have liked, but I could relate the islands to my aerial satellite image and plot my position along with a few route permutations that might allow me greater progress. My mind was still eager to explore all the possibilities, but with five and a half weeks of paddling behind me, my body – and my reason – had both reached the conclusion that plodding on and not trying to be clever was by far the most effective course of action. So, head down, paddle planted, and pick a point in the distance to aim for. It took me over three hours to get around the bend and into the final stretch.

Once I had rounded the bend, I had the wind on my rear left flank, and whilst it wasn't sweeping me madly toward my final destination, it was providing some gratefully received assistance. It made a most welcome change to not be battling into the wind, but whilst it was not in my face it certainly had the river's back up. Close to the left-hand bank I had about three metres of sheltered, relatively calm water with a clear delineation marking the point at which the wind started to agitate the river. Beyond that, I could see quite clearly the line of the current out toward the middle of the river with its snarling brown ridges and white tops of windswept foam.

These were the sort of conditions I had learnt not to paddle in, but this time it was slightly in my favour, and I was on the home straight. The downside was that the sheltered water closer to the bank was slack with little or no onward momentum. In order to gain any assistance, I had to drift away from the bank and out into the affected water, and there attempt to ride the choppy line between getting a slight boost from the river and wind or being blown further out to where the swell risked breaching my gunwales. I ended up zigzagging along the bank, letting the wind and current push me out into the torment and judging when to fight my way back toward the lee of the bank. It was workable but required a lot of concentration and effort.

I reached the entrance to the Tunurokpak Channel after a further hour or so of zigzagging and there made an interesting decision. The channel would offer 15 miles of sheltered water running parallel to the Yukon and would re-join the river about 30 miles before Emmonak, but it would mean 15 miles of solid paddling as there would be very little current to help me along. That would equate to at least three hours of paddling with little respite or the security of an island to camp on if required, not to mention possibly having to dodge skiffs hurtling up and down the protected route. I decided, instead, to use the wind on the main river and continue as far as I could with the aim of putting me within one day's paddle, in favourable conditions, from Emmonak. I'd identified a few islands for possible campsites and girded myself for another two to three hours zigzagging along the river's edge.

This worked well for a couple of hours before, once again, I became embroiled in another series of interminable mudbanks, none of which were obvious from my mapping and which either forced me into slack shallow channels between the riverbank and the mud, or out to the right and into the wind and choppier water. Inevitably, I always took the right-hand option in search of a way around the mud rather than risk meeting a dead end on the inside and having to retrace my paddle.

It has been a long day!

Mistakes
Creeping In

JOURNAL 31 JULY 2019: 12:10pm, I'm still in the tent, that storm that looked like it was coming last night did come in. I think it's starting to abate now and I hope to be on the water in an hour or so. I now doubt very much I'll make Emmonak today, so I need to look for somewhere to aim for this evening.

Negotiating the mudbanks sapped me of any remaining momentum and with 12 plus hours of paddling behind me, I was still just short of the point at which the Tunurokpak Channel rejoined the main river when I decided I'd had enough for the time being. I pulled in on a small grass-topped island with a terraced mudbank that looked like a low, tiered chocolate cake with a green iced topping. The island was the size of a small football pitch and stood about two metres above the river's surface which I assumed would afford me some security from any tidal flooding, albeit the island itself had no cover other than a thick succulent type of grass. Experience had taught me that grassy campsites usually equated to excessive mosquito activity, but the wind and, now, slight drizzle seemed to be keeping them down so I thought I'd risk a night.

The terraced bank was new to me; I assumed it had something to do with being cut this way by the tidal action of the Bering Sea which I knew was capable of reaching this far upstream. I'd seen a gillnet with buoy and bucket obviously stored by a fisherman for later use on a step just below the grass top of the island, so in my tired state assumed it would be safe to haul the canoe up onto the step just above the waterline. I didn't register fully that there would be more steps below the waterline nor that the water might rise up and down, as it normally does when affected by the tide. It probably would have been hard to tell that I live on an estuary at home in Devon or that I'd been sea kayaking around the British coastline for a number of years. In my semi-comatose, desperate-to-get-the-tent-up-and-get-some-sleep state, my analysis of my situation was sadly lacking.

This quickly transpired to bite me to comical effect when having made my first trip up the steps to put up the tent on the grass, I returned to get the satellite phone out of the boat only to find that there was another step below the waterline toward the back of the boat and I stepped off another ledge sending me sprawling into the murky water. Fortunately, I hadn't picked anything out of the boat so all that happened was I got a soaking and a wakeup call. Having recovered myself and got out of the water, I pulled the boat further up the step, collected the kit I was looking for and climbed back up to the tent, where I had to smile to myself ironically as I changed into some dry clothes. Lucky no one was there to see me make a prat out of myself again!

My soaking had at least woken me up to the fact that the water here ebbed and flowed, so having pulled the canoe up away from the water's edge, I used my folding shovel as an anchor, embedding it firmly in the mud and attaching the bow and stern lines securely to it. As usual, and just as I had been doing throughout my paddle, I had situated my tent so that, with a little craning of my neck, I could see the boat out of the flap and would whenever I woke during the night check that my transport was still where I'd left it, thus allowing me to sleep more securely. So, imagine my surprise when in the early hours I hoisted myself up onto an elbow to look out of the tent into the dank, drizzling gloom and down onto the mud step only to find that my lifeline, my steed, my bloody canoe was no longer there! Oh fuck! Oh Fuck! OH FUCK! was about all I could say. I'm not actually sure I said it out loud after nearly six weeks on my own, but I can assure you that whether it was out loud or in my head, I said it pretty loudly as I kicked my way out of my sleeping bag, tearing at the tent flaps and into the wet, windy and now fairly dark night.

In the seconds that it took me to get out wearing nothing but a T-shirt, most of the permutations of the implications of being canoeless on the Yukon went through my head. They ranged from trying to hail a lift from a passing skiff, all of which would probably use the Tunurokpak Channel so not see me; waiting for one of the fishermen to come along (how long would that be?); to calling the Anchorage Emergency Centre on the Sat-Phone. To be honest, my situation would not have been particularly life-threatening – uncomfortable, yes, but not immediately deadly – but more to the point for me at that time, was the sheer embarrassment of being the muppet that allowed his canoe to drift away nearly 1300 miles into a 1340-mile trip.

As my eyes adjusted to the mizzle, I looked into the distance downstream hoping to see 16ft of red moulded plastic bobbing around somewhere, with the thought at the back of my mind of swimming for it, but without any joy. It was then with my panic still mounting that I noticed a red prow poking out of the bank, about 50 metres along the step near to the end of the island; as I leant further over the top of the grass-covered bank I could, thankfully, see my boat. I scrambled along the top bank and leant over to grab a line from the boat and then dragged it back to a position just below the tent where I fastened it securely to the spade, this time planted firmly by the door of my tent and with another 30 metres of line attached (why hadn't I done this in the first place?). I could only assume that as the canoe had been picked up on the flooding tide, it had dislodged the spade and drifted with the wind but fortunately – very fortunately – the spade had dropped back onto the mud and had provided enough purchase as it dragged to swing the boat back toward the very end of the island and lodge itself against the bank.

How could I have been so stupid? I knew that it's always toward the end of journeys, expeditions, or operations that these sort of cockups happen. Just when you think you have finished or at least can see or smell the finish line, you stop focusing fully on the task at hand. I really needed to switch on.

Having checked my lines several times I got back into my sleeping bag and tried to nod off. In the morning when I eventually woke the wind was not too bad, but it was still raining so I decided to wait out the rain before making my final push up to Emmonak. I knew that once I set off, I would have stick to the left-hand bank, negotiate the dogleg immediately in front of me, and then I would be in the exposed main channel all the way up until I was opposite the entrance to Kwiguk Pass where I would need to dash across the mile-wide river and into Emmonak. I had read in Dan Maclean's guide, "The entrance to the Kwiguk Pass is a potential bad spot. Weird currents boil unexpectedly on the upstream side, so it works best to swing a little wide as you make the turn into the channel. If it's stormy, wait for the weather to settle before making the crossing".

So, it was with this thought in mind that I tried to get some more sleep. When I woke later that afternoon, the wind had picked up and the rain continued – I couldn't get back on the water. I was close, but I knew that with the exposed run up to Emmonak and conscious of the mistakes and misjudgements creeping in, I had to wait for better conditions. After another frustrating day of reading, sleeping and peering hopefully out of the tent, it appeared that the wind was settling by early evening. I had learnt along the way that a sudden drop in the wind didn't constitute a change in the weather, no matter how frustrated I was or how long I'd been waiting, or what I thought might be lurking in the bush behind me.

I eventually set off in the late evening with the thought of cracking a couple of hours of paddling and thereby getting myself a little closer to Emmonak ready for a final push the following day. I'd spied a possible campsite on the upstream end of an island using my satellite mapping, the last obvious site I could see before the exposure of the river and prior to trying to cross into the Kwiguk Pass and toward Emmonak. I continued to hug the left bank, passed the exit from the Tunurokpak Channel, slipped between one larger island and the shoreline before coming into a wider part of the river. The sun set at 10-ish and there was an eerie sense of approaching darkness, something I had not really experienced on this trip, along with a developing chill mist rolling over the water from the shore, all of which contributed to my uneasiness about this final leg.

As I approached my potential stopover, it was difficult to make out the lie of the land, given my low sightline, sitting just above the surface of the river, the now poor light and the encroaching mist. I could make out the silhouette of the little island I was aiming for, but I couldn't ascertain where the mudbank around it started or finished. I'd used a larger scale on my mapping for this leg, and the islands – and the higher, therefore drier and lighter-coloured, mudbanks – were obvious. What were not clear were the mudbanks just below the water which appeared to be the same colour as the water itself on the imagery. In addition, I had no idea whether the pictures were taken at low or high tide.

I hit the mud about 200 metres away from the island. I could see that there was a small channel between the island and the shore, which may have offered me another sheltered route, but in the twilight and mist I couldn't see if it was passable and really didn't fancy the idea of heading down it only to get stuck and having to lug my boat back out again. So, I turned right and started to negotiate the mudbanks around the island. This sounds pretty straightforward, and indeed I thought it would be, but in reality it became an almighty pain in the butt. Having therefore passed my intended camp, I decided that I was not going to stop at all but that I'd try and push on overnight to reach Emmonak.

The night was still darkening, colder than I'd experienced thus far, and increasingly misty, but mercifully it was not blowing a hoolie. In fact, I had again a slightly helpful south-westerly breeze behind me to my left. The mudflats turned out to be far more extensive than I had thought and selfishly they didn't offer any discernibly straight edges, but having been deposited by the rolling river, they formed a series of rolling banks and gullies which stretched away from the shoreline out toward the middle of the river. I spent a few hours constantly bottoming out, having to push myself off into deeper water and then start the process all over again, still very apprehensive about drifting out into the river and being exposed to any sudden changes in the conditions with no shelter other than the mud.

This exertion and fannying about came to a head near midnight when I stopped for a 'leg stretch' on one of the interminable expanses of mud. I thought that there was no way that anything could creep up on me out on this emptiness, so I simply stepped out of the boat without bothering with the usual drills. It was seriously quiet, but when I looked up from my fumbling relief, I saw, with incredulous surprise in the mid-distance, what I thought was a huge bear racing across the mud toward me. In the half-light and mist I took a second look: it was still there, still running, but not making any noise and weirdly not seeming to get any closer. I strained to make it out fully and, in my confusion, did entirely the wrong thing. I stepped back into the boat, not to grab my bear spray and make a stand, but to run it out into the deeper water, jump in and paddle like mad until I was sure nothing was behind me.

All the while I knew somewhere in the back of my mind that if a bear were after me it would have been further encouraged by my fleeing, followed me into the water, easily out run me and would, by now, most likely be hauling me ashore by my head. I was probably only waist deep in the river but nothing came. Only then did I look over my shoulder: there was nothing there, well nothing alive. In the spot where I'd seen the bear was the carcass of another large, washed-up spruce, the root system of which had been facing toward me whilst I was relieving myself. I was now drifting past it, about 50 metres downstream, and bemusedly trying to work out what had happened. Throughout the trip I'd been amazed by the shapes made by tree carcasses – many looked like real or sculptured creatures basking on the sandbars, but it was the root circles that threw up the most remarkable shapes, their tangled forms taking on life after being dragged from the soil.

Growing on top of a layer of permafrost meant that the root systems were often squashed into circles rather than ball shapes, the bases of which offered intricate, writhing patterns of polished wood, many of which had uncanny similarities to Celtic knots and the entwined snake designs of the Sutton Hoo treasures. I'd told myself that if indeed I were to make the trip again, I'd take a decent camera and try to capture some of the amazing forms. However, at this juncture, I could only imagine that I'd looked up and seen the distant root wheel which must have been nearly two metres in circumference and, to me, in the misty gloom – and given my lack of sleep – must have looked like the silhouette of the sharp end of a bear, head down, big round shoulders and in-turned paws. Added to this, the fact that I had been gently bobbing around on the river for quite a few hours meant the 'bear' looked to be swaying from side to side as if running toward me!

Embarrassed as I was at being chased by a tree stump, not to mention my inability to face down said stump with my bear spray and small knife, I was at least wide awake and so pumped full of adrenaline that I made one of the best decisions of my trip. I decided to escape from the mud and headed out into the middle of the river. This was the stretch of river that had been worrying me all the way through my planning and the trip itself; the stretch that I thought would be exposed to the winds straight off the Bering Sea; the stretch in which I would be subjected to conditions akin to sea kayaking with proper rollers threatening to swamp the exposed open canoe; the stretch for which I'd discussed with the guys back at Up North Adventures in Whitehorse, six weeks previously, the idea of buying some floatation bags for the canoe to keep it afloat when faced with being swamped by the expected conditions – that was until I saw how much the floatation bags cost. But here I was, out in the middle of the mighty Yukon in the middle of the night, close to the Bering Sea, utterly exposed, at the very end of an Alaskan July; and I felt brilliant!

I could no longer discern the riverbanks due to the mist which enveloped them but didn't seem to be making its way out into the middle of the river. I could just make out the outlines of treetops in the distance and above the mist. The wind was now cold, but gentle, regular and behind me. The sun had set in front of me to the northwest, but there was still a discernible, pale yellow glow on the horizon as I paddled contentedly toward it. Behind me it was black, and I could feel the darkness slowly creeping up and over me like the Grim Reaper's cowl, his icy breath now playing on my neck. I recollect it being quiet but can't remember whether it actually was. There must have been the occasional cry of a gull somewhere in the distant mist, but otherwise the only sound I was aware of was the rippling of the river as my canoe nosed its way forward, my paddle strokes rhythmically entering the water accompanied by the odd hollow knock of the paddle on the gunwale.

Ranging from the sun's dim ambient glow on the horizon, the night sky changed in colour from a pale yellow, flecked with a faded silver glint, turning into ever deepening hues of blue much like an old bruise: initially a soft, pastel light blue but then, as it moved up away from the horizon and over behind me, it graduated through the spectrum from violet to a deep indigo before becoming entirely black. Much like the transition of sky to space I imagine you would witness if leaving our planet's atmosphere. I was glad I was heading the way I was, into the remaining light; having looked over my shoulder I was sure that if I'd been heading in the other direction, into that blackness, any ambition, hope or desire to continue would have been quickly eaten.

But this was it, this is what I came for. I was in the middle of the mighty Yukon River being chased by the night and guided by the memory of one and the promise of a new day. The banks were shadows of land, mere ideas of safety, but I felt utterly at home; I was at ease, I was really on the Yukon River, immersed in its magnificence. I had my world, all 16ft of it, and was supremely conscious of the size of my being, diminished by the scale of my surroundings and magnified by my place within it. As if in agreement with my situation, the first star I'd seen since leaving the UK appeared against the encroaching night above me and to the west. I was tired, very tired, but also very, very happy.

It was cold now and I had on pretty much all my warm paddling gear, a stark contrast to the notion of paddling almost naked a few weeks before. My Jacques Cousteau, crew of the Calypso (or Pasquinel from Centennial) red woollen toque was pulled low over my ears. The sun had begun one of its few remaining attempts to beat back the night and stave off the encroaching winter that year and I found myself on a tranquil, misty, early morning river. Mindful of Dan Maclean's advice about reaching Emmonak by crossing the Yukon into the Kwiguk Pass and the unpredictable currents upstream of that junction, I thought about heading back to the left bank and following his advice to swing wide beyond the entrance to the pass, but I could see that I was as close to the right bank and as to the left and given the conditions and my energy levels it seemed counterintuitive to make a big loop; so, I simply allowed myself to ferry-glide toward the right bank.

An evening paddle on the delta

My Final Day on
the River

As I made my way along the bank in the early morning mist trying to find any helpful movement in the water, I was sure that I was close to Emmonak, but with the limited visibility, mixed with my extreme tiredness, I really had no idea; I just knew that all I had to do was keep on paddling: just keep paddling! As I strained for the sound of fishing boats ahead, hopefully moving in and out of the Kwiguk Pass, I glimpsed out of the corner of my eye what I initially took to be the first sizeable pollution I'd seen on the river. Ahead of me and slightly toward the centre of the river I saw a large white plastic container rolling along with the current and glinting in the low sun. It caught me by surprise and when I took a second better look it had gone. I presumed that yet again I'd been hallucinating; I'd been on the water for nearly twelve hours again and had been working my eyes hard trying to make out details as I'd paddled through the semi-darkness, and I was now negotiating my way through a low sun infused mist.

Having refocused on my paddling, I suddenly saw the round white shape reappear. This time as I turned, I saw two and then three containers gently break the water's surface and then roll under again. I was still of the mind that they must have been large, discarded plastic barrels but then one of them expelled a foam cloud which steamed in the cold morning air; it clicked, these were dolphins! No, wait a minute, they're too big to be dolphins – and they're pure white. Surely not...? I'm still over ten miles from the Bering Sea, but these must be beluga whales. Of course, I'd never seen a beluga whale in the wild before – or more correctly a belukha whale to distinguish them from the Russian sturgeon fish of caviar fame – and I'm not entirely sure I'd seen any in captivity, but they are so very distinctive.

I cautiously edged closer to the white shapes now barrelling nonchalantly alongside me no more than 20 metres away. They didn't have dorsal fins, rather small ridges along their backs, which added to their barrel-like appearance, but I could now see the slight change in the shape of their heads although I don't recall seeing their tail flukes break the surface. All thoughts of my long paddle, tiredness and pain disappeared as I watched these ephemeral, ghostly creatures effortlessly roll through the mirk of the morning river, hardly breaking the water. It's easy to understand why, for some of the Native Peoples of the Yukon, these whales have traditionally been associated with death. After the fleetest time and the faintest suggestion of eye contact from the nearest white shape, they dipped back below the polished flat brown surface and disappeared. I held my course in vain for a while in the hope of catching sight of them again but to no avail. All too quickly the weariness and pain reappeared to remind me where I was and why I was there; had I woken up? All I needed to do now was find the entrance to the Kwiguk Pass and reach Emmonak. Had I really just seen belukha whales?

A little later, once in Emmonak and in the community centre which doubled up as the hotel, I mentioned my sighting to Mona, the very efficient, and in my case, patient, Yupik clerk in the office. She was completely nonplussed and dismissed my excited sighting by saying, 'Oh, are they in the river again?' So, I had seen belukha whales. Nothing in my planning or research had prepared me for that; sighting those whales in the river was an absolute privilege and potentially the highlight of my journey. Mind you, Mona's reaction did remind me of an occasion, a few years ago, kayaking around the Sound of Jura in Scotland when I'd first sighted some sea otters in the wild. I naïvely and excitedly mentioned the sighting to a barmaid in the Tigh-an-Truish Inn, next to the Clachan Bridge on Seil Island, to a response that surprised me: 'otters, don't talk to me about fucking otters,' she said, 'the fuckers ate all of my goldfish!' She was a lovely-looking girl but clearly didn't like otters. I had to assume that when she said goldfish, she was actually talking about carp in a garden pond, unless the otters in question had in fact been caught with their heads in the goldfish bowl in her kitchen, in which case her vehemency toward them might have been justified. Either way, I guess one person's 'wow that's amazing' is another person's shoulder-shrugging 'whatever', or profane exclamation.

The entrance to the Kwiguk Pass was not as evident from the near bank as I'd hoped. It took a few skiffs running in and out for me to be sure of where it was, not that there was any real danger of passing it without noticing. Once at the entrance to the pass, Emmonak was there. The Kwik'Pak fish processing plant was right in front of me with the first vehicles I'd seen in weeks moving to and fro; boats of all shapes and sizes were busily moving about the pass. I am still not sure if the name of the processing plant, Kwik'Pak, was a comment on their packing efficiency or a derivation of the Alaskan Natives' former name for the Yukon River, Kwikhpak. On either side of the river there appeared to be industry or the remnants of such and behind it all I could see the large white wind turbines that should have led me to Emmonak many hours beforehand.

Dan Maclean writes in his guide that reaching Emmonak can be a bitter-sweet experience – I quickly understood what he meant. It was an alien world. I picked my way past the busy dock and then the array of skiffs pulled up on the foreshore, looking for somewhere to put ashore in my little boat. It was the 1st of August, about 9am. I'd been on the river overnight for over 12 hours and I had to find some coffee and breakfast before working out how I could cover the last 11 miles of river to the sea and hopefully arrange a pick-up to get me back to Emmonak. As with the majority of the villages and settlements I stopped at, Emmonak had a long, graded dirt road running parallel with the riverfront, with further tracks and buildings leading from there. For the visitor, there was no obvious sign as to which way would lead to a store; why should there be – how many visitors do they get!

In Emmonak it didn't really matter, as I was to discover there was a large Alaska Commercial (AC) store at one end of the shore road and the Emmonak Public Works store at the dock end of town about a mile apart; I had landed halfway between the two. I turned left and headed past a number of dilapidated barrack-type buildings, a few houses with quad bikes and snow mobiles in various states of repair outside. I stopped outside the large, dark wooden, slightly tatty-looking church with a long ramp up to the open door. Further along the road, opposite the church, was a lurid blue, corrugated iron building with a sign saying it was a woman's refuge.

As I passed the refuge a small officious-looking native woman was in the process of clambering onto the biggest quad bike I've ever seen. It was almost as if she were mounting a Shire horse. She caught me staring at her and before I had the chance to ask her if there was a store nearby, she drew first and asked me if I was the stand-in priest. The question caught me by surprise, not unsurprisingly, and it took me a while to answer in the negative, at which point she simply said, 'well, you look like a priest', as if her mistaken identification were my fault, and I was masquerading as the stand-in priest. I must admit that for a nanosecond the thought of becoming the Emmonak stand-in priest sounded rather appealing. The church, whilst tatty, looked cosy and besides – how difficult could it be? But, then the weird Father Ted, Craggy Island scenario whizzed across the emptiness of my brain and I realised that I was actually too tired to cope with that. As I left her, I found I was intrigued to find out what the real priest looked like.

Mind you, it got me thinking about exactly how I do appear to people at those moments when I think I'm probably looking a tad rough. I must have been in my mid-forties when after a good day's kayaking around St Michael's Bay in Cornwall, between The Lizard and Penzance, I was caught out by someone's reaction to me. It had been a blowy day and I knew I was covered in sea spray and probably looked pretty tired – I certainly felt it. I had finished my paddle on the beach at Marizion and, after sorting out my kit, went for a reinvigorating pint of Guinness in the Jig Bar downstairs at the Godolphin Arms just beyond the beach. It was dark in the bar, compared to the bright windy day outside, and having ordered my stout, I was busy sorting a few coins in my open palm ready to pay when, without warning, the young lady behind the bar reached over to grab the coins from my hand.

Instinctively I pulled away before realising that she was only trying to help and then, being so very English, apologised for my social indiscretion. I was confident that I hadn't been taking longer than necessary to count out my change but was gob-smacked when she looked at me and said, 'It's alright love, it's important that you keep your independence, good for you'. I was dumbfounded: just how rough must I have been looking to give the young lady the impression that I was fighting to take care of myself? She didn't seem so concerned when I went back for my second and third pints!

*"They say before entering the sea, a river trembles with fear.
She looks back at the way she has travelled, from the peaks, the
mountains, the long winding road which crosses forests and villages,
and sees in front of her such a vast ocean that entering it doesn't see
anything else than having to disappear forever. But there's no other
way. The river can't go back. No one can go back. Going back is
impossible in existence. The river needs to take the risk and to enter
the ocean. It's only when entering the ocean that fear will disappear,
because it's only then that the river will know that it's not about to
disappear into the ocean, but to become the ocean."*

Kahili Gibran, Fear

Once I'd established that I could stay at the community centre hotel, I then asked Mona about the potential of getting picked up from the coast. Having covered 1330 miles I didn't mind cracking the extra 11 miles to finish my journey actually on the Bering Sea, I just didn't fancy then having to schlep back to Emmonak. With her straightforward no-nonsense approach Mona pointed at the VHF handset on a sideboard in the office and said, 'why don't you ask?' I didn't know that pretty much all of the locals had VHF radios, but in hindsight, of course they would, and given further thought I would have taken my own VHF handset on the trip.

Now, you probably wouldn't believe that I'm trained in the use of several radio systems and how to use 'correct' voice procedure protocols, since when faced with having to talk to an unknown native and local audience and explain my request, I hesitated. I couldn't pick up the handset and launch into some pucker Brit military voice procedure. It would be a bit like when trying to ring a taxi in Bantry, in western Ireland, on an English mobile, or even with an English accent on the pub phone – no one responded. The taxi driver that finally answered did compliment me on my Dublin accent, who'd have known! So, I tentatively picked up the handset in the community centre office, conscious that much of the wonderful local chat and hubbub that had previously been occurring around me had now stopped to listen to this weird, dishevelled, tramp explain himself over the airways.

'Hello, my name's Richard, I've just arrived by canoe from Canada and would like to finish my trip at the sea. Is there anyone out there that could pick me and my boat up from the sea later today?' I put the handset down and, quick as a flash, nothing happened. I waited for a bit, still conscious of being the entertainment in the room, and was just about to launch into a discussion about how long it would take me to reach the sea and get back when the radio sprang into life with a voice saying, 'Hi Richard, I think I can help you'.

The release of tension from within my audience in the office, given that no one was really listening, was palpable and before I could pick up the handset there was a general murmuring of acknowledgement and recognition around the office toward the channel number that responded: 'that's Mario', 'yes that is Mario', 'I thought it might be Mario'. I clicked the switch and said hello to Mario, we had a quick chat about time and location. I was reluctant to discuss anything as filthy as money over the radio (too English again) and it was agreed that Mario would pick me up from the channel that led to the sea, north of Kawokhawik Island, at 6pm that evening.

Now here's where my deluded approach to the vinegar strokes of my epic journey comes in. It was still relatively calm and bright outside and, therefore, in my head, I had my accommodation sorted out, I had my lift back arranged, all I needed to do was take a leisurely paddle out to the shores of the Bering Sea where I would have all the time in the world to sort my kit out, have a final meal and coffee, maybe a celebratory whisky. I'd already, thankfully, given up on the idea of having a night camped under the stars on a beach overlooking the sea, but thought maybe I could have a swim and even try and film myself skinny dipping in the Bering Sea to show folks back at home. What a prat!

It took me four hard hours to reach the recommended channel out into the sea, north of Kawokhawik Island, using the sloughs for the final hour or so to protect me from what was now an increasingly strong south-easterly wind. It was a strange sensation, finally reaching the sea: I had spent six weeks on a powerful river, fed by glaciers high up in the mountains, the culmination of dozens of considerable tributaries all feeding this single mass of water over thousands of miles. There was no sign of the idyllic beach I had in my befuddled head. Somehow, I expected to see this force being disgorged into the sea and, in turn, see that force being reflected by a sea, throwing briny waves back at the silt-ladened river. But, no, the estuary, when I arrived, was still and unerringly calm, the only force at play was that of the wind, but even that coming from across the land as it was made little impression on the merging waters. This lack of conflict is, maybe, not so surprising if you take a look at a satellite image of the Yukon–Kuskokwin Delta: the delta spreads out over hundreds of square miles, looking much like the bronchi of a lung, dissipating the river's water across hundreds of miles of coast; I was bobbing along on one small vein of the delta.

There were just more mudflats, flats that went on and on, low and indiscernible. I could see white gulls or wading birds of some sort shimmering in the distance, but I couldn't reach them. I decided to paddle to the west, as far out as I'd dare given the building wind that was unhelpfully helping me out to sea. About 250 miles to my front was the eastern coast of the Russian landmass. At intervals I stuck my finger in the water to taste it, after what seemed like an age and with an ever-increasing sense of exposure; I thought I tasted salt. I took a second lick just to be sure it wasn't my sweat; no, it was salt, but then the salt water could have travelled much further upstream – I was just trying to justify the fact that I was on the Bering Sea and I could therefore turn back and head for land.

On the Bering Sea - next stop Russia

I took a quick photograph of nothing but sea – the Bering Sea – and sky (my mother-in-law would have been so impressed), then I turned the canoe around and started heading back for land. The wind had been building, it was now strong, and I had to work hard to get back into the shelter of the mudflats. I reached the channel that Mario had suggested, but only just, and it was still only 3pm. I tried making for the slough that I used for shelter on my way out but couldn't reach it. Instead, I got blown into a muddy inlet surrounded by low tufted grass. I reached a gulley, grabbed at some grass and pulled my boat alongside. I was stuck there, but it was not really a problem; I could see the channel where I was meant to meet Mario in three hours, so all I had to do was sit it out. It started raining. I pulled up the hood of my cagoule got my camping chair out of the boat, hopefully for the last time, put it on top of the tufted mudbank and started my vigil waiting for my agreed pick-up.

Within a few minutes a skiff appeared in the channel and stopped as if looking for someone – could this be Mario arrived early, having seen the conditions, to pick me up? I grabbed my paddle and put my yellow collapsible bucket over the blade and started waving it the air; the skiff saw me. It powered its way over and up onto the bank on the channel side of the mudbank. With almost effortless ease the young lad driving hopped off the front of his boat, chucking his anchor up on the bank as he did so, and introduced himself. His name was Jerome, he was about 5'6", compact with thick dark brown hair that surrounded a broad, open, kind face; he looked trustworthy. I was glad he was there.

As I explained my situation and we were discussing whether maybe he could take me back to Emmonak a second skiff arrived containing three more young lads. It transpired the pilot of the second skiff was Tyrone, Jerome's cousin. Tyrone was slightly taller than Jerome, thinner with darker hair and a tricky look; unlike his cousin he struggled with eye contact and seemed to be searching for something about me. The two lads with Tyrone were a little different, younger, they seemed innocent, both were white and looked like they were being led astray. They all sported sunglasses and were wearing similar clothes, variations of cagoules, jeans and calf length hide boots. They were, variously, at home and suited to the environment, but they were high and I felt a little outnumbered and slightly concerned by Tyrone as he and Jerome were having quiet whispers with each other.

None of the people I'd met on the Yukon had given me any cause for concern, not that I'd met many and not that I'm usually prone to being concerned by people. The majority of those I had met, the ones that did not treat me with indifference as is their right, were interested in my trip and friendly toward me and my endeavour. Being given an enthusiastic wave or a cheery shout of 'good luck' and 'stay safe' was always much appreciated. So, I was not overly worried by these guys, I was just conscious that I was tired and not wanting to put myself in a compromising position. They were just young lads with weapons, alcohol, drugs and huge, fast, skiffs!

Tyrone was becoming insistent that Jerome should take me back. I said I'd only go with him if they could contact Mario and tell him I was coming back with them, ostensibly to avoid him coming out and looking for someone that wasn't there but also to ensure someone else knew that I was with these lads. We finally agreed, I would let Jerome take me back. I offered to empty the canoe and help them drag it across the mudflat to Jerome's skiff. No need, before I could start, Tyrone and Jerome had lifted the boat, kit and all, and had it unceremoniously laid in Jerome's skiff, the nose pointing up and out of the front. They were Yupik lads and strong with it. I got into the skiff with Jerome and my boat and we powered off. I thought we were heading straight for Emmonak but no, they had decided I needed to see their Aunt's fish camp first. We disappeared into a maze of sloughs Tyrone and Jerome racing their skiffs at 30mph plus alongside each other around the bends. I was slightly concerned: after all I'd been through, I didn't want to die in a drunken skiff accident, but I was also happy that I'd finished paddling and, kind of, on my way back to civilisation. Kind of!

As it turned out, their Aunt's camp was actually a corrugated-tin-roofed, wooden-planked shack on stilts, hidden in the maze of the sloughs. It had seen better days but was somewhere they could escape and get stoned. Inside there was an old, iron-framed double bed, a table, and a number of chairs in various states of repair. On the walls there was an incongruous mix of religious iconography and hunting trophies, and scattered around the room was the equipment and paraphernalia for hunting, drinking and drugs – not a great combination. I wondered how many of the other fish camps looked like this.

The five of us went in, Tyrone confidently, Jerome also, but I could discern a touch of reluctance from the other two who both seemed nervous. Later, the taller white lad asked me not to tell his mother that he'd been smoking dope, a strange request given I didn't know who he was or where I was likely to meet his mum. I nodded paternally, and then relaxed in the realisation that these were like any other lads, anywhere in the world, trying to enjoy themselves, albeit with powerful boats, drugs, alcohol and guns. We sat in the shack, the four lads younger than my own boys; Tyrone passed me his treasured, lit, walrus tusk ivory pipe, and I had a heady drag to show willing. In truth I was in no real rush: I'd finished my paddle, I had a room ready for the night, I just wanted to get there.

They talked shit, occasionally in English, occasionally in (I assumed) Yupik. Tyrone was getting more animated as he got more stoned and pissed, which concerned me more. He still wouldn't believe that I didn't have a gun and kept asking if I'd give it to him. As it transpired, their original plan that day had been to go out hunting seals. I'd messed that up for them, but so had the weather, the rain outside getting heavier and now ricocheting off of the tin roof. I let them shoot the shit for a bit before making a pointed remark about having finished a very long trip, being very old and not having slept for nearly 24 hours (my main excuse for not joining them for a vodka and another puff) and that I had agreed to pay to be taken back to Emmonak. There was some further furtive discussion between Tyrone and Jerome before the vodka was passed around with a final toke on the walrus tusk and we headed out into the rain and toward their skiffs.

The ride back with Jerome was excruciating: the rain was horizontal and Jerome was again moving at 35mph plus – I could see the instrumentation on the console of his skiff. He had goggles on, so I pulled my cag hood low. It was, eventually, good to be back at Emmonak; once my canoe was ashore, we discussed the price. I think this is what the secretive chats had been about and where Jerome had taken Tyrone's advice. I made an offer, he trebled it; I split the difference and I assume my subsequent cursing as I tried to fish out my cash from deep within my baggage for the first time in months was enough to convince him he had a good deal. I think he had, but then again, I didn't really know what the score was, I just knew I was back at Emmonak, I had made it all the way to the Bering Sea, I was alive, I had finished but it was certainly a bitter-sweet moment!

It was just another classic, anti-climactic, ending to so many long and emotional journeys: the end, however strongly longed for, can so often be such a serious disappointment. Whilst maybe slightly different, the year before I'd cycled from John o' Groats to Land's End on a mountain bike with my tent following the national cycle network, so only using designated cycle paths, a distance just shy of 1200 miles. I reached Land's End to find the iconic 'finger signpost' situated in a bizarre, incongruous, amusement arcade on Britain's most south-westerly point – sacrilege! The end of my journey was fenced off and I was expected to pay to be photographed under it. How could anyone have ever agreed to the building of such a 'carbuncle' on such a sacred place? I plumped for having my picture taken under the Wallace & Gromit attraction entrance. Remember to enjoy the journey and not place all your expectations on the arrival.

So, my deluded idea of a final night on the shores of the Bering Sea didn't pan out – what the hell! As it transpired, I was so incredibly lucky. The weather that came in that evening and over the next few days was horrendous. Back in the community centre office they were using the VHF radio to transmit coastguard warnings of exceptionally strong winds and six-foot plus tidal surges along the delta for the next few days. So, if I had decided to spend another night on the river, after losing my canoe, or tried to spend a night on the coast, I'd still be there and would have been for another three or more, very wet, windy and hungry days; I was lucky.

I had planned to explore Emmonak the day after finishing, visit the community sauna, do my laundry and send a postcard or two from the post office, but the weather was so foul that once I'd found my boat again (which took another hour or so as it had been caught by the tidal surge and washed up in a culvert under the main drag), I spent the day in my room trying to extract Yukon silt from every nook and cranny of both my kit and myself. Down in the community centre office, with the wind raging down the corridors and rain battering the windowpanes, I arranged my flights out. Once again, I was conscious of what a jammy bugger I am, and that without any real rhyme, reason, or any pre-apprehension of what was going to happen, things worked out for me, to a fashion.

View from the Cessna as we leave Emmonak

Return from the Wilderness

"In wilderness is the preservation of the world."

Henry David Thoreau, The Wild (1851)

Alaska and the Canadian Yukon Territory are marketed as the 'Last Wilderness'. I can now say that I've been there, done that – although I suspect I'll be back for more – and yes, I do now have the T-shirt 'Alaska the Last Wilderness'. The region certainly has the environment and space to justify that claim, but I wonder for how long it will be able to maintain that. I saw no more than half a dozen other paddlers throughout my six weeks on the river, the majority of which were in the Yukon–Charley Preserve with no one at all beyond Yukon Crossing, although I did hear along the way that there were a few paddlers ahead of me. I understand this may have been Jason 'Foxy' Fox, another former Royal Marine, now of TV's Who Dares Wins fame, who I gather had kayaked with a mate all the way from Skagway.

In Emmonak the locals I spoke to all seemed particularly unconcerned and rather disinterested in who had arrived from upstream. This was probably a personal notion on my part, perceived betwixt my own singular focus at the time and their disconcertingly pleasant nonchalance, although I suspect that the community had tabs on me most of the way, sharing information as to who was about on the river as they passed in their skiffs between towns, villages and settlements. However, it did occur to me that, in my dotage –and given the combination of barely adequate planning, a degree of luck and some dogged determination – if I had considered and then actually managed to complete such a trip, surely many more will attempt do so. I wondered how any significant increase in 'adventure tourists' would affect the environment.

Certainly, there was a clear Alaskan state push to promote such along the Yukon–Charley Preserve, the region being served by road access from Fairbanks to both Eagle and Circle and with the provision of the public use cabins along the river. Back in the mid-1970s John McPhee was already alluding to the policy of managing – possible managing out – many of the miners, trappers and settlers and, indeed, the Native Peoples beyond their agreed established settlements.

The Yukon–Charley Preserve is now relatively easy to access and thereby, perhaps, could it be deemed as less 'wild', dependent on one's definition of 'wild' or, more pertinently 'wilderness'? Definitions of 'wild' range from 'uncontrolled, violent, or extreme' to 'being in a state of nature, not tamed or domesticated' whereas 'wilderness' is defined as 'a large area of land that has never been developed or used for growing crops because it is difficult to live there.' I noticed that none of the definitions I could find included 'where the wild animals/things live' – I would have hoped that wild creatures received some consideration in our concepts of such places, as their presence enhances any sense of wildness.

So, for how long can the Yukon River and the surrounding country remain a wilderness? If one accepts this definition of wilderness, then provided the country along the river is not developed or used for growing crops then, in theory, a wilderness it remains. But what if that development is the provision of tourist accommodation, and what if the 'crop' being grown is adventure tourists, backpackers and paddlers such as myself – would this challenge the wilderness status? That said, significant parts of the country along the Yukon have been previously developed and managed for the extraction of furs and minerals, most of which have now been fully or partially reclaimed by nature without damaging the idea of wilderness. I think Barry Lopez makes a valid point when he suggests that "what every culture must eventually decide, actively debate and decide, is what of all that surrounds it, tangible and intangible, it will dismantle and turn into material wealth. And what of its cultural wealth, from the tradition of finding peace in the vision of an undisturbed hillside to a knowledge of how to finance a corporate merger, it will fight to preserve". I guess it is down to a sense of perspective: what is really important to us and, perhaps more fundamentally, do we really know what is important to us?

I am confident that the Canadians and Alaskans are acutely aware of the potential impact of visitors to their precious and vulnerable 'wilderness' – the land, animals and the people – and are well placed to actively manage and protect these areas. My own concerns, as an outsider that 'came to the country' for such a short time, are most likely a product of my own background and experience coming from a land in which the pressures of development and growth now seem almost impossibly overwhelming; a land where it seems the relationship between nature and people has been strained and is now artificially one-sided, where the balance may have been irrecoverably tilted too far away from nature.

As I write, the UK Government has announced plans to replace the former European Union farm subsidies and is looking to provide funds for our farmers that encourage them to 'rewild' and restore our natural habitats. Hailed as the most important change in the UK's natural habitat management in four decades (so since the UK entered the EU), naturalists cautiously welcome the initiative, but want the government to 'act big and act fast'. Many, however, remain sceptical: Janet Street-Porter, the outspoken TV presenter, writer and rambler, is reported as saying, rather typically, that "rewilding is a fad for the rich that will turn our green and pleasant land into a theme-park wilderness covered in forests full of dangerous animals, wind turbines and solar farms". Whilst, perhaps, not everyone's cup of tea, personally I could live with forests full of dangerous animals: they might help us to be more conscious of our place on this planet and provide a us with a much-needed, heightened sense of awe toward nature; the wind turbines and solar farms I may have to learn to live with if we want cleaner energy.

In 1901, when talking about the establishment of national parks in the US, John Muir wrote, "Thousands of tired, nerve-shaken, over-civilised people are beginning to find out that going to the mountains is going home; wildness is a necessity". It begs the question why, over 120 years later, are we still having to re-learn this fundamental truth? Where and when did we forget or lose sight of the benefits of nature? In The Wild Places, Robert MacFarlane makes the point that "We have come to accept a heresy of aloofness, a humanist belief in human difference, and we suppress wherever possible the checks and balances on us – the reminders that the world is greater than us or that we are contained within it. On almost every front, we have begun a turning away from a felt relationship with the natural world." Macfarlane's 'heresy of aloofness' and 'turning away from nature' appears much like Alastair Bonnet's 'universal pretensions', the reasons why we have assigned 'place' to the parochial, preferring instead the hubris of 'space', the notion of mobility, the absence of restrictions and empty landscapes filled with promise.

In these terms, could the concept of 'place' be seen as our place within nature, our understanding of where we fit, an acceptance that we are contained within it? And if so, is the modern Western desire for the openness and freedom of 'space' in fact an existential fallacy that doesn't really exist? Perhaps what we are really seeking is an internal freedom from our own psychological relationship with nature, rather than seeking our real place within it: the curse of consciousness, the loss of Eden. Are we doomed to wander the face of our planet trying to control nature, trying to re-create it in our own image, seeking safety from our nightmares, demons and gods, rather than embracing our true place and the benefits we now know this will bring?

Heavy stuff, perhaps, and I apologise, because I did say that I would warn you before getting too philosophical, but whether the ideas of 'place' or 'space' work for you, I think for me the answer keeps coming back to that sense of awe and wonder, the sense of the sublime. Too often we forget or ignore the fact that nature, however small (or, for that matter, vast) – the frog and shrew, or the bear and whale, a ripple on the river's surface or the water's reflection of a sun-gilded bluff, a flower in a vase, or a walk in a wood – nature is not different from us, it is us: we are nature, and in turning away from nature we are probably turning away from ourselves, we are turning away from the fact that we are awesome and sublime.

"There is no real ending. It's just a place where you stop the story."

Frank Herbert, author of Dune

As I sat at my table in Gwennie's Old Alaska Restaurant and Bar, along Spenards Road in Anchorage, eating what seemed like an obscene amount of steak, curly fries and salad and having an ice-cold beer that really was nowhere near big enough, I was earwigging a conversation at the next table in which the waitress was desperately trying to find a different hotel for a couple that had just arrived in the bar. She was very concerned that the hotel

First meal in Anchorage

just down the road that the couple had checked into was, in fact, some sort of crack-den and was renowned for gang violence. I didn't want to tell them that that was the hotel I was already staying in.

The couple that the bar staff were trying to help had probably found out, just as I did 48 hours earlier, that it was the only place with rooms available in Anchorage that weekend. The hotel itself was nice enough, for the price, but I must admit there did seem to be a lot of random people hanging around cars with blacked-out windows in the parking lot and on the stairs at the back. I had stayed there the previous night and would be leaving for the airport at 4am the following morning, so I kept quiet.

It was, however, at that point where it dawned on me that my Yukon adventure was now well and truly over, and that the dualism, the juxtaposition between the pragmatic and the sublime, that had accompanied me throughout my time on the river, was rapidly dissipating. I was now well and truly back in the land of the practical, a less wonderous world which, sad to say for me, equated to the world of people. A world where there seems little place or time to stop and look for – and bathe in – that connection with our surroundings, our world, to seek out or be touched by any sense of wonder. I remember feeling robbed. As a relative 'newbie' to this dualism, I didn't want to just melt back into the world of people, I wanted to hang onto my place in the sublime, my place within nature.

As if to reinforce this sense of loss, I arrived at Anchorage airport at 4:30am the morning after overhearing the conversation in Gwennie's, feeling spiritually robbed but thankfully physically unmugged, although the entrance to the hotel was very busy for that time of the morning and the first 'taxi' I got into was not actually there for me. I couldn't work out who was more surprised, the guys furtively dealing inside the blacked-out cab or me. I think they took one look at me, the kit I was carrying and maybe the large wooden paddle in my hand, and thought it better to let me retire back into the hotel lobby and wait for my real taxi.

I arrived, tired and slightly discombobulated, at a very busy early morning airport to find out that the flight that I thought I had booked over the dodgy internet on my phone back in Emmonak had not actually been processed and I had no seat on the flight from Anchorage to meet my subsequent connecting flights. Step forward Poli, the petite, calm, check-in clerk, the angel of my morning. Despite the grumbling queue behind me and having worked out what had happened to my booking, Poli found me a seat on the plane, arranged for all my baggage to be forwarded onto my connecting flights, and found a protective bag for my paddle to ensure it would not be damaged. My faith in humanity temporarily restored, I filled out a customer feedback form praising Poli whilst having a relaxed breakfast in the airport lounge.

However, my smug feeling of relaxation and contentment was quickly burst when, sat on the plane just before take-off, having discerned that I was a Brit, the couple in the seats next to me asked what I thought about the outcome of the recent UK general election. I had, over the last few weeks, completely forgotten about domestic politics back home and as the couple enthusiastically told me that Boris Johnson was now my Prime Minister and enquired about my thoughts over Brexit, I wondered if it was too late to get off the plane and head back to the sanctuary of the Yukon.

Of course, I did make it home and was pleased to do so. My wooden paddle, my only physical memento from my adventure, which didn't arrive on the baggage carrousel at Gatwick, was delivered to my front door two days later, and I was so very grateful to all the people that had made that happen. I quickly settled back into life at home and even became a little more accepting of our national politics. Then, as I looked back on 2019 with a sense of fulfilment and satisfaction buoyed by the idea that I had achieved part of my reason for taking early retirement – to follow Edward Abbey's advice to get out there, to enjoy the land while I can and while it's still there – and looking forward to more adventures, COVID hit and we were all locked down!

I have found the necessary restrictions difficult, particularly the inability to immerse myself in nature (a sense so greatly heightened by my recent experiences on the Yukon) and as I have tried to seek out and open up to more dualism in my life. I now revisit the Yukon River in my mind when looking for a safe, peaceful place and more often than not, over these last few months and years, for me being in a canoe on the Yukon makes more and more sense. It had taken me forty days and forty nights to complete my trip – the river had let me.

Ultimately, I am an optimist and have faith in the future, and in people for that matter, so I leave you with the full version of Edward Abbey's 'final paragraph of advice'. These are words that have helped and inspired me and I hope that you might find something in them too:

*"Do not burn yourselves out. Be as I am, a reluctant
enthusiast, a part time crusader, a half-hearted
fanatic. Save the other half of yourselves and your
lives for pleasure and adventure. It is not enough to
fight for the land; it is more important to enjoy it
while you still can and while it's still there. So, get out
there and hunt and fish and mess around with your
friends, ramble out yonder and explore the forest,
encounter the grizzly, climb the mountains, bag the
peaks, run the rivers, breath deep the yet sweet and
lucid air, sit quietly for a while and contemplate the
precious stillness, that lovely mysterious and awesome
space. Enjoy yourselves, keep your brain in your head
and your head firmly attached to your body, the
body active and alive and I promise you this much;
I promise you one sweet victory over our enemies,
over those desk bound people with their hearts in
safe deposit boxes and their eyes hypnotized by desk
calculators, I promise you this; you will outlive the
bastards."*

Edward Abbey (1976)

OK, maybe you won't outlive anyone, but I can promise you that your life
will be richer for a little bit of adventure and a sense of wonder.

Bibliography

Alvarez, Al. Feeding the Rat, Bloomsbury, London, 2003.

Ansell, Neil. The Last Wilderness, Tinder Press, London, 2018.

Bonnett, Alastair. Off the Map, Aurum Press, London, 2015.

Brooke, Rupert. Delphi Complete Works of Rupert Brooke (Illustrated), Delphi Classics, 2013.

Burke, Edmund. A Philosophical Enquiry into the Origin of our Ideas of the Sublime and Beautiful. Oxford World Classics, 2015.

Deakin, Roger. Waterlog, Vintage Books, London, 2000.

Franklin, John. Thirty Years in Arctic Regions, University of Nebraska Press, Lincoln and London, 1988.

Hunter, Linda Jo. Lonesome for Bears: A Woman's Journey in the Tracks of the Wilderness, Lyons Press, London, 2008.

Jones, Lucy. Losing Eden, Penguin, 2020.

Krakauer, Jon. Into the Wild, Villard Books, New York, 1998.

Laing, Olivia. To the River, Canongate Books, Edinburgh, 2017.

London, Jack. To Build a Fire and other stories, Bantam Classics, New York, 2007.

Lopez, Barry. Arctic Dreams, Vintage, London, 2014.

MacFarlane, Robert. Underland, Penguin, 2020.

MacFarlane, Robert. The Wild Places, Granta Books, London, 2007.

Maclean, Dan. Paddling the Yukon River and its Tributaries, Publication Consultants, Anchorage, 2007.

McPhee, John. Coming into the Country, Travels in Alaska, Daunt Books, London, 1977.

Michener, James A. Alaska, Dial Press Trade Paperbacks, New York, 2014.

Muir, John. Travels in Alaska, Riverside Press, Cambridge, 1915.

Nelson, Richard K. Make Prayers to the Raven, A Koyukon View of the Northern Forest, The University of Chicago Press, Chicago, 1983.

Newby, Eric. A Short Walk in the Hindu Kush, Harper Press, London, 1959.

Pinker, Steven. Enlightenment Now, Penguin Random House, UK, 2018.

Pretor-Pinney, Gavin. The Wave Watcher Guide, Bloomsbury, London, 2010.

Rourke, Mike. Rivers of the Yukon Territory, Yukon River, Dawson City to Circle, River North Publications, Houston.

Russell, Andy. Grizzly Country, The Lyons Press, New York, 2000.

Service, Robert. Collected Poems of Robert Service, Dodd, Mead & Company, New York, 1940.

Webster, Len. Teslin River Guide.

Weymouth, Adam. Kings of the Yukon, Penguin Random House UK, 2018.